THE STOICS: A GUIDE FOR THE PERPLEXED

CONTINUUM *GUIDES FOR THE PERPLEXED*

Continuum's *Guides for the Perplexed* are clear, concise and accessible introductions to thinkers, writers and subjects that students and readers can find especially challenging. Concentrating specifically on what it is that makes the subject difficult to grasp, these books explain and explore key themes and ideas, guiding the reader towards a thorough understanding of demanding material.

Guides for the Perplexed available from Continuum:

Adorno: A Guide for the Perplexed, Alex Thomson
Deleuze: A Guide for the Perplexed, Claire Colebrook
Derrida: A Guide for the Perplexed, Julian Wolfreys
Descartes: A Guide for the Perplexed, Justin Skirry
Existentialism: A Guide for the Perplexed, Stephen Earnshaw
Freud: A Guide for the Perplexed, Celine Surprenant
Gadamer: A Guide for the Perplexed, Chris Lawn
Habermas: A Guide for the Perplexed, Eduardo Mendieta
Hegel: A Guide for the Perplexed, David James
Hobbes: A Guide for the Perplexed, Stephen J. Finn
Hume: A Guide for the Perplexed, Angela M. Coventry
Husserl: A Guide for the Perplexed, Matheson Russell
Kant: A Guide for the Perplexed, T. K. Seung
Kierkegaard: A Guide for the Perplexed, Clare Carlisle
Leibniz: A Guide for the Perplexed, Franklin Perkins
Levinas: A Guide for the Perplexed, B. C. Hutchens
Merleau-Ponty: A Guide for the Perplexed, Eric Matthews
Nietzsche: A Guide for the Perplexed, R. Kevin Hill
Plato: A Guide for the Perplexed, Gerald A. Press
Quine: A Guide for the Perplexed, Gary Kemp
Ricoeur: A Guide for the Perplexed, David Pellauer
Rousseau: A Guide for the Perplexed, Matthew Simpson
Sartre: A Guide for the Perplexed, Gary Cox
Spinoza: A Guide for the Perplexed, Charles Jarrett
Wittgenstein: A Guide for the Perplexed, Mark Addis

THE STOICS: A GUIDE FOR THE PERPLEXED

M. ANDREW HOLOWCHAK

continuum

Continuum International Publishing Group
The Tower Building   80 Maiden Lane
11 York Road   Suite 704
London SE1 7NX   New York NY 10038

www.continuumbooks.com

British Library Cataloguing-in-Publication Data
A catalogue record for this book is available from the British Library.

ISBN-10: HB: 1-8470-6044-7
PB: 1-8470-6045-5
ISBN-13: 978-1-8470-6044-0
PB: 978-1-8470-6045-7

Library of Congress Cataloging-in-Publication Data

Holowchak, Mark, 1958–
The Stoics : a guide for the perplexed / M. Andrew Holowchak.
p. cm.
Includes index.
ISBN-13: 978-1-84706-044-0 (HB)
ISBN-10: 1-84706-044-7 (HB)
ISBN-13: 978-1-84706-045-7 (pbk.)
ISBN-10: 1-84706-045-5 (pbk.
1. Stoics. I. Title.

B528.H73 2008
188—dc22
2007039299

Typeset by Servis Filmsetting Ltd, Manchester
Printed and bound in Great Britain by
MPG Books Ltd, Bodmin, Cornwall

In fondest memory of Gregory
Dies iste, quem tamquam extremum reformidas, aeterni natalis est.
Seneca, *Epistles*, CII.26

CONTENTS

ABBREVIATIONS

D.L.   Diogenes Laertius' *Lives of Eminent Philosophers*

ISA   Stobaeus' *Anthology* (*Ioannis Stobaei Anthologium*, ed. Curtius Wachsmuth and Otto Hense, Berlin: Weidmannos, 1884–1912).

SVF   *Stoicorum Veterum Fragmentus, Hans Friedrich August* von Arnim, *Irvington Publishers, 1986*

LIST OF TABLES

ACKNOWLEDGEMENTS

I would like to thank my wife Angela for her patience in this project, my students at Kutztown University and the fine people at Continuum for their invaluable assistance throughout this project.

INTRODUCTION

'Does not a good man consider every day a festival?'

Diogenes the Cynic

The final decade of the twentieth century was a time of unparalleled prosperity for the United States. With a robust economy, exceptional standard of living for most citizens and the world's most capable military force to protect them, Americans conducted their daily affairs with a smug indifference to events in other parts of the world. Americans felt safe, secure and invincible, though there was considerable global disconnection.

At 8.46 a.m. on 11 September 2001, without warning, American Airlines' Flight 11 crashed into the North Tower of New York City's World Trade Center, which collapsed over one and a half hours later. At 9.03 a.m., United Airlines' Flight 175 crashed into the South Tower, which toppled one hour later. A third plane, American Airlines' Flight 77, crashed into the Washington Pentagon at 9.45 a.m. A fourth plane, United Airlines' Flight 93, en route to Washington, crashed in a wooded area outside of Pittsburgh at 10.10 a.m. Overall, thousands were killed. A nation was horrified.

Americans responded to these tragedies with shock, disbelief and fear. The country was in panic. Within 24 hours, a few carefully orchestrated attacks by terrorists razed completely the inveterate belief, given global sanction, in American invulnerability.

In some ways, however, the events of 9/11 were good to America's president, George W. Bush. They gave him an identity that hitherto he lacked as a leader, and a common enemy toward which to direct US fear and anger. Because of 9/11, vulnerability became an issue of utmost significance to Americans. For example, in a talk in White Sulphur Springs, West Virginia, on 9 February 2003, Bush spoke, as he had often done before, of the impact of 9/11 on America, in an effort to gain support for the invasion of Iraq.

> The world changed on September the eleventh. Obviously, it changed for thousands of people's lives for whom we still mourn. But it changed for America, and it's very important that the American people understand the change. We are now a battle-ground. We are vulnerable. Therefore, we cannot ignore gathering threats across the ocean. It used to be that we could pick or choose whether or not we would become involved. If we saw a threat, it may be a threat to a friend, in which case we would be involved, but never did we realize the threat could be directed at the American people.
>
> And that changed. And therefore, when we hear of stories about weapons of mass destruction in the hands of a brutal dictator, who hates America, we need to take that seriously, and we are.[1]

What Americans became aware of with the events of 9/11 is what most other countries and their people acknowledge as a part of everyday living – misfortune and vulnerability to it. Should that have been such an astonishing lesson for Americans to learn?

I can try to answer this question through a story, passed on to us from antiquity by the Roman emperor Julian. The great Persian king, Darius, was bemoaning to the noted Greek philosopher Democritus the loss of his wife. After more conventional means of appeasing the king failed, Democritus challenged the king to find three persons in the whole of his great kingdom who had never suffered from grief and to inscribe their names on to the tomb of his departed wife. This once done, he promised to bring his queen back to life. When Darius could not name three persons, Democritus thereafter laughed heartily at the great king for thinking that he alone suffered such grief and undeservedly so.[2]

Though Democritus was no Stoic, his reply to Darius was Stoic-like and incisive. Moreover, since its message is as plain today as it was then, it sheds considerable light on the shock, disbelief and bitter grief with which Americans reacted to the events of 9/11. Like Darius, from the Stoic perspective, Americans suffered mightily because they entertained three foolish notions. First, they suffered in thinking that they were invulnerable. Next, when reality sank in, they suffered in thinking that such attacks were undeserved. Finally, they suffered in thinking that they were alone in their grief. Democritus, like a Stoic sage, would have laughed at all three misjudgments, as he understood that human wisdom is just awareness of human vulnerability.

The events of 9/11, just like the story of Darius and Democritus, show that Stoicism is needed in today's world: when one comes face to face with misfortune, Stoic wisdom gives one invaluable succour. On the one hand, Stoic indifference, as the Greek word *apatheia* is often translated (see Chapter 1), is a way of keeping a clear head through ever-shifting circumstances. For instance, Winston Churchill is often described as a leader whose Stoic demeanour in the face of the devastating German assault pulled his nation through the horrors of World War II. Stoic indifference is also widespread in the world of competitive sport, where reversals of fortune are commonplace and many players and coaches deal with such reversals by cool acceptance of them. On the other hand, in extreme situations, Stoic indifference may mean the difference between life and death. I give two examples. First, there are prisoners of war who recount that they could not have survived being tortured without adoption of a Stoic attitude. Most notable is James B. Stockdale, a senior Navy pilot who was shot down over Vietnam on 9 September 1965. He spent over seven years as a POW and he survived this ordeal chiefly on account of his internalization of Stoic principles of endurance. He says:

> I took those core thoughts into prison; I also remembered a lot of attitude-shaping remarks. Here's Epictetus on how to stay off the hook: 'A man's master is he who is able to confer or remove whatever that man seeks or shuns. Whoever then would be free, let him wish nothing, let him decline nothing, which depends on others; else he must necessarily be a slave.'[3]

Second, Navy SEAL (sea, air, land team member) Richard Marcinko writes, in a Stoic-like manner, that a true 'Warrior' has a 'spiritual and moral gyroscope' that keeps his soul functioning constantly at a high plane, under the most adverse conditions, and makes him invincible.

It is this gyro that makes it possible to endure. You endure, because you know you are a better man than your opponent – purer, more consecrated, and sanctified . . . You can suffer, tolerate, or undergo anything.

It is my unshakable belief that when these two intrinsic values – the total acceptance of death as a natural condition of life, and the total acceptance of an absolute moral code – are combined, the Warrior becomes invincible.[4]

Examples such as these show clearly that Stoicism may be an appropriate philosophical attitude in response to troublesome or extreme circumstances today. I suspect, however, that one would need much more convincing before being persuaded that Stoicism could be a suitable way of life. The aim of this book is to show that it can.

WHY STUDY STOICISM?

It is difficult to explain the appeal of Stoic ethics. Aristotle's ethical views grip people easily on account of his stark, common-sense ethical realism. His ethics are demanding, but reasonable, and in reasonableness common sense finds a useful ally. Yet it is just because Stoic ethics are not so reasonable, that they are too demanding – what is considered a major defect of an ethical system – that, I suspect, many are attracted to them, at least as a curiosity. One has only to consider the following Stoic paradoxes, which seem prima facie extremely outrageous:[5]

- Virtue is sufficient for happiness.
- All virtuous persons are equally virtuous and all non-virtuous persons are equally vicious.
- Only a Stoic sage is free, rich, beautiful, loyal, sublimely happy and invincible – even while tortured on the rack.

Of these, let us examine the first paradox – known as the 'sufficiency thesis'. The sufficiency thesis entails that one's happiness is entirely a matter of one's psychical disposition, one's virtue, and for a Stoic sage that is completely unaffected by external circumstances. Virtue is wholly a matter of indifference to all things that are a matter of fortune: health and illness, wealth and poverty, and even life and death. Virtue is wholly an internal matter. Thus, a Stoic sage, being tortured on a rack, will never admit to being anything but happy. His invincibility is his virtue.

The Stoics also buy into some rather unfashionable metaphysical theses. These are perfectionism, fatalism, teleology and Stoic psychotherapy.

First, there is Stoic perfectionism. Who would sensibly be moved to strive to live virtuously, when it may reasonably be doubted that anyone has ever lived up to the Stoic standard of wisdom and all who fail to achieve complete virtue are said to be equally vicious? The Roman philosopher Seneca speaks voluminously of the celebrated Stoic sage. He writes freely about what a Stoic sage would do in varied scenarios and his words are inspiring and moving. Still, all of this, we admit, must be highly speculative, because no sage has presumably ever existed. We come to realize that we are then dealing with thought experiments – nothing more. So, the promise of invincibility to fortune seems nothing more than a false promise. At day's end, one feels cheated.

Even if one could attain invincibility through complete indifference to what fortune brings, why would anyone want to be *completely* indifferent? Fortune brings not only ills, but good things, and Stoicism seems to license no enjoyment of good fortune. Would not a father celebrate greatly the birth of a daughter? Would not he be exceptionally proud of her on her graduation from college? Great celebration and exceptional pride are not only socially expected here, but they seem to be the morally correct responses to such events. Aristotle at least would think so. Stoicism seems to make sense, however, only if fortune is known to be chiefly a harbinger of bad things.

Second, there is Stoic fatalism. Who could reasonably be enticed to accept an ethical system that presupposes a universe where all events are preordained and completely determined by deity? The Stoic Chrysippus, Epictetus tells us, grappled mightily with this difficulty. He said that if he could know his fate and it was his fate to be ill, then he would choose illness over health.[6]

Third, there is Stoic teleology. Humans are animals that strive to live, as best they can, toward their own proper end. Most Stoics agree that this end is a life 'in agreement with nature' – both their own human nature and the nature of the cosmos. The notion of teleology today has generally fallen into disfavour in scientific and philosophical discourse, mainly because essentialism – the notion that humans have an essence that separates them off from all other things, living and not living – has fallen into disfavour with the emergence of evolutionary biology and non-essentialist ways of thinking. In addition, the problems with trying to tease out a reconciliation of the different Stoic senses of 'nature', as we shall see in Chapter 1, are ponderous.

Finally, there is Stoic psychotherapy, which is not quick and simple, but Herculean and hard. Yet this Herculean path, difficult as it may be, is said to lead to complete psychological security from ill fortune. Stoics relate that the bad and good things that happen to one are really neither bad nor good, when seen from the Stoic point of view. If that were the only justification one could give, one that is essentially pragmatic, then Stoicism would be no better a remedy than any other school of thought that promises similar psychical security upon adoption of their principles of living. Epicurean hedonism, the acquisition of pleasure through avoidance of pain, springs to mind here. However, Stoic psychotherapy promises not just psychical strategies for dulling pain, as it were, but also the possibility of complete invincibility in face of whatever fortune brings one's way. The invincibility promised is supposedly not only a workable remedy, but also the only correct one. In short, one becomes indifferent to whatever things fortune throws one's way not only because indifference gets one through the day better than other 'remedies', but because, as a Stoic sage, one comes to realize that the things that fortune brings *really are* neither ill nor good. The only good for Stoics is a virtuous soul – invincible to the exigencies of fortune and perfectly self-controlled.

Such difficulties notwithstanding, can one draw from canonical Stoicism, as it existed in antiquity, sensible ethics for today, if one can extract from the various Stoic philosophers over the centuries a consistent ethic? I think that one can, and, in doing so I hope to show that what initially appeared to be outrageous is really quite sensible.

THE STOIC PHILOSOPHERS

The ancient chronicler of Greek lives, Diogenes Laertius (*fl. c.* AD 225), relates that Stoicism began with Zeno of Citium (*c.* 334–262 BC). Under the spell of Plato's dialogues and their stories about Socrates, Zeno came to Athens to study philosophy. On his way to

Athens, he met the Cynic philosopher Crates (*fl.* 325 BC) and became his pupil. He immediately adopted Crates' complete disregard both for the conventions of their day and for conservative values like financial status and social standing. He also learned what he could from such notable philosophers as Xenocrates, Polemo, Stilpo and Crantor of Plato's Academy. It was from these 'Academics' that Zeno developed the notions that no good other than virtue exists and that morally appropriate acts must agree with nature. In around 300 BC, Zeno founded his own school in Athens, and his pupils eventually came to be called 'Zenoians' or 'Stoics' – the last, on account of the 'Painted Porch' (*Stoa Poikile*) at which they met. Some of his most noteworthy pupils were Persaeus of Citium (306–*c.* 243 BC), Aristo of Chios[7] (*c.* 320–250 BC), Herillus of Carthage (*fl.* 260 BC), Dionysius of Heraclea[8] (*c.* 330–250 BC) and Sphaerus of Bosporus (*fl.* 220 BC). As one can plainly see, the school, due especially to the Hellenizing conquests of Alexander the Great (356–323 BC) in Persia and India, was quite cosmopolitan.

Upon the death of Zeno, Cleanthes of Assos (*c.* 331–*c.* 232 BC) became the new head. Though Cleanthes began his life as a boxer, he was a gentle and industrious philosopher, who showed little aptitude for the rigours of physics and logic. Though he wrote many works, none were outstanding. He was considered by some merely to be the 'amiable dullard' who followed Zeno, though that is certainly unjust.

It was with Chrysippus of Cilicia (282–206 BC) that Stoicism became one of the great schools of antiquity. Thought unimpressive in person, he had a keen mind and was a voluminous writer with over 700 publications, of which nothing but fragments survive. He also developed a formal approach to propositional logic that has only recently begun to receive due attention.

Zeno and Chrysippus divided philosophy into three parts: logic, physics and ethics. Suggestive of the sort of organic unity that characterized their cosmos as a living deity (see Chapter 1), none of the parts of philosophy were deemed foundational; all were said to be interdependent. Diogenes Laertius writes:

Philosophy . . . is like an animal: logic corresponding to the bones and the sinew; ethics, to the fleshy parts; physics, to the soul. Another simile the Stoics use is that of an egg: The shell is logic; next comes the white, ethics; and the yolk in the centre is physics. Or again, they liken philosophy to a fertile field: logic being the encircling fence; ethics, the crop; physics, the soil or the trees.[9]

Table 1. Egg/Body/Field Analogies

Philosophy	Egg Analogy	Body Analogy	Field Analogy
Logic	Egg-Shell	Bones & Sinews	Field's Fence
Ethics	Egg-White	Fleshy Parts	Crop
Physics	Egg-Yolk	Soul	Earth/Trees

A second wave of Stoicism, which may be called Middle or Platonic Stoicism, began in the second century BC, perhaps with Diogenes of Babylon (c. 240–152 BC), but more likely with his pupil Antipater of Tarsus (fl. 145 BC). In this wave, the two most famous philosophers were Panaetius of Rhodes, who introduced Stoicism to Rome, and his pupil, Posidonius of Apamea, both of whom were unorthodox Stoics. The works of Panaetius and Posidonius do not survive. What we do know of them comes to us from authors like Cicero (106–43 BC) and the physician Galen (AD 129–200). These writers indicate that their works were a syncretism of Platonism, Peripatetism and early Stoicism.

Panaetius (180–110 BC) ignored Chrysippus' logic and rejected Zeno's notion of a phoenix cosmos[10] for one that was unregenerated and eternal. His focus was on ethics, and he deviated from early Stoicism here as well. Impacted by Plato, Panaetius developed a new, bipartite (i.e., rational and desiderative) view of the soul to supplant the view of a uniform, rational soul of prior Stoics. With a desiderative faculty of the soul, there came the notion that wickedness was not due to misjudgments of reason, but was in us by nature. He also maintained that the human end was not to live in agreement with nature, but to achieve full human potential. To this end, he argued that humans were guided by four impulses: that toward self-preservation; that toward truth; that toward self-sufficiency; and that toward order, fitness and beauty.

Posidonius (135–55 BC), using Plato's Timaeus as his guide, moved even closer toward a complete revival of Platonism. First, he separated Deity, Nature and Fate, which were thought to be identical for the earlier Stoics. Zeus or Deity was deemed an active principle that permeated the cosmos and bound matter like glue, but predominantly sat at the outmost regions of the cosmos to constrain things geometrically. In addition to this active principle, there was also a passive principle: Nature (i.e. Body or Matter), given form by Zeus. Finally, Fate was said to correspond to Plato's concept of Necessity – a principle that worked on the lowest level of material things. Secondly, like Panaetius, Posidonius rejected the early Stoic notion of a uniform soul. Here he followed Plato to the letter in positing rational, spirited and desiderative faculties of the soul. In spite of the complexity of the human soul, the end of each person, he thought, was participation in truth – that is, participation in the order and regularity of the cosmos.

As time passed, interest in physics and logic waned, and ethical speculation became the predominant interest of Stoic thinkers.[11] There began the third and final wave of the early Stoic movement – Roman Stoicism. Its main philosophers were Seneca the Younger, Gaius Musonius Rufus (*c.* AD 30–110), his pupil Epictetus and the Roman emperor Marcus Aurelius. Fortunately, we possess complete works of many of these authors.

Seneca (1 BC–AD 65) was a tremendously significant political and philosophical figure in the early Roman Empire. He was tutor and advisor to the young Nero, until he eventually fell into disfavour with the emperor and committed suicide to escape his wrath. While he lived, he wrote letters and moral essays prolifically and on a large variety of ethical issues, such as benefits, leisure, suicide and anger. Epictetus (*c.* AD 50–130), a former slave from Phrygia, was a disciple of Musonius in Rome before he set up his own school in Nicopolis. He wrote nothing, but his ethical teachings were preserved by a pupil, Arrian, in eight books called *Discourses* and a short manual called *The Handbook*. His consistent message of freeing oneself by surrendering completely to one's fate bears the mark of his former slavery. Finally, Aurelius (AD 121–180) was the Roman emperor from AD 161 to 180, whose work, *Meditations,*[12] proves that Stoic principles could be as serviceable for an emperor as they were for common persons.

EARLY INFLUENCES ON STOICISM

The Stoic founder, Zeno, upon being shipwrecked in the Athenian port Piraeus and reading about Socrates in Xenophon's *Memorabilia*, asked the bookseller where he could find a man such as Socrates. At just this time, the Cynic philosopher Crates happened to be passing by and the bookseller told Zeno to follow the Cynic. Thereafter, Zeno became a pupil of Crates and took up Cynical philosophy.[13]

Cynicism was an ancient 'school' of thought maintaining, following Socrates, that a virtuous lifestyle was sufficient for one's happiness. Virtue, for Cynics, was a matter of simple living through following nature and despising fortune[14] and the conventions of humans. Instead of withdrawing from the society of humans, however, they chose to live in cities. They dressed simply, rejected book-learning, preferred not to work, favoured homelessness and lectured on virtue on street corners or in marketplaces. Virtue, for Cynics, was not a matter of having book-smarts, but street-smarts, as it were, through triumphing over daily hardship. In some sense, it is not unfair to say that they lived parasitically on the very lifestyle they habitually condemned.[15]

The first Cynic was Antisthenes[16] (c. 446–c. 366 BC), a 'student' of Socrates (469–399 BC), who, as is commonly known, voluntarily lived an impoverished life and spent all of his time in pursuit of virtue, which he identified with knowledge. From Socrates, Antisthenes learned hardihood, disregard of feeling, toleration of pain and piety,[17] though he rejected the Socratic notion that virtue consisted of knowledge.

The most prominent Cynic was Diogenes (404–323 BC), son of Hicesius and pupil of Antisthenes.[18] Diogenes was an older contemporary of Aristotle and a native of Sinope. From Antisthenes, Diogenes learned to live simply, without ornament. From watching a mouse scampering about, Diogenes learned to avoid pleasantries, to be unafraid of the dark and to adapt to existing circumstances.[19] He had an abhorrence of luxury, extravagance and custom. He is said to have acquired the name 'cynic' because his manner of living emulated that of a dog (kyon).[20]

Outside of Cynicism, Stoicism was impacted significantly by Plato and later Platonists. Plato (427–347 BC), another pupil of Socrates, depicts his mentor as someone who, though he professed to know nothing, was nonetheless tirelessly in pursuit of knowledge to improve his soul and others'. Plato's Socrates discoursed each day on issues such as piety, self-control, courage and justice.

What the Stoics inherited from Plato was, most significantly, his insistence on the possibility of knowledge. Astonishingly, Plato's own Academy in the third century BC turned Plato on his head, so to speak. From Plato's dogmatic insistence on the possibility of knowledge, his Academy, several decades after his death, developed an equally dogmatic insistence on the impossibility of knowledge. The Academy turned sceptical. Academic philosophers rejected certainty for what-is-probable (*eulogon*). Arcesilas (*c.* 315–241 BC) and Carneades (*c.* 213–129 BC) delighted in arguing both sides of an issue with command in an effort to show that each could be equally defended and that dogmatism on such matters was fool-hardy. Academic Sceptics' main target was Stoicism and its notion of the cataleptic sensory impression (Chapter 1) that attempted to give epistemology a firm footing. It is likely that each school bene-fited greatly from their vigorous exchanges and debates over the years. What is strange, however, is that the Stoics were truer to the spirit of Plato's thought than were Plato's own pupils.

The impact of Plato's thinking on the Middle Stoics, especially Panaetius and Posidonius, as we have already seen, was substantial.

A third prominent influence was Aristotle (384–322 BC). Stoic epistemology was not radically different from that of Aristotle, with the notable exception that the Stoics, because of attacks by Sceptics, had to grapple with a systematic defence of epistemology, whereas Aristotle faced no such organized and persistent epistemological opposition. In some measure, Stoics' ethics too were not radically dissimilar from Aristotle's ethics. Whereas Aristotle argued that a virtuous state of soul was the chief component of a happy life, the Stoics maintained that virtue was sufficient for happiness.[21] For Aristotle, goods such as health, wealth, fine looks and good fortune were needed in some measure for happiness; for Stoics, such things added fullness to one's life, but nothing to one's happiness. For all practical purposes, the disagreement may have been slight, which is why Cicero in *On Ends* stated that the disagreement was more one of words than of principles.[22]

METRIOPATHEIA AND *ATARAXIA*

Two popular alternatives to Stoic indifference to all things other than virtue and vice (*apatheia*) were Aristotle's conception of mean states of affection (*metriopatheia*) and the psychical-equilibrium view (*ataraxia*) adopted by Epicurus and his followers. Since I shall be referring to them abundantly throughout this book, I give a brief sketch of each overleaf.

The pursuit of happiness for Aristotle involves the acquisition and exercise of virtue (*arete*) at two distinct levels: one corresponding to virtue of thought, the other corresponding to virtue of character. Virtue of character (*ethike arete*) is a certain stable state of soul that comes about through being habituated to cultivate virtue and avoid vice – primarily under the guidance of good laws. Virtue of thought (*dianoetike arete*), in contrast, comes about mostly through education over time and involves contemplation of eternal, ungenerated and incorruptible things (i.e. the objects of theoretical science).

It is virtue of character with which Aristotle's *Nicomachean Ethics* is principally concerned. Aristotle spells out his catalogue of virtues and his well-known doctrine of the mean in Books II–V. Virtue of character comes through striving for the mean (*to meson*) between two vices: one of excess (*hyperbole*) and one of defect (*elleipsis*). Each virtue, then, is the intermediate between two vices.

Aristotle gives a list of particular virtues and their corresponding vices of extremes at II.7.[23] There are, one finds, virtues regarding attitude toward battles, pleasures and pains, handling of money, honours, anger, truth-telling, amusement, and attitude toward others.[24] Two examples will suffice. Courage is virtuous and it lies between the vices of foolhardiness (i.e. excess) and cowardliness (i.e. defect). The courageous person, described from III.6 to III.9, will exhibit fear, but in the correct amount, towards the right things, in the right place and at the right time. Yet he will also face dangers if reason dictates, even to the extent of confronting death. Magnanimity, which he explicates at IV.3, is 'a certain ornament of the virtues'. Its vice of defect is pusillanimity, where one regards himself as worthy of much less than he is, while the vain person (vice of excess) believes himself worthy of what is great when he is not.

Not all (perhaps no) contrary vices are to be regarded as equidistant from their corresponding excellence. Sometimes the vice of defect is farther from the mean. For magnanimity, the pusillanimous person (vice of defect) is more of an extreme than one who is vain (vice of excess). At other times, the vice of excess is farthest from the mean, just as, with respect to pleasure and pain, the self-indulgent person is more vicious than one insensible to pleasures and pains. Consequently, in aiming for the mean in all excellent activity, one must first steer clear of the most contrary vice, which is often the best one can do to come as near to excellence as possible. What guides us throughout is correct reason.

In contrast to Aristotelian *metriopatheia* is Epicurean *ataraxia*. In contrast to Stoicism, where part of the aim of living is to buffer oneself from pain through rational recognition that pain cannot impact one's happiness, for Epicureans, the ultimate goal or the highest good of life is pleasure (*hedone*), which they define as the absence of pain or the privation of the fleeting pleasures that bring greater pain as a consequence. One strives for pleasure not by actively seeking it, but by employing reason to avoid all pain, inasmuch as that is possible. Through the eradication of both bodily and psychical pain, one attains freedom from bodily disturbance (*aponia*) and freedom from psychical disturbance (*ataraxia*). All other contenders for the good life – even the most celebrated virtues such as courage, moderation, wisdom and justice – are themselves desirable only because they lead to pleasure. The chief agitators of psychical equanimity are mistaken beliefs about how the world works. People suffer mental agitation because they believe that the gods intervene in human affairs, that death is something to be feared, and that there are no limits to their desires.

Overall, Epicurus deems epistemology and metaphysics worthy of serious study mostly insofar as they contribute toward the practical aim of psychical pleasure through the removal of unsettling, irrational beliefs. A true philosopher is really a practising physician of the soul. In Epicurus' own words: 'Empty is the argument of the philosopher by which no human disease is healed; for just as there is no benefit in medicine if it does not drive out bodily diseases, so there is no benefit in philosophy if it does not drive out the disease of the soul.'[25]

OUTLINE OF THE BOOK

The Stoics: A Guide for the Perplexed comprises five chapters. In them, I sketch out a view of what I roughly take to be canonical Stoicism that accepts the following Stoic theses.

Sufficiency Thesis: Virtue, which is identical to equanimity, is the sole human good. This runs against current strains in contemporary philosophy – e.g., discourse ethics, utilitarianism, relativism and postmodernism – that forbid saying anything definitive about some things being unqualified goods.

Indifferents Thesis: External goods, such as health and wealth, are human indifferents. Canonical Stoicism says that such things are not goods, but indifferents that one prefers not to be without (G., *proegmena*, L., *commoda*). When present, they add nothing to one's happiness, but can be useful ornaments to one's life. I call these 'conveniences' throughout. Contrariwise, 'ills' such as poverty, illness and even death are indifferents that one prefers to be without (G., *apoproegmena*, L, *incommoda*). When present, they take away nothing from one's happiness, but make for an unembellished life. I call these 'inconveniences' throughout.

Herculean Thesis: A simple, hardy life is preferable to a soft life. Consistent with the Socratic/Cynical strain in Stoicism, the best life entails a certain amount of hardship, as virtue is best tested by trying circumstances. Since every life will be fraught with trying circumstances, a soft life is poor preparation for such difficulties. One wishing to make progress toward virtue will even practise hardship, when times are favourable.

Rationality Thesis: A happy life is one that strives to remove, not moderate, wrong emotion as much as possible to allow utmost rational activity. If equanimity through rational activity is the best human life for a human to live, then the Stoics are right to insist that any amount of cultivation of the wrong sort of emotional activity impedes this end.

Oikeiotic Thesis: Virtue is a matter of striving for what is one's own, staying away from what is not, and helping others to do the same. Wisdom comes through knowing one's place in the overall scheme of cosmic affairs, insofar as this is possible. One progressing toward virtue will therefore strive for self-knowledge, which includes knowledge of one's physical and psychical capacities and awareness of one's particular circumstances. Following Panaetius, a progressor strives to realize his potential as a rational human being through developing his capacities to their fullest and best extent. As that process is essentially social, in fully realizing himself, he helps others to do the same. This I call the *Oikeiotic Thesis* from the Stoic term *oikeiosis*, examined fully in Chapter 2.

I turn now to a synopsis of the book:

Chapter 1, 'The Stoic Sage', illustrates what may be taken as canonical Stoicism. I begin with a sketch of Stoic cosmology and epistemology, and then turn to ethical issues. The aim here is to come to grips with the ideal of Stoic perfectionism, embodied in the celebrated, flawless and elusive Stoic sage. Among the subjects covered are the sufficiency thesis, Stoic indifferents, the Stoic view of nature, the

Stoic view of emotions, fatalism and determinism, self-knowledge and rules of right conduct.

Chapter 2, 'The Stoic Progressor', is an attempt to show how Stoicism can be made relevant today. The perfectionist ideal of canonical Stoicism is discarded for Stoic progressivism – the view that the best life is one in which an apprentice strives for daily progress towards the perfectionist ideal. Among the topics are Stoic cosmopolitanism, truth, freedom, capabilities, life and death, Stoic *oikeiosis* and authenticity. In addition, I articulate a model for what it means to be wise in the Stoic progressivist sense – what I call the Peak-Performance Model.

Chapters 3 and 4, 'Equanimity in Adversity' and 'Equanimity in Prosperity', look at Stoic arguments for bearing hardship with courage and magnanimity and for enduring success without losing one's virtue. Topics in Chapter 3 include illness, pain, anger, grief and death. Topics in Chapter 4 include benefaction, revelry, friendship, books, gormandizing, restlessness and retirement.

Finally, in Chapter 5, 'The Heroic Course', apprenticeship in Stoicism takes centre stage. First, indoctrination in Stoicism is likened to confession of illness, where a student assumes the role of patient and his teacher assumes the role of physician. Second, indoctrination in Stoicism is likened to athletic training, where ethical progress is compared to athletic progress. The chief aim here is to give textual confirmation of the Peak-Performance Model of virtuous activity that is sketched in Chapter 2. Next, I list epistemological and ethical 'curatives' for psychical illness: doctrines, precepts, reminders and exhortations aimed at right acts through improved judgments of reality and equanimity. I end with signs that an apprentice is making progress.

ADDITIONAL COMMENTS

Before ending, allow me a few additional words about *The Stoics: A Guide for the Perplexed*.

First, the translations of Greek and Latin throughout are principally drawn from the Loeb translators, though I make significant modifications. The sole exception is the translation of Aurelius, where I usually follow Long's translation. Overall, I tend to break up lengthy English sentences and add to translations what is implicitly, though unambiguously, assumed. Furthermore, I take certain liberties with the ancient languages. For example, beyond Chapter 1, I often use 'Stoic', not 'sage', where the Latin *sapiens* or the Greek *phronimos* occurs, since I reject the canonical Stoic notion that sagacity as complete invincibility is possible. Moreover, to be as egalitarian as possible – and Stoicism is nothing if not egalitarian – I tend to shy away from literal translations that seem to do more to obfuscate than clarify what I take to be the intended meaning for us today. For instance, where a masculine subject such as the Latin *vir* or the Greek *aner* occurs and the point being made is meant to be applicable to all human beings, I tend to choose a gender-neutral term such as 'one', 'everyone' or 'a person' instead of 'man'. Finally, as my aim is philosophical and not philological, I offer little in the way of criticism of existing translations and manuscripts throughout.

Second, as *The Stoics: A Guide for the Perplexed* is an attempt to bring Stoic ethics alive today, I assume that one can sketch, from Zeno to Aurelius, a rough framework that captures the tenor of Stoic ethical thinking. In doing so, I acknowledge philosophers who called themselves 'Stoics' but were obvious exceptions. However, because little survives of earlier Stoic writers and because the focus of later authors, whose texts we have, is ethics, I draw chiefly and abundantly from the readily available works of Seneca, Epictetus and Aurelius. To make these ancient texts more accessible to readers unfamiliar with Stoicism or Greek thinking, I give many ancient and modern-day examples of relevant or significant events to illustrate Stoic principles. I also use excerpts from today's poetry, films and novels to exemplify key arguments or themes. Finally, while I do often refer to the secondary literature on the Stoics, my focus is not on criticism of that literature. My main goal throughout is to present Stoicism as a substantive, not cosmetic, cure for psychical malady today.

NOTES

1 http://www.whitehouse.gov/news/releases/2003/02/20030209-1.html
2 Democritus was known as the 'laughing philosopher', presumably because, when he saw stupidity all around himself, he preferred to laugh rather than to weep. Julian, *Epistles,* 201B–C.
3 Nancy Sherman, *Stoic Warriors: The Ancient Philosophy behind the Military Mind* (Oxford: Oxford University Press, 2005), p. 6.
4 Richard Marcinko and John Weisman, *Rogue Warrior* (New York: Pocket Books, 1997), p. 146.

5 The outrageousness of Stoic paradoxes is in part due to the impact of Cynicism on early Stoic development.

6 Epictetus, *Discourses,* II.iii.9–10.

7 A colleague, with a mind of his own, who completely shunned logic and physics and whose views on indifferents we shall see in Chapter 1. D.L., VII.160.

8 Called 'Renegade'. He dissented from Zeno's views because he suffered violently from ophthalmia and could not accept the notion of pain being something indifferent. D.L., VII.166.

9 There are the usual dissenters, like Cleanthes, who divided philosophy into six parts: dialectic, rhetoric, ethics, politics, physics and theology. D.L., VII.40–1.

10 Stoics believed in world-cycles, each identical with the previous one, where the world periodically burned itself up in a massive conflagration and then was reborn. E.g., Eusebius, *Evangelical Preparation*, XV.xiv.2 and D.L., VII.141.

11 At least, this view is justified by the surviving texts of this third period. One exception is Cleomedes' (*c.* AD 100) *The Heavens.* See John Sellars, *Stoicism* (Berkeley: University of California Press, 2006), p. 19. Long believes that cosmological disagreement after Posidonius caused neglect of cosmology and a focus on ethics thereafter. A. A. Long, *Epictetus: A Stoic and Socratic Guide to Life* (New York: Clarendon Press, 2002), p. 151.

12 Acquiring the title *To Himself,* because of its self-reflective nature.

13 D.L., VII.2–3.

14 With the exception of Bion of Bosysthenes (335–245 BC), whose attitude to fortune was remarkably Stoic-like.

15 See R. Bracht Branham and M.-O. Goulet-Cazé (eds), *The Cynics: The Cynic Movement in Antiquity and Its Legacy* (Los Angeles: University of California Press, 1996).

16 Antisthenes initiated the Cynical movement, but Diogenes acquired the name for the movement and is generally regarded as the first 'Cynic'.

17 D.L., VI.2.

18 Socrates too. D.L., VII.91.

19 D.L., VI.22. Cynics in the main rejected the traditional view of humans as beings somewhere between gods and animals, for the view that animals were more godlike than humans given that their needs were fewer than those of humans (i.e., gods need nothing, animals need few things and humans 'need' many things) (D.L., VI.105).

20 It may also be that Cynics acquired their name because they would meet at the *Kynosarges*, a gymnasium outside of Athens for those not of pure Athenian blood. The eminent Athenian general Themistocles attended this gymnasium.

21 Panaetius and Posidonius being dissenting voices and maintaining that health, wealth and strength were also needed. D.L., VII.128.

22 Cicero, *Ends*, III.iii.10.

23 Spelled out more elaborately and with some inconsistencies from III.6 to IV.7.

24 The mean also figures crucially in political harmony. Whoever pushes deviant forms of constitutions (e.g., oligarchies and democracies) to extremes, loses sight of proportion and leads to what is no longer a constitution (Aristotle, *Politics*, V.9)

25 Epicurus, *Marcella*, XXXI.

CHAPTER 1

THE STOIC SAGE

'We must accept what happens as we would accept the fall of dice, and then arrange our affairs in whatever way reason best determines.'

Plato, *Republic*

For Stoics, invincibility is a matter of complete virtue, which seemingly requires that one suffer one's share of misfortunes along the way. Complete virtue is not, then, invulnerability to what fortune brings. Stoics did not think that one fully versed and practised in Stoic principles would literally suffer no wounds as 'invulnerability' implies. They merely thought there was no wound that could affect a sage's equanimity.[1] Thus, invincibility, not invulnerability, is the aim of a good life for Stoics, and the simple formula for that is summed neatly by the Stoic Epictetus' famous dictum, 'Bear and renounce' (*anekhou kai apekhou*).

This first chapter is a summary of what I take to be canonical Stoicism – a view that is, I believe, untenable. Nonetheless, here and throughout, I accept and defend five essential Stoic claims:

- Virtue, as equanimity, is the sole human good.
- External goods, such as health and wealth, do not affect human happiness.
- A simple yet hard life is preferable to one that is soft and secure.
- A good life strives to remove, not moderate, emotions, to allow utmost rational activity.
- Virtue is a matter of complete cosmic integration – that is, knowing what is one's own and what is not one's own, insofar as one is capable of doing so – and helping others to do the same.

19

A COSMIC SPIDER'S WEB: THE STOIC COSMOS

The earliest Stoics were chiefly cosmologists. The word 'cosmos', Diogenes says, relates to deity himself – the artificer of the cosmos who at times absorbs into himself all of creation and recreates later; to the orderly arrangement of the heavenly bodies; and to the whole which comprises the first two.[2] The Stoic cosmos, taken in the third sense, was believed to be both a plenum and an animal, which was interchangeably called Reason, Fate or Zeus.[3] Writes the Roman Stoic Seneca, 'All that you see – that which comprises both god and man – is one; we are parts of one great body.'[4] Nature (*physis*), regarded universally, was a generative force, responsible for all growth, life and order within the cosmos. As an animate body, the same principles that were responsible for animal vitality were responsible for the life of the cosmos, which continually came to be and passed away in recurrent cycles. Behind the vitality of their phoenix universe were two material principles: god, a fiery and powerful active force; and a type of passive watery matter without attributes that the active force fashioned. These two material principles were not separable natures; they described two aspects of the same material thing.[5]

Like a human embryo, for Stoics the cosmos was thought to develop through various stages over time. At the first stage, a fiery god acts on the precosmic water. That interaction results in the generation of the four elements – fire, air, water and earth – arranged in spherical tiers in the spherical universe.[6] With the birth of the elements, the cosmos comes into being.

Pervasive throughout the cosmos and vitalizing it throughout all of its cycles, there is a tenuous matter called *pneuma*, a vital but tenuous breath or wind of sort – the same sort of breath that permeates and vitalizes the body as soul.[7] *Pneuma* is a material principle that is responsible for coherence and order in the cosmos. Chrysippus states that *pneuma* does this by effecting a certain tension (*tonos*) within the cosmos.

Chrysippus appeals to the analogy of a spider and his web to describe the tension that unifies a human being and coordinates activity between his various parts: When any insect lands in the web, the tension of the web conveys this motion to the spider.[8] That tensional force is responsible for seeing, hearing, moving, sleep, death and even desire in humans.[9] The same analogy can also be used to understand cosmic unity and the coordinated activity of its various parts as well.

From the cosmic tension, there comes to be a vital, material unity and coherence to the cosmos as there is with all things that are its parts. Animals have a soul (*psyche*). Plants have an analogous binding agency (*physis*). Even inorganic things have a fiery principle (*hexis*) that, turning back toward itself, holds them together. Consequently, even the most lifeless of things, like rocks, were thought to be vital in some sense.[10]

In time, the cosmos matures to such a state that the fiery deity is in perfect command and what is moist is entirely consumed. The cosmos is now a complete conflagration. Yet in the conflagration are the seeds for regeneration of all past, present and future things. All events, then, are predetermined by deity, which is the cosmos. Until such time that a new cosmos is born, identical with the previous one, all evil is vanquished. The cycle is eternal.[11]

PULLED BY THE HAIR: HOW KNOWLEDGE IS POSSIBLE

For Stoics, invincibility through virtue is essentially linked to the possibility of knowledge, because invincibility is possession and right use of knowledge.

Knowledge begins through sensation (*aisthesis*), which Diogenes Laertius says has four meanings for Stoics – the vital force that passes from the principal part of the soul to the senses, discernment through the senses, the apparatus of the sensory organs, and, more generally, the activity of sensory organs.[12] The Stoic standard of truth relates to the second of those. It is a specific type of sensory impression, whose likeness to its object is so plain that one who is virtuous is literally forced to assent to the impression being true. This criterion of truth, the cognitive or cataleptic[13] impression (*kataleptike phantasia*), is used as their standard of judgment to serve as a foundation for knowledge. The Sceptic Sextus Empiricus (*c.* AD 160–210) writes:

A cataleptic impression is one that (1) arises from what is, (2) is stamped and impressed exactly in accordance with what is, and (3) is of such a kind that it could not arise from what is not. Since the Stoics hold that this impression is capable of precisely grasping objects and is stamped with all their peculiarities in a crafts-man-like way, they say that it has each one of these peculiarities as an attribute.[14]

Sextus says the relationship between a cataleptic impression and its object is isomorphic, like a signet ring on wax, for a perceiver. Though we are free to renounce any impression, a cataleptic impression 'all but seizes us by the hair and pulls us to assent'.[15]

Cicero, whose philosophical works are an invaluable source for Stoic thought, says of the Stoic cataleptic impression:

> Just as a scale must sink when weights are placed in the balance, so the mind must give way to clear presentations. Just as no animal can refrain from seeking what appears suited to its nature – which the Greeks call *oikeion* – so the mind cannot refrain from assenting to a clear object.[16]

Epictetus adds that it the nature of the intellect to assent to what is true, to be dissatisfied with what is false, and to withhold judgment on what is unclear.[17]

Of course, not all impressions are cataleptic in nature.

> An impression [*phantasia*] is an imprint on the soul: the name having been appropriately borrowed form the imprint made by the seal upon the wax. There are two species of impression – the one is cataleptic, the other is non-cataleptic. The cataleptic impression [*kataleptike*], which the Stoics take to be the test of reality, is defined as what (1) proceeds from a real object, (2) agrees with that object, and (3) is imprinted in seal-like fashion and stamped on the mind. The non-cataleptic impression [*akatalepton*] either does not proceed from any real object or, if it does, fails to agree with the real object itself, because it is not clear and distinct.[18]

The similarities to Cartesian epistemology should be obvious.

In all, virtue for the Stoics is a matter of being cataleptically disposed to the cosmos and everything in it. Stoic wisdom comes by assenting to those perceptions that are cataleptic in nature and refusing to assent to all others that admit of any doubt.[19] Thus, living invincibly requires a cataleptic disposition to reality.

What was at stake for the Stoics with their notion of a cataleptic impression? The Stoics could not merely have been making important practical points for ethically disposed living, as only a sage would have been capable of assenting infallibly to cataleptic impressions and no such person, we are often told, has ever existed.[20] What was at stake was theoretical 'turf', and the Academic Sceptics most notably were fighting the Stoics for that turf. While Academic Sceptics rejected the possibility of knowledge and put in its place a probability calculus for practical decision-making, the Stoics wanted to show that knowledge was possible. Stoics needed the cataleptic impression to show that.

At VII.177 of his *Lives of Eminent Philosophers*, Diogenes Laertius tells us a story that gives us some notion of the extent of this disagreement between the two schools. The Stoic Sphaerus, a disciple of Cleanthes, was staying at King Ptolemy's court in Alexandria. One day while there, the king brought in some wax pomegranates to show Sphaerus. To the king's delight, the Stoic philosopher assented to the wax replicas being pomegranates. Sphaerus, however, defended himself cleverly by replying that he had not assented to the proposition that the wax replicas were pomegranates, rather to the proposition that there was good reason to think that the wax replicas were pomegranates. Thus, he maintained that he assented correctly.[21]

Throughout their long history, the Stoics never wavered on the notions that virtue is knowledge and that the cataleptic impression, being essentially propositional, is the base of wisdom. Their model for attaining knowledge is essentially that of Aristotle.[22] Gathering together raw perceptions, people form memories; gathering together memories, they form experiences; and gathering together experiences, they finally arrive at knowledge. Assenting carefully to the simplest cataleptic impressions, a person can thus build up a store of knowledge and attain wisdom.

Epictetus relates that there is no greater task for a Stoic than to test and discriminate between impressions.[23] He adds that there are three fields of study for one progressing toward wisdom – the Stoic apprentice or progressor – and each field requires the development of reason. The first concerns desires and aversions. An apprentice aims to have his desires and aversions square with things worth desiring and avoiding. The second concerns duty (i.e., impulses to act and refrain from action), which allows an apprentice to act with good reasons and in an orderly manner. The last concerns assent. An apprentice aims to avoid rashness and error in judgments.[24] Yet one must be cautious not to confuse acts of a progressor with those of a Stoic sage. Though a progressor may often act behaviourally identical to a sage and even with identical intentions, his actions are not virtuous, as he acts from an unsettled psychical disposition.

How do impressions stir one to act? For Stoics, there are two sorts of rational mental activities. First there is thinking – an activity that has truth and not physical action as its aim. Then there is impulse – an activity that has physical activity and not truth as its aim. For physical activity, one first is stirred by an external impression, which leads to an impulse to act in a specific way. Next, the impulse to act is given rational confirmation or disconfirmation: One assents or refuses to assent to it. Overall, the process of rational confirmation or disconfirmation is a voluntary process that leads, to one of suitable psychical disposition, to correct action. The key to controlling impulses so that humans may act virtuously, Seneca warns, is to disallow vicious thoughts.[25]

VIRTUE AND INVINCIBILITY

The power and nature of the soul, Cicero writes of the Stoics, are twofold. First, there is appetite, mistakes of reasoning that lead a person any which way. Next, there is reason, which guides a person through knowledge and explains what he ought to do and to avoid doing. In one whose soul is properly disposed, reason presides and rules; appetite obeys.[26] It follows that knowledge, being stable, is the sole Stoic good; ignorance, its lack, is vice.[27]

Given the status of knowledge as the sole good, it is indispensable as a guide for appropriate human action. Thus, all actions are to be judged by three principles in accordance with reason: the obedience of impulse to reason, action directed at an object in proportion to its worth, and action with due moderation.[28]

How is an agent, upon acting, to be judged? Stoics consistently state that one is to be judged virtuous not by the effects of one's actions, but instead by one's moral worth (G., *kalon*, L., *honestum*). Moral worth, Cicero says, has these considerations. It is concerned with the full and rational perception of what is true. It is also concerned with the conservation of organized society, justice within that society, and the faithful discharge of all obligations therein assumed. Finally, he adds, it is concerned with the magnanimity, nobility, orderliness and self-control of an indomitable spirit.[29]

Overall, moral worth is measured by 'excellence' (G., *arete*), which for Stoics was deemed equivalent to knowledge. Excellence, in general, relates to the perfection of anything – such as perfection of physical attributes, like health or strength, or perfection of moral attributes, like self-control or justice. It also relates to perfection in inanimate objects. The Stoics, however, were principally interested in psychical excellence, hence the customary translation of *arete* as 'virtue'.

Not only is virtue thought to be the sole good for Stoics, it is also thought by most Stoics to be sufficient for happiness.[30]

Does virtue alone suffice for happy living? Perfect and divine as it is, why should it not suffice – better yet, why should it not over-flow? If a person has been placed beyond the reach of all desires, what can he lack? If a person has gathered into himself all this is his own, what need does he have of anything outside of himself?[31]

Virtue, as a whole, requires full possession of the particular virtues – especially prudence, justice, courage and self-control[32] – which are sought because they are goods, not for their effects. Each is com-pletely choice-worthy and admits of no change.[33] Moreover, the virtues are mutually entailing. He who has full possession of one virtue has full possession of all others, and a fully virtuous person who performs an action with one virtue performs it with all other virtues.[34] Full possession of the particular virtues is full possession of virtue itself, which is 'true and unmovable judgment'.[35] It seems likely, following Aristo, that the Stoics thought virtue is a state of the soul and the particular virtues are the actualization of the soul in particular circumstances (i.e. when it controls desire, virtue is self-control; when it acts rightly in relations with others, it is justice).[36] In contrast, foolishness, injustice, cowardice and immoderation are vices due to ignorance.

Diogenes Laertius relates that full possession of virtue requires not only equanimity, but also equanimity over a lifetime.[37] Con-sistent with that, some Stoics believe that virtue, once attained, cannot be lost. Others disagree.[38] Yet all acknowledge that a key to becoming virtuous is inflexibility of character. Wisdom is a matter of always desiring the same things and always shunning the same things. What a virtuous person desires should be good, since no one can always to be satisfied with the same thing, unless it is good, and what is good does not change.[39]

Once wise, a Stoic possesses virtue fully and to the same extent as all others.

The power and greatness of virtue cannot rise to greater heights, as increase is denied to what is superlatively great. You will find nothing straighter than the straight, nothing truer than the truth, and nothing more self-controlled than what is self-controlled. Every virtue is limitless [*sine modo*], as limit is a definite measurement. Constancy cannot advance any more than fidelity, truthfulness, or loyalty. What can be added to what is perfect? Nothing, otherwise that to which something was added was not perfect. Nothing can be added to virtue either, since if anything can be added to it, it must be defective . . . The ability to increase is a sign that a thing is imperfect.[40]

Though virtue, fully possessed, cannot be increased or diminished, Stoics did believe that it can be expanded. The scale of one's virtuous actions can always be made larger or smaller, depending on circumstances.[41]

In summary, the happiness of a Stoic sage is complete, perfect and without reproach. Cicero in his *Tusculan Disputations* says that a Stoic sage does nothing against his will, but always acts honourably, consistently, seriously and rightly. Nothing shocks him, as he fears nothing and is prepared for everything. He sums:

[T]he Stoics . . . perceive the final good to be agreement with nature and living consistently with nature, which is not only a sage's settled duty [*officium*], but it is also in his power [*in potestate*]. It follows that the greatest good is in the power of the person whose happiness is in his power. Therefore, a sage's life is always happy.[42]

In stark contrast to sages are non-sages, who come in all shapes and sizes, as it were, though they have vice in common. Strangely, the Stoics thought that failure to possess virtue fully is to be vicious and that each vicious person is equally vicious, regardless of how near to or far from virtue one might be. Virtue and vice admit of no degrees. That, of course, differs from the view of Aristotle and his Peripatetic disciples.

It is the Stoics' tenet that there is nothing between virtue and vice, whereas for the Peripatetics, there is the state of moral improvement [*prokope*]. The Stoics say just as a stick must be either straight or crooked, so a man must be either just or unjust. Again, there are no degrees of justice or injustice, and the same applies for the other virtues.[43]

Plutarch (c. AD 45–120), a philosopher and chronicler of Greek and Roman lives, offers helpful analogies. A person in the sea, not more than an arm's length from the surface of the water, may be drowning every bit as much as another 500 fathoms under the sea. Again, one who is blind is still blind, even though he may recover his sight later. Likewise, one close to virtue is no less in a state of vice than one far from it, and he remains foolish and vicious right up to the time that he attains virtue.[44]

These paradoxical propositions – that sagacity is a state of psychic perfection and that all other states are equally imperfect and vicious – had their detractors in antiquity. Plutarch was one.[45] Cicero was another, and he offered analogies of his own in an effort to show the mistakes of the Stoics. When physicians apply remedies to people with poor eyesight or poor health, their defect gets better each day. We say that they progress, and progress is a matter of getting closer to good health. Strangely, Stoic teachers acknowledge progress towards virtue, but they deny diminution of vice on the way to virtue. While closer to virtue, they are somehow no less vicious than they were before, and that is absurd.[46] Progress toward virtue without diminution of vice is certainly a strange sort of progress. Still, however queer their notion of progress was, the Stoics did hold on to it, for they needed to show how the leap from non-virtuous to virtuous could be something up to each person and not something arbitrary or due to nature.[47]

What distinguishes a Stoic sage from a progressor? Both a sage and a progressor are capable of doing the right sort of moral action – what the Stoics called an 'appropriate act' (L., officium, G., kathekon). Cicero states: 'Now an appropriate act is an act so performed that a reasonable account can be rendered of its performance.' It is, he adds, neither a good nor a bad thing, but rather something intermediate.[48] However, only a Stoic sage is capable of grasping that his action is not only appropriate, but completely correct. Such perfect activity, done with full knowledge of its perfection, is called a 'right act' (L., recte factum, G., katorthoma or teleion kathekon).

We notice that something exists which we call 'right action'. This is an appropriate act performed perfectly [*perfectum officium*]. Still, there will be an imperfect appropriate act [*inchoatum*]. Thus, if *to restore a trust as a matter of principle* is a right act, *to restore a trust* must be counted as an appropriate act. The addition of the qualification 'on principle' makes it a right action. The restitution in itself is counted as an appropriate act.[49]

The Stoic Panaetius adds, Cicero tells us, that a Stoic sage's virtue is also maximally and perfectly expeditious. Whatever is morally right (*honestum*) is expedient (*utile*) and whatever is not expedient is not morally right.[50] More than that, the relationship between actions that are morally right and those that are expedient, when each of these is grasped rightly, seems to be biconditional: all right actions are expedient and all expedient actions are right.

How does one become fully virtuous, insofar as full virtue is attainable? Seneca offers this advice.

> An action will not be right, unless the will is right, for that is the source of action. Again, the will cannot be right, unless the attitude of mind is right, for that is the source of the will. Moreover, such an attitude of mind will not be found even in the best of persons, unless that person has learned the laws of life as a whole and has worked out a proper judgment about everything and unless he has reduced everything to [the standard of] truth. Equanimity is enjoyed only by those who have attained a fixed and unchanging standard of judgment. The rest of mankind – afloat in a condition where they alternately reject things and seek them – continually ebb and flow in their decisions.[51]

Overall, the happiness of a Stoic sage is a result of perfect equanimity by means of complete integration – personally, locally and cosmically – through self-knowledge, fulfilling one's capacities and living according to providence (i.e. in agreement with cosmic nature). A Stoic sage is free of the disturbances of emotion and in full compliance with what providence has in store for him. In such freedom from emotional disturbance and full compliance, he knows precisely what is his own and what providence forbids him.[52] We may call this the 'Perfectionist Thesis' and state it as an ideal for a Stoic initiate:

Perfectionist Thesis: The proper end for a Stoic initiate is to live a life completely free of emotion[53] and in full awareness of what is and what is not one's own.

What binds virtue-driven persons to providence is what both persons and deity share – reason. Complete invincibility, on this account, is complete rational integration – complete accord with what deity has preordained. As Aurelius sums:

> It is characteristic of a good person to delight in and welcome what happens to him and what is spun for him by destiny, and not to contaminate the divine that sits in him or confuse it with an abundance of impressions. A good person, uttering no word that is untrue and doing no deed that is not just, maintains his divine element to the end in a gracious serenity and in orderly obedience to deity.[54]

NO PLACE TO SHIT: THE GOOD AND 'CONVENIENCES'

The Stoics were inescapable naturalists: Their notion of good could not be divorced from some conception of nature. As they were fond of saying, what is good is in agreement with nature. Seneca, however, tells us that there is more to the story than that.

> Attend to what I say: 'What is good is in agreement with nature, but what is according to nature does not also become immediately good.' Many things harmonize with nature, but are so trifling that it is not suitable to call them 'good'. They are trivial and ought to be despised. Still there is no such thing as an insignificant and despicable good, for if it is insignificant, it is not good, and if it begins to be good, it ceases to be insignificant.[55]

What are the trifles that agree with nature, but are not 'goods'? Diogenes Laertius relates that 'good' generically grasped is 'that from which some advantage comes'. He adds, virtue itself or whatever partakes of virtue is good in three ways: being a source from which benefit results (i.e., virtue itself), being an action that results in benefit, and being a particular agent who participates in virtue. Specifically, 'good' for man is 'the active exercise of his soul's rational faculties in conformity with virtue'.[56]

Aristotle says that the number of 'goods' are three: external goods

Table 2. Aristotle's Three Types of People

	Complete Virtue	Incomplete Virtue
Complete Stock of Other Goods	Happy	Miserable
Incomplete Stock of Other Goods	Neither Happy Nor Miserable	Miserable

(e.g. wealth and fame), bodily goods (e.g. health and beauty) and psychical goods (e.g. courage and justice). The perfectly happy person has the right admixture of each of these goods. First and most significantly, he is fully virtuous. That entails that he has a correct and full amount of each particular virtue.[57] Secondly, he has the needed complement of lesser goods – bodily and external goods – though these goods are not needed in abundance.[58] As such, he can be shaken from happiness, if he falls into gross misfortune through loss of external or bodily goods at some point in his life. Though he will not be happy, such a fall, however, will not make him miserable. Only a fall from virtue could do that.[59] Thus, for Aristotle, the different types of goods make for three types of people: those happy, those miserable and those neither happy nor miserable (see Table 2).

The Stoic attitude toward 'goods' is different, if not radically different. For Stoics, virtue is the sole good[60] and it consists of a life in accordance with nature.

> The greatest good [*summum bonum*] consists in applying knowledge of the working of natural causes to the conduct of life, in choosing what is in accordance with nature, and in rejecting what is contrary to it. In other words, the greatest good is to live in agreement and in harmony with nature.[61]

Living in complete agreement with nature – that is, being in possession of the greatest good, virtue, suffices for happiness. External and bodily benefits, since they do nothing to make the mind better, are not goods.[62] Why should that be? Seneca elaborates, 'We deem nothing as good that someone can put to wrong use.'[63] For Stoics, then, a sage may be called 'miserable', but he can never really be anything but happy.

Though Stoics did not consider external and bodily benefits to be goods, they did not consider them valueless. These were labelled 'things preferred' (G., *proegmena*) or 'conveniences' (L., *commoda*[64]). Seneca says, 'Bodily goods are indeed good for the body, but they are not good categorically. They will have some value, however they will not have merit. They will differ significantly among themselves – some will be lesser, others will be greater.'[65] Thus, conveniences, like bodily goods, have value that is not fixed and absolute, like the virtues, and that is proof sufficient for Stoics that they are not goods.

In contrast to Aristotle, for Stoics, given their adherence to the sufficiency thesis, there are merely two types of people: those happy and those miserable (Table 3).

Table 3. Stoics' Two Types of People

	Complete Virtue	Incomplete Virtue
Complete Complement Other Goods	Happy	Miserable
	Happy	Miserable
Incomplete Stock of Other Goods		

Why is it that nothing affects a person's happiness in the least other than virtue? Cicero offers a Stoic argument, in which bodily 'goods' are added to psychical goods to illustrate.

> If wisdom and health are both desirable as goods, a combination of the two would be more desirable than wisdom alone. Yet it is not true that, if both are deemed valuable, then their conjunction [i.e., wisdom plus wealth] is more valuable than wisdom by itself. We Stoics deem health as deserving of a certain value, but we do not reckon it as a good. At the same time, we rate nothing so valuable that it can be put before virtue.[66]

Moreover, virtue's value annihilates the value of any mere convenience, just as the sun overpowers a lit lamp and a drop of honey is drowned by the Aegean Sea.[67] Furthermore, if something is good, it must be an unqualified good, yet when it comes to non-internal 'goods', one could easily have too much of a good thing, so to speak.

In addition, indifferents can be put to good or bad use. For instance, wealth or even health in the possession of an incurably vicious person does neither that person nor any other person he encounters good.[68] Finally, true goods are complete and cannot, like health or wealth, be made better (or worse) by increase.[69] Aurelius makes the same point in a somewhat vulgar manner: We should never value all such things 'whose abundance leaves their owner with no place to shit'.[70]

CANONICAL STOIC VIEW OF INDIFFERENTS

Overall, the Stoics' point is that all such things that do not have an internal origin are things that are not up to us. All such things, whether they are conveniences, like health and wealth, or inconveniences, like illness and penury, are indifferents.

Diogenes Laertius relates that 'indifferent' (*adiaphoron*) has two distinct meanings. First, there is a trivial sense of 'indifferent'. One is indifferent to the exact number of hairs on one's head, for instance, because that number ought not to lead anyone towards any sort of impulse for action. Second, there is a non-trivial sense of 'indifferent'. One is indifferent to health, for instance, because health does not contribute to one's virtue or happiness, but concern for health does activate an impulse to act. Examples of preferred indifferents include health, pleasure, beauty, strength, wealth, reputation, good birth and life. Indifferents are dispreferred, when they, contributing neither to happiness nor unhappiness, activate repulsion. Examples include disease, pain, ugliness, weakness, poverty, low repute, bad birth and death.[71]

Cicero tells us that Zeno's terms for the two indifferents were *proegmenon* (preferred) and *apoproegmenon* (dispreferred) respectively.[72] He explains:

In a royal court, Zeno says, no one speaks of the king himself as 'promoted' to honour, for that is the meaning of *proegmenon*, but the term is applied to those holding some office of state whose rank most nearly approaches, though it is second to, the royal pre-eminence. Similarly, in the conduct of life, the title *proegmenon* – that is, 'promoted' – is to be given not to those things that are of the first rank, but to those that hold the second place. For these, we may use either the term suggested, for that will be a literal translation. We may also use 'advanced' [*promota*] and 'degraded' [*remota*], or the term we have been using all along, 'preferred' [*praeposita*] or 'superior' [*praecipua*]. For the opposite, we may use 'rejected' [*reiecta*] . . . But since we state that everything that is good occupies the first rank, it follows that what we call 'preferred' or 'superior' is neither good nor ill. Accordingly, we define it as being indifferent but possessed of a moderate value, as it has occurred to me that I may use the word *indifferens* to represent the term *adiaphoron*.[73]

Seneca says that preferred indifferents – which I shall hereafter call 'conveniences', because they not at all impact one's happiness, though they make one's life easier – are not 'goods' because they are not the result of reason, but of opinion, and are not in our power. Being external to us, they are not up to us, but rather due to fortune.[74] Something is 'indifferent', then, when it is neither good nor ill – such as wellness, pleasure, wealth, fellowship, life and their contraries. None of those things is intrinsically magnificent, but one must recognize that there is nothing magnificent without them. One does not praise poverty, he adds, but the man whom poverty cannot bend or cower.[75]

Though they are not goods, conveniences are still choice-worthy. Seneca adds, 'Should I have a choice, I would choose health and strength, but the good involved would be my judgment about such things and not the things themselves.'[76] This indicates starkly that what is up to one is not the actual having of certain conveniences or the not having of certain inconveniences, but rather one's mental disposition toward them. One cannot control fate, but one can control one's mental disposition toward it.

Overall, as Seneca's use of *media* to describe indifferents indicates, they lie somewhere between virtue and vice. They exist, in a manner of speaking, as the matter for virtuous activity.[77] In *On Ends*, Cicero calls them the 'primary things of nature' (*prima naturae*).[78] A virtuous person, like any other, must act on these primary things. The way he acts in some sense shows his virtue.

What is in itself in agreement with nature or what produces something else that is in agreement with nature and is deserving of choice, because it possesses a certain amount of value, the Stoics call it *axian*, and declare that it is 'valuable' [*aestimatione*]. Its contrary is declared 'invaluable' [*inaestimabile*], because it is contrary to what is superior. The initial principle is established thus: Things in agreement with nature are 'things to be taken for their own sake' and their opposites, similarly, 'things to be rejected'. The first 'appropriate act' [*officium*] – as I translate *kathekon* – is to preserve oneself in one's natural constitution. The next is to retain those things that are in accordance with nature and to repel those that are not. Then when the principle of choice and avoidance has been discovered, there follows next in order, choice conditioned by 'appropriate action', then such choice as a fixed habit, and finally choice fully rationalized and in harmony with nature.[79]

On Ends III.vi.20 is a very dense passage, about which I shall have more to say shortly. For now, let us chiefly note that the model is developmental.

How is one to grasp the correct Stoic attitude toward indifferents? Epictetus offers a helpful analogy of playing with dice. When one plays with dice, one cannot control the faces on the dice, once thrown, but one can control how one responds to the faces on the dice, once motionless. With indifferents, since they are externals, it is the same. One cannot control them, but one can control one's attitude toward them, since moral judgment (G., *prohairesis*) is fully under one's control and most completely one's own. Thus, good and ill are entirely within one's control; good and ill are entirely one's own. Yet, he cautions, one ought never to use the words 'good' or 'evil', 'benefit' or 'injury', or similar words about what is another's.[80]

Goods that are under the governance of reason, Seneca says, relate to the exercise of virtue and are of two types. The first type, relating to the exercise of specific virtues upon the having of certain conveniences (e.g. the right show of cheer after victory), 'governs the indulgences of Fortune'. The second type, relating to the exercise of virtues upon the having of certain inconveniences (e.g. equanimity in the face of adversity), 'subdues Fortune's impetuosity'.[81] The having of inconveniences, he often stresses, allows for a greater display of one's virtues.[82]

While the having of some indifferents is convenient and the having of others is inconvenient, by activating impulse, a sage does not literally seek out conveniences and shun inconveniences from the full stock of those indifferents accessible to him, as he took himself to be doing when his rational faculties were in the process of developing. Once fully rational and self-sufficient, a Stoic merely takes what fortune gives and lives to the best of his ability under existing circumstances. He accepts gratefully those blessings he is awarded at any particular time. He resigns himself and strives to endure the misfortunes that befall him.

Thus, conveniences for Stoic sages have some 'selective value', though they are not valued as ends. 'Selective' here implies only inner impulse and choosing, not physical activity directed towards conveniences in the manner that one could have *acted* otherwise. For Stoics what is up to each person is not activity towards indifferents, but his mental disposition towards them. That is chiefly what the Stoics mean by *prohairesis.*

Overall, indifferents were a problem for the Stoics. They had a queer status. On the one hand, they were said to contribute nothing to the happiness of a virtuous person, but were still worthy of selection or avoidance. That made them seem like lesser goods of an Aristotelian sort – a view the Stoics disallowed. On the other hand, all indifferents were said to be equally indifferent insofar as none could have any direct impact on one's virtue. The Stoic Aristo, a maverick pupil of Zeno, took that to its logical conclusion by positing that all indifferents had precisely the same status: Wealth was no more worth choosing than poverty; poor health was no more worth avoiding than good health. For Aristo, virtue was just a matter of complete indifference to indifferents.[83] Antiochus, a critic of the Stoics, argued that the Stoic view was actually a middle position between Aristotle and Aristo and that such a position was untenable. I sketch out a different view of indifferents in the second chapter.

LIVING IN AGREEMENT WITH NATURE

For the Greek Stoics Zeno, Cleanthes, Chrysippus, Posidonius and Hecato, the aim of life was to live in agreement with nature, which was to live virtuously.[84] Chrysippus added that living virtuously was 'living in accordance with our experience of what happens by nature', as our individual natures are parts of the nature of the whole universe. Diogenes Laertius says:

> This is why the end may be defined as 'life following nature' or, again, 'in agreement with our own human nature as well as that of the universe'. In such a life, we refrain from every action

forbidden by the law common to all things – that is, by right reason that both pervades all things and is identical with Zeus, lord and ruler of all that is.[85]

For the Stoic Cleanthes, Diogenes adds, universal nature alone was the appropriate guide to virtue.[86]

Overall, there was general agreement among the Stoics that the primary human impulse, dictated by nature, was self-preservation. Chrysippus states, 'The dearest thing [*oikeion*] to every animal is its own constitution and its consciousness of it.'[87] Seneca writes:

> Each animal at the same time consults its own safety, seeks what helps it, and shrinks from what will harm it. Impulses towards useful objects and revulsion from the opposite are according to nature. Without any reflection to prompt the idea and without any advice, whatever nature has prescribed is done.[88]

Zeno, Cleanthes and Posidonius add that the end of human life is living in agreement with both the nature of the cosmos and our own human nature, which inclines us, upon rational maturity, toward virtuous activity.[89]

Toward what does a life in agreement with nature incline people? Seneca says that virtue, nature's end, entails contemplation of things and action.[90] Nonetheless, virtuous activity has a humble origin in self-directed activity, as self-love and self-preservation are immediate impulses for Stoics. I return to *On Ends*, where Cicero's Stoic spokesman, Marcus Cato, says:

> It is the view of the Stoics . . . that immediately upon birth . . . a living creature feels an attachment for itself and an impulse to preserve itself. It feels affection for its own constitution and for those things that tend to preserve that constitution. On the other hand, it feels an antipathy to destruction and to those things that appear to threaten destruction.

As proof, Stoics appeal to infants, whose actions show that they pursue self-preservation and reject self-destruction, prior to pleasure or pain. Thus, infants have self-affection and self-consciousness. Therefore, self-love, not pleasure, is the primary impulse to action.[91]

What rouses the social impulse is more complex. Cicero tells us that for Stoics nature creates parental affection for their children, and parental affection is the foundation of communal living. From the impulse of parental affection, there springs the mutual attraction that unites all human beings. In such a manner, people are by nature fitted to form unions, societies and states.[92] Overall, the developmental picture goes something like this: Self-affection branches out into mutual affection and friendship with others, which develops into a sense of patriotism, of care for posterity, and even of fit into the cosmos itself.[93] Here Aristotle's political animal has become cosmic.

Chrysippus suggests that this late-budding sense of other-concern is just the maturation of our rational faculties, recognizing a code of law that unites all human beings. Whoever upholds this code is deemed just; whoever departs from it, unjust.[94] Seneca states that this code of law has its base in nature:

> Nature produced us as kinsmen, as she created us from the same source and for the same end. She engendered in us mutual affection and made us prone to friendships. She established fairness and justice. By her ruling, it is more wretched to commit, than to suffer, injury . . . Let us possess things in common, for birth is ours in common. Our relations with one another are like a stone arch that would collapse, if the stones did not mutually support each other and that is upheld in this very manner.[95]

It is thus recognition of natural law, upon the maturation of humans' rational faculties, which enables humans to have a fuller, cosmic sense of justice.

Nature has a hand in moral progress too. It guides each person to virtue through proper assent, as a good and excellent person orders his impressions according to nature.

> The function of one who is good and excellent [*kalou kai agathou*] is to deal with his impressions in accordance with nature. Just as it is the nature of every soul to assent to the true, dissent to the false, and withhold judgment in matters of uncertainty, so also it is the nature of every soul to be moved by desire toward the good and by aversion toward the evil, and to feel neutral toward what is neither good nor evil.[96]

It is clear from this that Stoics speak of 'nature' both normatively and descriptively. Normatively, they speak of 'nature' as an anthropological and a cosmological regulative force. The ambiguity is captured in two senses of Stoic naturalism in today's literature – cosmological and anthropological naturalism.

Cosmological naturalists appeal to cosmic reason to ground human ethical behaviour.[97] Humans, developing as individuals prior to full rationality, begin by choosing what is natural and advantageous for themselves considered as self-interested beings – conveniences – and end by choosing what is natural and advantageous for themselves considered as complete rational beings – virtue. Thus, living in agreement with nature is seeing oneself as an indivisible part of the cosmic whole, of deity, and acting in strict obedience to the dictates of cosmic law as a moral imperative relating to what is divine and eternal. Epictetus says:

> Instruction consists precisely in learning to desire things exactly as they happen. And how do they happen? They happen as he who ordains them has ordained . . . Mindful of this ordaining, we should go to receive instruction not in order to change the constitution of things – for that is neither vouchsafed us nor is it better that it should be – but in order that, things about us being as they are and as their nature is, we may, for our own part, keep our wills in harmony with what happens.[98]

Anthropological naturalists, drawing chiefly from Cicero's *On Ends* III, maintain that human nature does not surrender itself to cosmic fate when one becomes fully rational. Once rational, self-interest may become subordinate to divine prescription, but that does not entail abandonment of self-interest. Living in agreement with nature here is a matter of committing to a rational lifestyle, characterized by regard for consistency in thought and action. Ethical principles are universal insofar as they are dialectically driven by human discussion of and agreement on first principles; they are not universal because of a cosmic foundation.[99]

Hereafter, I sketch a view of cosmological naturalism that reconciles self-regarding activity with the cosmic demand for Stoic detachment. We shall see that following nature requires not detachment or indifference, but complete cosmic integration. Following the *oikeiotic* principle, it is a matter of knowing precisely what things are and what things are not one's own.

HOMOLOGIA: GROWING TOWARD THE GOOD

To make sense of Stoic naturalism, one has to have some story to tell, and a convincing one, about how humans go from beings who are pre-eminently preoccupied with self-preservation, to beings whose rational element predominates and has such regard for other- and cosmic-concern that it may even subordinate the self-preservative instinct to a cosmic ideal. What is most unusual about this story is that, for infants, the preservation of one's life is an all-consuming, in-accordance-with-nature drive, while for virtue-embracing adults the drive for self-preservation takes a back seat to a newly found cosmic awareness of one's duty. The story is this. Virtue-cultivating rationality, during human maturation, takes one from a local and selfish perspective of appropriate action that involves only acting on conveniences for self-preservation, which is all that a youth can manage, to a global perspective of appropriate action that involves acting virtuously, which requires the right amount of other-concern and a cosmological perspective. Rational maturation is a shift from 'recognition' of a duty to preserve oneself at all costs to recognition of a duty to act with full expression of excellence as cosmic awareness.

To grasp the enigma, we must study Nature as it plays itself out locally and cosmically. (Hereafter, I adopt the convention of distinguishing nature as a cosmologically regulative force by 'Nature' and nature as a locally regulative force (e.g. human nature) by 'nature'.) Seneca tells Lucillius that virtue begins locally, by examining one's own nature.

> When I seek the reason why Nature brought forth humans and why she set them above other animals, do you, Lucillius, suppose that I have left the study of character behind? Of course not. How are you to know what character is desirable, unless you have discovered what is best-suited for humans or you have studied human nature? You can find out what you should do and what you should avoid, only when you have learned what you owe to your nature.[100]

Seneca writes that Nature's gifts to us are immediate and instinctual. All animals come into the world with an immediate understanding of how to use their body. They manifest this knowledge slowly, but persistently, even when they are obviously in pain. One observes that in the case of children, who try for the first time to stand. They test their weight, then fall, and with tear-filled eyes they test their weight again. Such instinctual restlessness is a gift of Nature.[101]

An immediate grasp of how to use one's body is an instance of the first and most primitive instinct – self-regard. Infants, Seneca acknowledges, seek pleasure and shrink from pain, and they do each because of self-regard. They know what is harmful and they shrink from it in an effort to cling to life. Self-regard is not acquired from experience, however. It is inborn, not learned.[102]

> Each animal, instinctively consults its own safety, seeks what benefits it [*iuvantia*[103]], and shrinks from what will harm it. Impulses toward useful objects and revulsions toward their opposites are in agreement with Nature. Without any reflection to prompt the notion and without any advice, whatever Nature prescribes is done.

One has only to consider bees, building their cells, or spiders, constructing their intricate and delicate webs. Thus, animals too and even plants are capable of action in agreement with Nature or appropriate action. 'Since Nature has communicated to each nothing but the duty of caring for itself and the skill to do so, learning and living begin at the same time.'[104]

How do infants go from self-preoccupation, which is purely ego-oriented, to rationality, which in extreme circumstances seems to work against self-preservation and even countenances suicide?

Seneca's answer is, in part, that humans always possess some form of rationality – even in infancy, where it is inchoate. The self-preservative instinct is knowledge that is inscribed on the souls of humans, though knowledge of which no child is consciously aware. Children know their own nature, though not as 'cradle-bound logicians'. For instance, they cannot have a grasp of the definition of their constitution, though their every action speaks of an intimate acquaintance with it. How that is so is inexplicable, Seneca says, but is graspable by way of analogy. Though no one knows the nature, place, quality or source of the human soul, each knows that he is with soul.[105] Consequently, the base for conscious rational reflection exists inchoately in childhood and it provides a platform for subsequent rational development.

Yet that is merely part of the answer – a very small part. It fails to disclose how and why humans go from a natural inclination to act selfishly, regardless of circumstances, to a natural inclination towards optimizing virtuous activity, which may even countenance the taking of one's life in extreme circumstances.

In agreement with Aristotle, for Stoics, virtue can only be housed in a fully mature, fully functioning human specimen, which rules out children, whose rational faculty is underdeveloped. 'Just as Nature in general does not produce her good, unless she is brought to completion, so too the human good is not in a person (i.e. not fully in a person), unless reason has been perfected in that person.'[106] However, that is where agreement ends. For Aristotle, practical excellence is unique to humans and foreign to gods, though humans share contemplative activity (*theoria*), void of practical consequences, with the gods. For the Stoics, it is otherwise. The universe, of which humans are a part, is itself a divine and rational animal, and the best human life is one that emulates divine activity, which acts always in the most rational manner. For Stoics, the aim of human activity literally is to be like god. Just how that process of divine emulation occurs is a matter of what it means to act in *complete* agreement with Nature.

What is valuable, Stoics believe, is what is in agreement with Nature or what produces something in agreement with Nature. Thus, one's first duty is to preserve oneself and to act thus is to act appropriately. So far, that is just what humans share with other animals, even plants. We need now to move toward what humans share with the gods. I return to Cicero's *On Ends*, where he outlines five steps for progress toward virtue.[107]

What is in itself in agreement with Nature or what produces something else that is in agreement with Nature and is deserving of choice, because it possesses a certain amount of value, the Stoics call it *axian*, and declare that it is 'valuable' [*aestimatione*]. Its contrary is declared to be 'invaluable' [*inaestimabile*], because it is contrary to what is superior. The initial principle is established thus: Things in agreement with nature are 'things to be taken for their own sake' and their opposites, similarly, 'things to be rejected'. The first 'appropriate act' [*officium*] – as I translate *kathekon* – is (1) *to preserve oneself in one's natural constitution.* The next is (2) *to retain those things that are in accordance with Nature and to repel those that are not.* Then when the principle of

41

choice and avoidance has been discovered, there follows next in order, (3) *choice conditioned by 'appropriate action'*, then (4) *such choice as a fixed habit*, and finally (5) *choice fully rationalized and in harmony with Nature*. It is at this final stage that the Good properly so-called first emerges and comes to be understood in its true nature.[108]

Let us tease out the developmental process here. First, humans begin, as do other living things, with the instinct of self-preservation. They soon come to value all such things that are in agreement with Nature, and avoid all such things that are contrary to Nature, and they pattern their actions, through choice, thus. Next, progressors learn to choose by considering what is appropriate. Continued choice becomes fixed habit to do what is right – to act appropriately. Appropriate action[109] (G., *kathekon*, L., *officium*) does not imply that one's actions must have the right outcome, but only that one's actions must be properly motivated. Purity of intention is everything. Cicero gives the example of spear-throwing. One's purpose is to have true aim. It is desirable, not necessary, to hit the target.[110] When habit harmonizes perfectly with reason and duty, there is *homologia* – conformity or complete integration with divine or cosmic design. *Homologia* is sagacity. As intention is perfectly in keeping with cosmic intention, action and outcome converge and all of one's actions now, as it were, hit the mark, because all of one's intentions are perfectly virtuous.

Diogenes Laertius says that action based on *kathekon* is action in agreement with Nature – prompted by reason toward one's true end. He states that there are three types of acts: appropriate acts, inappropriate acts and acts neither appropriate nor inappropriate.

Of the acts done at the prompting of impulse, some . . . are fit and right; others, the opposite; while there is a third class that is neither the one nor the other. (1) Appropriate acts [*kathekonta*] are all those that reason prevails on us to do. This is the case with honouring one's parents, brothers, and country, and intercourse with friends. (2) Inappropriate [*para to kathekon*] are all acts that reason forbids – that is, to neglect one's parents, to be indifferent to one's brothers, not to agree with friends, to disregard the interests of one's country, and similar things. (3) Acts that fall under neither of the classes above are those that reason neither urges us to do nor forbids, such as picking up a twig, holding a style or a scraper, and similar things.[111]

Moreover, some appropriate acts – concern for health and sensory organs – are unconditionally prevailing, while others – maiming oneself and sacrifice of property – are merely conditionally prevailing. Additionally, there are duties always prevailing, such as regard for virtue, and those that are not always prevailing, such as the practise of dialectic or walking for improved health.[112]

Whereas we are duty-driven or act appropriately when we choose self-love and those things in agreement with Nature, to do so on account of virtue is to engage in 'right actions' or absolute duty (L., *recta facta*, G., *katorthomata*). Cicero explains through a distinction between mean duty and absolute duty:

> We distinguish between so-called 'mean appropriate act' [*medium officium*] and 'perfect appropriate act' [*perfectum officium*]. A perfect appropriate act we may presumably call 'right' [*rectum*], for the Greeks call it *katorthoma*, while the mean appropriate act they call *kathekon*. The meaning of those terms they fix thus: Whatever is right duty they define as 'perfect appropriate act', but 'mean appropriate act', they say, is duty for the performance of which an adequate reason may be given.[113]

Cicero says that the moral worth of a sage is its own reward, whereas appropriate acts are done for the sake of the primary things of Nature – attaining conveniences.

> Nevertheless, moral worth [*honestum*] is the sole thing that is desirable for its own worth and value, whereas none of the primary objects [*prima naturae*] of nature is desirable for its own sake. Yet since those actions that I have termed 'appropriate acts' are based on the primary natural objects [*initiis naturae*], it follows that the former are means to the latter. So, it may correctly be said that all appropriate acts are means to the end of attaining the primary things of Nature.[114]

In such a manner, mean appropriate acts differ from right acts or perfect appropriate acts in that only the latter are done because of virtue and in accordance with right reason. Right acts are acts

Table 4. Stoic Character and Intentionality

	Sage	Progressor	Wicked Person
Right-Intended Act	Perfect Appropriate Act (virtue; always)	Mean Appropriate Act (vice; frequent)	Inappropriate Act (vice; infrequent)
	IMPOSSIBLE SCENARIO FOR SAGE	Inappropriate Act	(vice; frequent)
Wrong-Intended Act		Inappropriate Act (vice; infrequent)	

performed only by a Stoic sage. The former, being performed by one who is less than fully virtuous, are strictly speaking vicious actions. Table 4 is offered as an illustration.

As Table 4 shows, only perfect appropriate acts, performed by sages, are virtuous acts, as mean appropriate acts are performed by persons aspiring to virtue. Thus, a mean appropriate act, to all intents and purposes for the Stoics, differs not at all from an inappropriate act performed by one who is wicked, as all acts that are not right are vicious acts. Moreover, there is no room here for what Diogenes Laertius labels 'acts that are neither appropriate nor inappropriate', as even picking up a twig for a sage would have to be a virtuous act, and the same act for someone who is not a sage would have to be vicious.

If all of a progressor's actions are just as vicious as those of a wicked person, how then does progress toward virtue occur? Cicero outlines the intellectual maturation that occurs with the five steps for progress toward virtue.

A man's first attachment [*conciliatio*] is toward the things in accordance with Nature. Yet as soon as he acquires understanding or rather, perhaps, the capacity to form concepts [*notio*], what the Stoics call *ennoia*, and sees the order and as it were the harmony of actions, he values those things far more highly than those earlier objects of his love. He concludes by thought and reason that this is the greatest good of a person – what is praiseworthy and desirable for its own sake. That consists in what the Stoics call *homologia* and we may call 'agreement' [*convenientia*] with order and harmony. In *homologia* resides that good to which everything must be referred – morally worthwhile actions and moral worth – the last of which alone is counted among good things, though of a later development.[115]

As a progressor develops a sufficiently large base of concepts, he comes to see cosmic harmony as conformity of one's thoughts and actions with the Good and the divine cosmos as a whole. Such a large, cosmic perspective also convinces him that sometimes choices that may have once seemed to be ill-suited to him, from the provincial perspective of one's own nature viewed apart from the cosmos – for example, pain or self-sacrifice – are often precisely those things that are most in keeping with cosmic order and divine preordination.

> If you see yourself as a thing detached, it is natural for you to live to old age, be wealthy, and be healthy. But if you see yourself as a human being and as a part of some whole, then for the sake of that whole it is appropriate for you now to be sick, now to set sail and take risks, now to be in need, and now maybe even to die before your time. Why then are you upset?[116]

Having one's reason accord with the cosmic flow of events is *homologia*. That is just how a progressor goes from the natural instinct of self-love to virtue-love by the exercise of reason and choice. *Homologia*, then, implies not cosmic indifference, but complete cosmic immersion or integration.

FATE AND THE 'LAZY ARGUMENT'

As we have seen, the Stoic cosmos was thought to be a self-contained, completely deterministic system in which all events were preordained through the providential planning of Zeus. Seneca writes: 'Everything proceeds according to law, fixed and enacted for all time. Fate guides us and the length of time each has was settled at the first hour of birth. Cause is linked with cause and all public and private issues are directed by a long sequence of events.'[117] The long sequence of events, linking all things causally, leaves no room for anything but a trivial sense of human agency, where the best one can do is fix one's mind to assent to events as they must play themselves out according to Zeus' preordination. 'A good man . . . must have the highest piety toward the gods. Hence, he will endure with an unruffled soul whatever happens to him, as he will know that it has happened as a result of divine law by which everything in the universe advances [*procedunt*].'[118]

One troubling consequence of Stoic fatalism is culpability. If cause is linked with cause and all events are fated, then why is one responsible for anything one does? Diogenes Laertius illustrates the problem by relating an amusing story of Zeno's slave, who cunningly said, as he was about to be whipped for stealing, that his stealing was fated. Zeno replied baldly that the whipping too was fated and went on to whip the slave.[119]

Critics were fully aware of this difficulty, expressed neatly in what is called the 'lazy argument' (*argos logos*). Summarily expressed as a hypothetical syllogism:

1 If it is your fate to recover from this illness, you will recover, regardless of whether or not you call a doctor.
2 If it is your fate not to recover from this illness, you will not recover, regardless of whether or not you call a doctor.
3 One or the other is your fate.
4 Therefore, it is pointless to call a doctor.[120]

The Stoic Chrysippus attempted a refutation of the lazy argument. Assent, according to Chrysippus, requires an antecedent impression (*visum*) as a proximate cause, but that is not its principal cause. The principal cause is within the agent. He uses the examples of a roller and a top. Each needs a proximate cause to begin motion, but once moving, both move of their own nature, which is their principal cause. With a person, the beginning of a movement requires sense impressions, but they are not the cause of his capacity for movement.[121] Chrysippus' strategy seems to be in part that we are somehow responsible for our actions and the type of nature that we have. Just as a well-fashioned roller will roll smoothly and for a long time over the right surface, given the right impetus, thus will a virtuous person assent to and act in the right, most efficient manner in a given set of circumstances.[122] What Chrysippus suggests perhaps is a type of cosmic fatalism, without strict determinism. Put simply, one cannot avoid one's end, though there are many paths one can take to arrive at one's end.[123]

The analogy, I think, should not be taken thus. Chrysippus' argument is that, as a push is needed for a roller's roll, so too is an antecedent impression needed for assent. He makes no mention of subsequent action. What is implicit here is that rollers roll due to their nature, given a proximate cause, and that people assent or withhold assent due to their nature, given a proximate cause. It is the nature of the good roller to roll well and a bad roller to roll poorly; it is the nature of a sage to assent only in the right conditions and a non-sage to have a subjective or arbitrary sense of assent. The focus is not on physical activity, but on assent, which is somehow seen by Chrysippus and probably most other Stoics to be outside of the chain of necessitated events and the only thing that is within our power.

Overall, the Stoic focus on assent should come as no surprise. For Stoics, it is assent, not action (i.e. physical action), that is up to us.[124] Conveniences are 'selected' and inconveniences are avoided only insofar as one would in the main prefer to live with health and wealth and prefer not to live with sickness and penury, were such things up to us. In other words, the 'selective' value of indifferents is merely a cognitive disposition towards them. People choose to have joy, when healthy and moderately wealthy, because those conveniences are not up to them; people choose to be courageous, not fearful, when at sea during a violent storm, because that inconvenience is not up to them. Thus, virtue for a sage is full understanding and free rational acceptance of one's circumstances, cosmically regulated, at all times.

If that is correct, virtuous activity comes in accepting just the things that Nature as cosmic regulator has preordained. That alone is a full expression of virtue and makes humans kin to gods.

> What is the role of a good man? It is to offer himself to Fate. We are swept along together with the universe and that is a great consolation. Whatever it is that has ordained us to live and die thus, by the same necessity it binds also deities. An unalterable course drives along the affairs of men and gods alike.[125]

It is also an account of 'selecting' indifferents that seems to be inconsistent with anthropological naturalism as sketched above.[126]

ON DRY GROUND: STOIC *APATHEIA*

The demand for moderate living was a staple of most Greek ethical systems. So imbued was the plea for moderation in all actions that the Oracle of Apollo at Delphi had 'Nothing too much' inscribed on a wall.

The Stoic view is not one that demands moderation in all actions as some sort of loose regulative principle that advises a person to live not too large or not too small. It advises, in effect, that he takes things as they come to him, without judging them to be good or bad and without developing an affective disposition towards them. That is Stoic *apatheia* – one of the most misunderstood terms in Stoicism.

Apatheia is often translated as 'apathy' or 'indifference', but neither translation suffices. Seneca writes of the difficulty of trying to translate into Latin what the Greeks meant by *apatheia*:

> We are bound to meet with ambiguity, if we try to express summarily the Greek term *apatheia* in a single word by the Latin word *impatientia*. It may be understood to have a contrary meaning to what we wish it to have. What we mean to express is a soul that spurns [*respuo*[127]] any sensation of ill. Yet people will [mistakenly] interpret the idea as that of a soul that can endure no evil. Consider, therefore, whether it is not better to say [as did the Epicureans] 'an invulnerable soul' [*invulnerabilem animum*] or a 'soul placed beyond all suffering' [*animum extra omnem patientiam positum*]. There is this difference between us and the Epicureans. Our ideal sage feels his troubles, but triumphs over [*vincit*] them. Their sage does not even feel them.[128]

As Seneca states, *apatheia* seems to be a sort of invulnerability of soul, but that is not quite correct, as a Stoic sage, like anyone else, certainly feels his troubles. He differs from others in that he endures his troubles and, thus, they not at all affect his happiness. Therefore, *apatheia*, properly grasped, is invincibility, rather than invulnerability, to fortune.

In addition, *apatheia* does not imply detachment, as many insufficiently familiar with Stoicism are wont to think. A Stoic is not only a citizen of his community, but also a citizen of the cosmos – grasped as a community of humans and a community of humans and gods. Each realm involves duties, which integrate him fully in the affairs of both humans and gods. Epictetus elaborates, 'I ought not to be unfeeling [*apathes*] like a statue, but I ought to maintain my natural and acquired relations, as a duty-bound man as well as a son, brother, father and citizen.'[129] *Apathes* here means not so much that one should not be completely unfeeling like a statue, but rather, less literally, that one should not be unmoved or uninvolved like a statue, as some affections, as we shall see, are admirable for Stoics.[130]

Nonetheless, the Stoic view differs remarkably from that of

Aristotle, who maintains that an affective disposition towards people, objects and events is needed by complete virtue. Peripatetics assert that one's affective disposition must be moderate, regulated by reason, and proportioned to circumstances. Seneca succinctly sums the debate in one of his letters to Lucillius: 'The question has often been raised whether it is better to have moderate emotions or none at all. We Stoics reject the emotions; the Peripatetics keep them in check. I do not grasp how any halfway disease [*mediocritas morbi*] can be wholesome or helpful.'[131] The difference is that the Peripatetics, in keeping with Aristotle's view of catharsis,[132] considered a moderate display of emotion to be purgative and healthy. In contrast, the Stoics thought that emotion was a disease of sorts and any amount of it would thus be debilitating. Seneca illustrates emotional debilitation through the Stoic Panaetius' view of love. Panaetius maintains that love – because it leaves us uncontrolled, disordered and enslaved – ought to be shunned completely. What applies to love, Seneca sums, applies as well to all other emotions: 'Insofar as we are able, let us step back from a slippery place, because even on dry ground it is hard enough to take a solid stand.'[133]

The Stoics thus considered emotions to be disturbances of the soul. Precisely how did they disturb the soul? The soul for Stoics is not a distinct, immaterial substance that is conjoined to the body. Being complete physicalists, the soul too is physical. Thus, the state of complete virtue is characterized by internal, physical harmony of a physical soul within a physical body – the harmonious coexistence of a tenuous material substance within another material substance, less tenuous. Disharmony of the two substances is due to emotional disturbance of their psychical equilibrium – that is, disobedient-to-reason and contrary-to-nature movements in the body.

Cicero states that emotional disturbance, for Stoics, is not a natural condition, but a pathological one, that is brought on by false opinions about reality.

The disturbances of the mind harass and embitter the life of the foolish. The Greek term for these is *pathe*. I might have rendered this literally and styled them 'diseases' [*morbos*], but the word 'disease' would not suit all instances – i.e., no one speaks of pity or anger as a disease, though the Greeks call each of these *pathos*. Let us then accept the term 'disturbance' [*perturbatio*], the very sound of which seems to denote something vicious, and these emotions are not excited by any natural influence . . . All of them are mere opinions and frivolous judgments. Thus, a sage will always be free from them.[134]

Diogenes Laertius states that for Stoics there are four main emotions: distress, fear, pleasure and desire. Distress (*lupe*) is a fresh opinion that some ill is present, while fear (*phobos*) is an avoidance of some anticipated ill. Pleasure (*hedone*) is a fresh opinion that something good is present, while desire (*epithumia*) is pursuit of some anticipated good. Distress and fear are irrational bodily contractions, while pleasure and desire are irrational bodily swellings. None is, strictly speaking, a mere bodily movement; each is a *judgement* that has concomitant or subsequent bodily movements.[135] Desire and pleasure are fresh judgements concerning the present; fear and distress are judgements concerning the future (see Table 5). All are irrational judgements insofar as the objects deemed worth pursuing or avoiding are not really worth pursuing or avoiding.

Table 5. Stoic View of Emotions

		ORIENTATION	
		Present	Future
		Distress/ Body Contracted	Fear/ Body Contracted
JUDGMENT	Ill	Pleasure/ Body Swollen	Desire/ Body Swollen
	Good		

Seneca illustrates by the example of anger. There are three movements (*motus*) involved with anger.

In order that you may know how emotions begin, grow, or are run riot, the first movement is involuntary, like a preparation for emotion and a kind of threat. The second movement is accompanied by an act of will, not an unruly one, which assumes it is right for me to avenge myself, since I have been injured, or it is right for the other person to be punished, since he has committed a crime. The third movement is now beyond control [*impotens*] in that it wishes to take revenge, not if it is right to do so, but come what may, and it has vanquished reason.[136]

Of these, the first is unavoidable, as it is involuntary. The second and third motions, requiring the consent of reason, are wholly avoidable. Consequently, only the latter two are constitutive of anger – a sort of reasoning gone awry.

The example of anger illustrates that emotions are impulses to which the soul assents. Nonetheless, sometimes even a sage will be nudged by emotion – for instance, first motions concerning sexual arousal or sorrow – but he will not assent to them. Instead, he will quickly gain his composure so that the initial motion does not lead to a second and third. Therefore, though a sage will sometimes be momentarily moved by impressions, failing to assent to them, he will not experience genuine emotions. That is Stoic *apatheia*.[137]

One under the spell of emotion, Seneca says, is like one who cannot wake from a deep slumber, where the deepness of the slumber represents the extent to which one's soul is overcome by emotion or vice.

> In diseases of the soul, the worse the disease is, the less one perceives it. You need not be surprised, for he whose sleep is light has dreams during sleep and sometimes, though asleep, is conscious that he is asleep. Yet sound slumber annihilates our very dreams and sinks the spirit down so deep that it has no perception of self. Why will no man confess his faults? He will not, because he is still in their grasp. Only he who is awake can recount his dream. Similarly, a confession of wickedness is an indication of a sound mind.[138]

Thus, for Stoics, an invincible life entails taming emotion through right use of reason. Once tamed, through endurance, a person may suffer a wound but he cannot be conquered. 'There are more things likely to frighten us than there are to crush us. We suffer more often from imagination than from reality.'[139]

How is one to attain *apatheia* through endurance? Seneca offers two ideas, both of which suggest exposure to hardship and practice in overcoming it. First, he gives illustrations of inclement weather and illness. A Stoic endures such misfortunes in the same manner that he submits to the rigours of winter, other sorts of severe weather, fevers and disease, and other things that are the result of chance.[140] Second, he gives an analogy of athletic competition. 'In the sacred games, many have won victory by wearing out the hands of their assailants through stubborn endurance [*abstinata patientia*]. Reckon, then, a Stoic in this class of men, who by long and faithful training has attained the strength to endure and tire out any assault of an enemy.'[141]

Does that show that a Stoic's life is wholly without emotion? That is anything but the case, for the Stoics recognize three types of good emotions (*eupatheiai*), which a progressor will want to have – joy, caution and wishing – as well as several subtypes.

> Joy [*chara*], the counterpart of pleasure, is rational elation. Caution [*eulabeia*], the counterpart of fear, is rational avoidance, for though a wise man will never feel fear, he will still use caution. They make wishing [*boulesis*] the counterpart of desire, insofar as desire is irrational appetite. Just as certain other emotions are under the primary passions and subordinate to them, so too is it with the primary *eupatheia*. Thus, under wishing, they subordinate well-wishing or benevolence, friendliness, respect, affection; under caution, reverence and modesty; under joy, delight, mirth, cheerfulness.[142]

When we compare the three *eupatheiai* (see Table 6 opposite) to the four emotions (see Table 5), we see there is no counterpart to the emotion distress – an opinion of some present ill. That makes some sense, when one considers that whatever happens to a sage is neither a good nor an ill.[143] Along such lines, it is understandable why a sage will feel no discomfort, brought on by a slight contraction of the soul, at a present inconvenience.

Like emotions, *eupatheiai* are impulses toward things deemed good and away from things deemed ill. The difference is that *eupatheiai* are impulses directed toward or away from things that really are good or ill. Here the concomitant expansion with joy and shrinking with caution are in accordance with reason; they are not irrational. Of joy, Seneca writes, 'Joy is an elation of spirit that trusts in the goodness and truth of what is its own.'[144] Thus, Stoic *apatheia* involves rising above matters of indifference – like fame, lust and death – so that reason is unimpeded and free in its proper activity. Pursuit of virtue, then, does not involve a lifestyle that is completely emotion-free.[145]

Thus, when grasped aright, *apatheia* does not imply a passionless pursuit of knowledge and a retreat from the vagaries of everyday human affairs. Like others, a Stoic feels his pains and those of his fellow human beings; yet unlike others, he refuses to allow misfortune to impact his happiness. A sage's happiness, as a rational

Table 6. Stoic View of Eupatheiai

		ORIENTATION	
		Present	Future
	Ill	———	Caution/ Slight Contraction
JUDGEMENT			
		Joy/ Slight Swelling	Wishing/ Slight Swelling
	Good		

matter, is complete acceptance of what Nature bestows and is entirely up to him. Thus, *apatheia* is not a retreat from, but utmost immersion and integration in, human and cosmic affairs.

JAVELIN-THROWING: RULES OF RIGHT CONDUCT

Though the Stoics did not believe that any one science – logic, physics or ethics – was foundational for the others, later Stoic thinkers focused on ethics. For Seneca, Aurelius and Epictetus, it was not merely the acquisition of knowledge that was the aim of life, but the assimilation of knowledge – knowledge that sticks to one's ribs, as it were, and guides one's daily thoughts and activities. In short, the aim of life was not mere wisdom, but practical wisdom. Seneca makes this point in a way that is critical of the philosophers in his time and, eerily enough, relevant to philosophers in our time.

> I have mentioned all this just to show you how eager beginners are with respect to their first impulses towards the highest ideals, provided that someone plays a role in encouraging them and in kindling their zeal. There are indeed mistakes made, through the fault of our advisors, who teach us how to debate and not how to live. There are also mistakes made by students, who come to their teachers to develop, not their souls, but their wits. Thus, philosophy, the study of wisdom, has become philology, the study of words.[146]

Once a Stoic has attained wisdom, he does everything well, as the full possession of virtue entails the full possession of each of the particular virtues. According to Chrysippus, Apollodorus and Hecato, the virtues are mutually entailing and virtue enables a sage to know what he is supposed to do in all circumstances.

> The Stoics maintain that the virtues involve one another and that whoever possesses one virtue possesses all of them, insofar as they have underlying principles in common [*theoremata koina*] . . . If a man possesses virtue, he is at once able to discover and to put into practice what he ought to do. Such rules of conduct [*poieta*] are rules for right choosing (*hairetea*), enduring [*hypomenetea*], remaining steadfast [*emmenetea*], and distributing things rightly [*aponemetea*] with the result that, if a man does some things through right choosing, some by courage, some by right distribution, and some things steadfastly, he is at once prudent, courageous, just and self-controlled.[147]

Just how does a Stoic do everything well? A sage has dispositionally innate preconceptions (*proleipseis*) that guide his behaviour.[148] Epictetus states that these preconceptions – such as the good is profitable and something to be chosen – are common to all men and consistent with each other.[149] He adds that each person has natural conceptions (*ennoiai physikai*) in some unspecified sense of 'good', 'bad', 'just' and 'unjust'. Why then is there error in ethical judgments? His answer is that each person needs to learn how to apply correctly the natural conceptions to particular cases in conformity with Nature. To do that correctly, one needs a full grasp of the things that are within one's control and those that are not. That entails a certain amount of open-eyed living and, of course, right choice (*prohairesis*).[150]

Epictetus mentions two principles each person ought to have readily at hand: 'There is nothing good or bad outside of right choice' and 'One ought not to lead, but follow, events'.[151] The first, by reaffirming that disturbances fall outside moral choice, is a principle usable mainly for disturbing news. The second is a general principle usable for all actions.[152]

The maverick Stoic Aristo likened the acquisition of knowledge and virtue to practise in javelin-throwing.

> When a man has gained a complete understanding of this definition of the greatest good and has thoroughly learned it, he can frame for himself a precept, directing what is to be done in a given

case. It is just like the student of javelin-throwing. He keeps aiming at a fixed target and thus trains his hand to give direction to the javelin. When, by instruction and practice, he has gained the desired ability, he can then employ it against any target he wishes, as he has learned to strike not any random object, but precisely the object at which he has aimed. Similarly, he who has equipped himself for the whole of life does not need to be advised concerning each separate item, because he is now trained to meet his problem as a whole, as he knows not merely how he should live with his wife or his son, but how he should live aright. In this knowledge, there is also included the proper way of living with wife and children.[153]

In general, there can be no wisdom of practical affairs for Stoics, without principles of philosophy to dictate right action. Here we come to a distinction between basic principles of right conduct (*decreta philosophiae*) and specific rules of right conduct (*praecepta philosophiae*) – hereafter doctrines and precepts – that Seneca examines in *Letters* XCIV and XCV. 'Both deal with advice – doctrines through the universal, precepts through the particular.'[154] The indispensability of such principles to guide action need not commit anyone, however, to the view that these principles are indefeasible guides of human activity.[155]

Of the reliance of precepts on doctrines, Seneca writes:

Philosophy, being theoretical, must have its doctrines. Why? It is because no one can correctly perform right actions, except one who has been entrusted with reason, which will enable him, in every case, to fulfil all the categories of duty. He cannot obey these categories, unless he receives precepts for every occasion, not just for the present. However, precepts by themselves are weak and as it were rootless, if they are assigned to the parts and not to the whole. Doctrines will strengthen and support us in peace and calm and will include simultaneously the whole of life and the universe in its completeness. There is the same difference between philosophical doctrines and precepts as there is between elements and members:[156] Precepts depend on doctrines, while doctrines are the source both of precepts and of all things.[157]

Doctrines are the most general principles of human activity for these reasons. First, they ground all activity and even ground reason. They allow agents a common base for consistent moral action, though they need not tell us just what it is we have to do in particular cases. Seneca says, 'If you would always desire the same things, you must desire the truth. But one cannot attain the truth without doctrines, as doctrines bind together one's life.'[158] Second, doctrines ground precepts. The reason is as follows. To one who knows, precepts add nothing. To one who does not know, they are insufficient guides of action, as they do not tell the uninformed why they ought to do what they ought to do. Doctrines do.[159] Finally, one doctrine can only be dismissed by another doctrine, not a precept. For instance, those who say, 'Precepts are sufficient for moral actions' or 'Doctrines are superfluous', are themselves giving one doctrine to eliminate another. Doctrines, then, are ethically indispensable.[160]

What, however, of specific principles of right conduct? Do they add to a good life or are they superfluous?

Precepts do more than rid a person of false opinions about specific affairs. They give him insight into those affairs. Also, though many precepts may be obvious, it often does a considerable amount of good to point out what is obvious.

> Precepts do a great deal of good, for we sometimes know facts without paying attention to them. Advice [*admonition*; i.e., in the form of precepts] is not teaching. It merely engages the attention and rouses us. It concentrates one's memory and keeps it from slipping away. We miss much that is set before our very eyes. Advice is, in fact, a sort of exhortation. The mind often tries not to notice even what lies before our eyes. We must therefore force upon it the knowledge of things that are perfectly well known.[161]

Moreover, precepts reinforce memories and enable people to disentangle knotty matters. In addition, they also help one manage complex and challenging affairs,[162] and they encourage the growth of virtue. Seneca says, 'Souls bear seeds of everything that is morally correct and such seeds are encouraged to grow by advice, just as sparks, fanned by a gentle breeze, develop their natural fire.'[163] Finally, precepts set duty in order and reinforce our notion of appropriate acts.

> For although we may be convinced by arguments just what things are goods and ills, still precepts have their proper role. Prudence

and justice consist of certain duties [*officia*] and duties are set in order by precepts. Moreover, judgment of good and evil is itself strengthened by following up our duties, and precepts conduct us to that end. Both are in accord with each other, and precepts cannot take the lead unless duties follow. Precepts observe their natural order. Hence, they clearly come first.[164]

Overall, the effect of good precepts is like the sting of a tiny insect. The sting is perceptible only insofar as there is swelling, but the effect, however unnoticeable, is unmistakable.[165]

Unlike doctrines, precepts may perhaps be best formulated conditionally, as Seneca illustrates:[166]

- If you wish to be self-controlled, do such-and-such things.
- If you wish to be happy, do not cause the unhappiness of another.
- If you wish to quash desire, do not give it a venue for display.

Overall, Seneca states, progress toward virtue requires practice through appropriate acts, and both doctrines and precepts are the most suitable guides to appropriate acts.

Virtue depends partly on instruction [*disciplina*] and partly on practice [*exercitione*]. You must learn first and then strengthen your learning by action. If this is true, not only do the doctrines of wisdom help us, but so do the precepts, which check and banish our emotions by a sort of official decree [*edicto*].[167]

In addition to doctrines and precepts, there are what the Greeks called *khreiai*.[168] *Khreiai* are simple, witty or clever sayings that aim at reinforcing certain points. For example, a particular *khreia* might remind one to recall what Zeno or Chrysippus did on a particular occasion in order to justify one's actions. Unlike doctrines and precepts, *khreiai* are especially suited for developing young minds that cannot hold much or use reason well. For such young minds, *khreiai* are to be repeated as a means of early mental conditioning. Seneca says that they are not recommended for adults, who should be concerned with action, not words. He adds that it is shameful for adults, especially the elderly, to have mere 'note-book knowledge', since while the young are learning, the old ought to be using.[169]

One could certainly spend the whole of one's life memorizing principles and repeating *khreiai* to no fruitful end. Yet the end of life is action, not repetition, and so Stoic progressors must have exemplars of virtue.[170] Seneca tells his friend Lucillius:

> The living voice and the intimacy of a common life [i.e., exemplars] will help you more than the written word. You must go to the scene of action, first, because men put more faith in their eyes than in their ears, and second, because the road is long through precepts, short and manageable through examples.[171]

Like the production of a fine work of art as compared to the production of a sock, the goodness in exemplars is not just thought-inspiring, but also awe-inspiring.[172]

Given the Stoic emphasis on action, principles ought to be internalized only insofar as they may be serviceable for appropriate acts. How many principles of philosophy ought to be internalized? Following the Cynic Demetrius, Seneca says it is better to possess a few serviceable maxims than many that are impracticable.[173]

Cicero agrees with Seneca. He lists several serviceable *khreiai* in *On Ends*. First, he gives four principles of Natural Justice:[174]

- Never wrong or harm another.
- Never befriend a wrongdoer.
- Always prefer truth to falsehood.[175]
- What is fair and just is honourable and what is honourable is fair and just.

Then follow four principles of cosmic significance, as 'he who is to live in agreement with Nature must base his principles on the system and government of the entire world'.[176]

- Prepare yourself for circumstances.
- Follow deity.
- Know yourself.
- Nothing too much.

Overall, to be invincible is to be completely one's own person and a needed part of that is knowledge. Yet knowledge is more than an uncanny capacity to spew forth the right words at the right time and in the right manner; it is a matter of having these words become a part of one's being. Wisdom, for Stoics, is equanimity.

Khreia for 'Rules of Right Conduct'

■ 'Contrary to recollection, knowing is making everything yours – not depending upon an exemplar and not always looking back at the teacher.'[177]

STOIC PARADOXES: THE STOIC 'LAPITH'

Plutarch relates a story, originally given by Pindar,[178] of Caneus the Lapith, who was said to be completely invulnerable. Though avowedly invulnerable, centaurs, with green fir-trees, beat Caneus into the earth, which he split with his foot. Plutarch states that reasonable persons consider the story to be a most implausible piece of fiction, yet the Stoics, with their far-fetched description of their sage, give people a story even more incredible.

> The 'Lapith' of the Stoics, whom they have constructed from insensitivity, as if they had forged him from steel, is not immune to wounds, disease or pain, but remains fearless, without distress, invincible and unconstrained, while he is wounded, in pain, on the rack, in the middle of his country's destruction or in the middle of his private disasters. While Pindar's Caneus is not wounded when he is hit, the sage of the Stoics is not impeded when confined, not under compulsion when flung down a precipice, not in torture when on the rack, not injured when mutilated, invincible when thrown in wrestling, not blockaded by circumvallation, and is not confined while his enemies are selling him into slavery. He is just like the boats that are storm-tossed, shattered and capsized, while they bear the names inscribed on them 'Bon Voyage', 'Providence', 'Protectress' and 'Escort'.[179]

As Plutarch's account illustrates, there was much resistance to Stoicism in antiquity, some of which was hostile. Why? Canonical Stoicism, we have seen, embraces a number of propositions that seem to be greatly at odds with common sense. They were even called 'paradoxes' (*paradoxa*) by the Stoics themselves.[180] In *On Ends*,

Cicero says:

> The same verbal legerdemain supplies the Stoics with their king-
> doms, empires and riches, so vast that they declare that everything
> the world contains is the property of the Stoic sage. Moreover, he
> alone is handsome, free and a citizen, while the foolish are the
> opposite of all these things and, according to them, insane as
> well. They call these *paradoxa*, as we might say, 'astonishing
> truths' [*admirabilia*].[181]

That Stoics used the word 'paradoxes' is itself sufficient proof that
Stoicism was either a radical departure from extant norms or an
attempt to re-establish a pre-existing ethos that had been long abandoned.

Cicero adds that Stoic paradoxes were often set out in quick syllogistic fashion so as not to make their case ornamentally, but by
minute and minuscule interrogatory pinpricks (*minutis interro-
gatiunculis punctis*).[182] Examples of such syllogisms abound in the
works of Seneca and Cicero, and Stoic paradoxes are routinely
stated non-syllogistically in Aurelius and Epictetus. I give one
example of the syllogistic sort from Seneca:

1 All benefits are goods.
2 A bad man cannot receive a good.
3 Therefore, a bad man does not receive a benefit.[183]

In *Stoic Paradoxes*, Cicero, whose attitude to Stoic thought is not
always so friendly,[184] lists and explains several Stoic paradoxes as
would a Stoic. Such paradoxes are not only 'Socratic', but, he adds,
'far and away the truest'.[185] I list five of the six below.

Paradox 1: Only moral worth is good.
Cicero illustrates with the story of Bias, whose city Priene was being
sacked by an enemy. While others were flitting around in an effort to
escape with as many of their belongings as possible, Bias replied to
one, who had suggested he do the same: 'I am doing just that, as I
have all my belongings with me.' Bias refused to consider such toys
of fortune (*ludibria fortunae*) as fitful belongings.[186]

Paradox 2: Virtue is sufficient for happiness.
Cicero writes syllogistically that as no wicked, foolish or idle person
can live well, so too can no good, brave and wise person be wretched.

As no wicked, foolish and idle person can be happy, so too the good, courageous and wise person cannot be miserable. Again, he whose virtue and character deserve praise cannot fail to live a life that is praiseworthy, and that is not a life from which to flee. Yet it would be a life from which to flee, if it were miserable. Therefore, whatever is praiseworthy must also be happy, prosperous and desirable.[187]

Paradox 3: All wrong actions are equal; all right actions are equal.
Wrong actions are large concerns, Cicero states, as they are not measurable by their results, but rather by the soul of the agent.[188]

If good acts are acts done rightly and if nothing is more right than what is right, undoubtedly too nothing can be found that is better than what is good. Thus, vices are also equal, insofar as they are correctly termed 'deformities' [*pravitates*] of the mind. Yet insofar as virtues are equal, right acts must be equal, as they proceed from virtues; similarly wrong actions must be equal, since they come from vices.[189]

Paradox 5: Only a sage is free and every fool is a slave.
Cicero asks: What is freedom? It is the power to live as one wills, he replies decisively. Yet no one lives as he wills, except he who follows what is right, who enjoys duty, who correctly maps out his path, who obeys the laws because of justice and not fear, whose every utterance, action and thought is voluntary, and whose conduct begins from within. It follows that a sage alone is free from compulsion. If so, then wicked persons are slaves, for they act from a broken and abject spirit, without volition.[190]

Paradox 6: Only a sage is rich.
For a fool, wealth is a matter of abundance and abundance is a full and overflowing supply of goods. Yet no one can have a full and overflowing supply of goods. Thus, a fool cannot be wealthy.[191]

For a sage, having money is not being covetous. Having an income is not enjoying buying things. The only fortune he needs is contentment with what he already has. Thus, only a sage is rich.[192]

Overall, Seneca cautions that some of the paradoxical content of Stoic paradoxes may be due to tendentious exaggeration. *On Benefits* talks of the usefulness of hyperbole to get across a point.

'When we say, "Let him who gives a benefit forget it", we mean, "Let him seem to have forgotten it; do not let his memory of it appear or obtrude".'[193]

Khreia *for 'Stoic Paradoxes'*

■ 'The wise too are the only priests, for they have made sacrifices their study, as also the building of temples, purifications, and all the other matters relating to the gods.'[194]

USELESS WEAPONS: KNOWING ONESELF

Alexander of Macedon, it is commonly known, was one of the world's greatest conquerors. With a modest army that generally numbered between 30,000 and 45,000, he consistently overwhelmed and put to flight much larger armies in Persia and India and eventually conquered the mighty Persian Empire. Yet as he raged against his enemies, he also raged against his friends and himself. He had Callisthenes, his campaign chronicler and Aristotle's nephew, put to death. In a drunken rage, he also killed Clitus, who once in battle saved Alexander's own life. Moreover, Alexander constantly exposed himself and his entourage to needless danger in his effort to conquer all nations and rival even the gods in greatness. Seneca states:

> Alexander himself, as he slew one friend or lost another, would lie in the darkness and lament sometimes his crime and sometimes his loss. He, the conqueror of so many kings and nations, was laid low by anger and grief! He had made it his aim to win control over everything, except his emotions . . . Self-command [*imperare sibi*] is the greatest command [*imperium*].[195]

What Alexander lacked was a needed component of Stoic invincibility – self-understanding – which, for Epictetus, is knowledge of the strength of one's governing faculty (*hegemonikon*)[196] and which, for Cicero, begins with an examination of Nature. The latter writes for a Stoic progressor:

> We must thus penetrate into the nature of things and come to grasp thoroughly its requirements, otherwise we cannot know ourselves. That maxim was too lofty for it to be thought to have emanated from a human being and it was therefore ascribed to a

deity. Therefore, the Pythian Apollo enjoins us, 'Know ourselves', but the sole road to self-knowledge is to know our powers of body and mind and to follow the path of life that gives us their full employment.[197]

Without self-knowledge, even precepts are unavailing, as precepts cannot help a person who is in no condition to accept them. It will not help to give precepts, says Seneca, without first trying to eliminate those conditions that lie in the way of precepts. That is like having weapons at one's side as one confronts an enemy without having one's hands free to use the weapons. The first course of action is for one's soul to be set free.[198] Setting free one's soul is a matter of having control over one's emotions and that means knowing one's capabilities fully. One must take up, not shun, difficulties to come to know one's capabilities – especially as they relate to the soul. That, in time, with the development of the right mental disposition, makes one invincible in the face of the many obstacles that fortune sets before oneself.

When a Stoic gains control over his emotions, he becomes as divine as is humanly possible and even has this one advantage over deity. Seneca elaborates:

There is one point in which a sage has an advantage over deity. A god is free of terrors by the benefit of Nature, whereas a sage is free of terrors by his own benefit. What a wonderful privilege to have the weakness of a man and the serenity of a god![199]

Given the Stoic aim of self-understanding through complete cosmic integration, it is queer, Aurelius notes, how often people look to others for validation. While a person loves himself more than he loves anyone else, he tends to value the opinions of others more than his own.[200] With a sage, things are otherwise. 'The prosperity of wealthy people looks to public opinion. Yet a sage, whom we have snatched from the control of the masses and fortune, is inwardly happy.'[201] A sage finds validation in his own virtue – an internal standard that finds confirmation in the orderliness and regularity of Nature, not the masses.

Khreiai *for 'Knowing Oneself'*
■ 'As a musical ear detects even the slightest falsity of tone in a harp, so we shall often draw important conclusions from trifles,

if we wish to be keen and careful observers of moral faults.'[202]
■ 'It is not enough for a man to have the wish, without having done a service; it is not enough to have done the service, without having had the wish.'[203]

NOTES

1 Seneca, *Epistles*, IX.
2 D.L., VII.137–8.
3 *SVF*, II.633 and D.L., VII.135, 140 and 142.
4 Seneca, *Epistles*, XCV.52.
5 *SVF*, II.300–1, 1045, 1132 and D.L., VII.134–6.
6 Similar to the Aristotelian cosmos, except that all four of the elements had a natural tendency toward the centre of the cosmos – both bodies without weight and especially heavy ones (*SVF*, II.555 and D.L., VII.137).
7 *SVF*, I.135–8, II.634, and D.L., VII, 138–9.
8 *SVF*, II.447, 556, 826 and 879.
9 *SVF*, III.220.
10 Philo, *God's Immutability*, 35–6.
11 *SVF*, I.98, 102, II.604, 606 and 1052 and D.L., VII.141.
12 D.L., VII.52.
13 'Cataleptic' indicates grasping.
14 Sextus Empiricus, *Against the Professors*, VII.247–52.
15 Sextus Empiricus, *Against the Professors*, VII.255.
16 Cicero, *Academics*, II.38.
17 Epictetus, *Discourses*, I.28.i–ii.
18 D.L., VII.45–6. Diogenes adds that Chrysippus did not take this imprinting literally, as it would make no sense to suppose a number of such impressions on the soul at the same time and each being clear and distinct. D.L., VIII.50.
19 The Stoics thought that such perceptions had propositional content.
20 Marcus Cato, however, was said by Seneca to have exceeded a sage in excellence. *Firmness*, VII.1.
21 D.L., VII.177.
22 *Metaphysics*, .1.
23 Epictetus, *Discourses*, I.20.vii.
24 Epictetus, *Discourses*, III.ii.1–2. Hadot argues that these fields are related to the three Stoic fields of study: physics (to desires and aversions), ethics (to duty) and logic (to assent). Pierre Hadot, *La Citadell intérieure: Introduction aux 'Pensées' de Marc Aurèle* (Paris, 1992), pp. 98–115.
25 Seneca, *Epistles*, CXIII.18 and Cicero, *Duties*, I.xxxvi.132.
26 Cicero, *Duties*, I.xxviii.101.
27 Seneca, *Epistles*, XXXI.6, LXXXV.17, LXXXVII.11, XCII.23, and *Good Life*, XVI.3 and Cicero, *Duties*, II.ii.5.

28 Cicero, *Duties*, I.xxxix.141.
29 Cicero, *Duties*, I.v.15.
30 The Middle Stoics, Panaetius and Posidonius, denied this sufficiency thesis and argued, similar to Aristotle, that certain other goods, like strength and health, were needed as well. D.L., VII.128.
31 Seneca, *Good Life*, XVI.3.
32 For Stoics, these are the four primary virtues. E.g., D.L., VII.92.
33 D.L., VII.101.
34 Plutarch, *Stoic Self-Contradictions*, 1046d.
35 Seneca, *Epistles*, LXXI.32.
36 Plutarch, *Moralia*, 441a.
37 D.L., VII.89. Seneca, queerly enough, argues that virtue is alive. Virtue is a state of a living thing. The soul, people agree, is a living thing and virtue is just the soul in a certain state. Since the soul is a living thing, virtue too, as the state of that thing, must be a living thing. Seneca, *Epistles*, CXIII.2.
38 E.g., Cleanthes maintained that a wise person's virtue was unshakeable, while Chrysippus thought he could slip away from virtue by intoxication or depression. D.L., VII.127.
39 Seneca, *Epistles*, XX.5.
40 Seneca, *Epistles*, LXVI.9.
41 Cicero, *Ends*, III.xv.48.
42 Cicero, *Tusculan Disputations*, V.81–2.
43 D.L., VII.127.
44 *SVF*, 1063a–b. See also Cicero, *Ends*, III.xiv.48.
45 Plutarch, *Progress in Virtue.*
46 Cicero, *Ends*, IV.xxiv.65–7. See also Seneca, *Benefits*, V.xv.2.
47 Seneca, *Epistles*, LXXV.7–14. See also *Epistles*, LXXII.8–10.
48 Cicero, *Ends*, III.xvii.58. Epictetus adds that appropriate acts are determined by one's relationships with others – whether, for instance, one is a father, brother or friend. *Handbook*, 30.
49 Cicero, *Ends*, III.xviii.59.
50 Cicero, *Duties*, III.iii.11.
51 Seneca, *Epistles*, XCV.57.
52 The Stoic notion of *oikeoisis*, covered fully in Chapter 2.
53 We shall see shortly that Stoics did think there were good emotions (*eupatheiai*) that were to be embraced.
54 Aurelius, *Meditations*, III.16.
55 Seneca, *Epistles*, CXVIII.12.
56 D.L., VII.94.
57 Irwin and Kraut offer radically different interpretations. T.H. Irwin, 'Permanent Happiness: Aristotle and Solon', and Richard Kraut, 'Aristotle on the Human Good: An Overview', in *Aristotle's Ethics*, ed. Nancy Sherman (New York: Rowman & Littlefield Publishers, Inc., 1999), pp. 1–34 and 79–104.
58 Aristotle, *Nicomachean Ethics*, I.7 (1098a 15–18).
59 Aristotle, *Nicomachean Ethics*, I.10.
60 Chrysippus and Hecato presumably held that the good was equivalent

to the beautiful. D.L., VII.101.
61 Cicero, *Ends*, III.ix.31.
62 Seneca, *Benefits*, V.xiii.2.
63 Seneca, *Epistles*, CXX.3.
64 I.e., 'conveniences' or 'advantages' or, more technically, 'preferred things' (*producta*). Seneca, *Epistles*, LXXIV.17.
65 Seneca, *Epistles*, LXXI.33.
66 Cicero, *Ends*, III.xiii.44.
67 Cicero, *Ends*, III.xiii.45.
68 Plutarch, *Stoic Self-Contradictions*, 1048c.
69 Seneca, *Epistles*, LXVI.45–6.
70 Following Hays' translation here. Aurelius, *Meditations* V.12.
71 D.L. VII.104–5. The queer pair is life and death. Seneca recognizes death does not seem to fit so neatly with the other things inconvenient. 'There are vast distinctions among these qualities that we call 'indifferents' (*media*, literally 'middle things') For instance, death is not as indifferent as the question whether your hair should be worn evenly or unevenly. Death belongs among those things that are not indeed ills, but still have in them a semblance of ill'. Seneca, *Epistles*, LXXXII.15. See M. Andrew Holowchak, 'Carrying One's Goods from City to City: Seneca on Friendship, Self-Sufficiency, and the Disdain of Fortune', *Ancient Philosophy*, XXVI.1 (2006): 93–110.
72 Cicero, *Ends*, IV.xxv.xxvi.72.
73 Cicero, *Ends*, III.xvi.52–3.
74 Seneca, *Epistles*, LXXIV.17.
75 Seneca, *Epistles*, LXXIII.10-1.
76 Seneca, *Epistles*, XCII.13.
77 Seneca, *Epistles*, LXXXII.15.
78 Cicero, *Ends*, III.xviii.61.
79 Cicero, *Ends*, III.vi.20.
80 Epictetus, *Discourses*, II.v.3–5.
81 Seneca, *Epistles*, LXVI.36–39 and 44.
82 E.g., Seneca, *Epistles*, LXVI.44 and XCVI.5.
83 See J. I. Porter, 'The Philosophy of Aristo', in *The Cynics: The Cynic Movement in Antiquity and Its Legacy*, ed. R. Bracht Branham and M.-O. Goulet-Cazé (Berkeley: University of California Press, 1996), pp. 156–89.
84 D.L., VII.87.
85 D.L., VII.88.
86 D.L., VII.89.
87 D.L., VII.85.
88 Seneca, *Epistles*, CXXI.21.
89 D.L., VII.85–88. Diogenes and Antipater phrase the end as rational behaviour through selecting what is natural.
90 Seneca, *Leisure*, V.1.
91 Called the 'cradle argument'. E.g., Cicero, *Ends*, III.v.16.
92 Cicero, *Ends*, III.xix.62–3.
93 Cicero, *Ends*, III.xix–xx.64–6.

94 Cicero, *Ends*, III.xx.67.
95 Seneca, *Epistles*, XCV.52–3.
96 Epictetus, *Discourses* III.iii.2–3.
97 Michael Lapidge, 'Stoic Cosmology', *Phronesis*, 18 (1973): 161–85; R. D. Hicks, *Epochs of Philosophy: Stoic and Epicurean* (New York: Russell & Russell, Inc., 1962), pp. 76–85; Anthony A. Long, 'Stoic Eudaimonism', in *Proceedings of the Boston Area Colloquium in Ancient Philosophy, Volume IV*, ed. John J. Cleary and Daniel C. Shartin (Lanham, NY: University Press of America, 1986), pp. 85–7; John M. Cooper, 'Eudaimonism, the Appeal to Nature, and "Moral Duty" in Stoicism', in *Aristotle, Kant, and the Stoics*, ed. Stephen Engstrom and Jennifer Whiting (Cambridge: Cambridge University Press, 1996), pp. 261–84; Michael Gass, 'Eudaimonism and Theology in Stoic Accounts of Virtue', *Journal of the History of Ideas*, 61 (2000), 19–37.
98 Epictetus, *Discourses*, I.xii.15–17.
99 Julia Annas, *The Morality of Happiness* (Oxford: Oxford University Press, 1993), pp. 165–79, and Troels Engberg-Pedersen, 'Discovering the Good: *Oikeiosis* and *Kathekonta* in Stoic Ethics', in *The Norms of Nature*, ed. Malcolm Schofield and Gisela Striker (Cambridge: Cambridge University Press, 1986), pp. 145–83.
100 Seneca, *Epistles*, CXXI.2–3.
101 Seneca, *Epistles*, CXXI.6–9.
102 Seneca, *Epistles*, CXXI.17–18.
103 *Iuvantia* also conveys the notion of 'pleasant things', so the sense is that each animal instinctively seeks what is at once advantageous and pleasant.
104 Seneca, *Epistles*, CXXI.22–4.
105 Seneca, *Epistles*, CXXI.11–13.
106 Seneca, *Epistles*, CXXIV.11.
107 This shows that Latin was ill-equipped to translate Greek Stoicism.
108 Cicero, *Ends*, III.vi.20.
109 Because other animals are capable of a *kathekon* or *officium*, 'duty' and 'appropriate act', which are often used as suitable translations, when it comes to humans, are not ideal.
110 Cicero, *Ends*, III.vi.22.
111 D.L., VII.108–9. We shall see that this cannot be quite right for Stoics.
112 D.L., VII.109–10.
113 Cicero, *Duties*, I.iii.8.
114 Cicero, *Ends*, III.xxii.
115 Cicero, *Ends*, III.21–2.
116 Epictetus, *Discourses*, II.v.25.
117 Seneca, *Providence*, V.7.
118 Seneca, *Epistles*, LXXVI.23.
119 D.L., VII.123.
120 Cicero, *Fate*, XII.28. The same tension is present in the 'Master Argument' (*kurieuon logos*), a collection of three incompatible premises:

1) Every past event is necessarily true.
2) What is impossible does not follow from what is possible.
3) What is not now and never will be true is possible.
Cleanthes and Antipater, Epictetus relates, get around the tension by rejecting premise one, while assenting to premises two and three. Others, he says, reject premise two. Having more interest in practical rather than foundational issues, Epictetus' own strategy is not to fret over which premise to reject. 'Show me how you are in the habit of conducting yourself in a storm on board ship'. There are many who can recite the 'petty arguments' of the Stoics; there are few who, through their actions, demonstrate virtue. Epictetus, *Discourses*, II.xix.20–6.

121 Cicero, *Fate*, XIII–XIX, 42–3.
122 Carneades simply rejected strict determinism on account of the seeming absurdity that nothing could be in our power, if it were true. Cicero, *Fate*, XIV.31.
123 Bobzien has argued convincingly that the modern and ancient understandings of culpability are radically different. Today, an action is considered up to us, if we could have done otherwise. In antiquity, an action was considered up to us, if it had an inner cause. Susanne Bobzien, *Determinism and Freedom in Stoic Philosophy* (Oxford: Oxford University Press, 1998).
124 Epictetus tells us that *prohairesis* and its acts are up to us, while the body, parts of the body, possessions, parents, brothers, children and country are not up to us. Epictetus, *Discourses*, I.xxii.10.
125 Seneca, *Providence*, V.8.
126 For a spirited defence of anthropological naturalism, see Engberg-Pedersen, 'Discovering the Good', p. 172.
127 Literally, 'spits out'.
128 Epicureans will not feel their troubles insofar as the hedonistic aim of Epicureanism is pleasure through avoidance of pain. Seneca, *Epistles*, IX.2-3.
129 Epictetus, *Discourses*, III.ii.4.
130 Following Long. A. A. Long, *Epictetus: A Stoic and Socratic Guide to Life* (New York: Clarendon Press, 2002), p. 232.
131 Seneca, *Epistles*, CXVI.1.
132 Aristotle, *Politics*, VIII.V.1339a25 and 1341b32–1342a16.
133 Seneca, *Epistles*, CXVI.6.
134 Cicero, *Ends*, III.x.35.
135 D.L., VII.111–14. Cicero lists sorrow (*aegritudo*), fear (*formido*), lust (*libido*) and pleasure (*voluptaria*). Cicero, *Ends*, III.x.35.
136 Seneca, *Anger*, II.iv.1. Seneca also calls the first motion a 'blow' (*ictus*, II.ii.2 and II.iv.2) or an 'agitation' (*agitatio*, II.iii.5). For a thorough analysis of these three motions, see Richard Sorabji, *Emotion and Peace of Mind: From Stoic Agitation to Christian Temptation* (Oxford: Oxford University Press, 2000).
137 Cicero, *Tusculan Disputations*, IV.14 and Seneca, *Anger* II.iii.1–2.
138 Seneca, *Epistles*, LIII.7-8.
139 Seneca, *Epistles*, XIII.4.

140 Seneca, *Equanimity*, IX.1.
141 Seneca, *Equanimity*, IX.5.
142 D.L., VII.116.
143 For further discussion, see John Cooper, 'The Emotional Life of the Wise', *The Southern Journal of Philosophy*, XLIII (2005): 176–218.
144 Seneca, *Epistles*, LIX.2.
145 Aurelius, *Meditations*, X.8.
146 Seneca, *Epistles*, CVIII, 23.
147 D.L., VII.125-5.
148 See Matt Jackson-McCabe, 'The Stoic Theory of Implanted Perceptions', *Phronesis*, 49.4 (2004), 323–47.
149 Epictetus, *Discourses*, I.xxii.1.
150 Epictetus, *Discourses*, I.xxii.9–11 and II.xvii.5–13.
151 Epictetus, *Discourses*, III.x.18.
152 Epictetus, *Discourses*, III.xviii.1.
153 Seneca, *Epistles*, XCIV.3.
154 Seneca, *Epistles*, XCIV.31.
155 Rules for ethical conduct are justificatory, not prescriptive in that they tie together particular circumstances to the whole of one's life. See Bran Inwood, 'Rules and Reasoning in Stoic Ethics', in *Topics in Stoic Philosophy*, ed. Katerina Ierodiakonou (Oxford: Oxford University Press, 1999), pp. 95–127. For the view that rules function indefeasibly for the Stoics, see Gisela Striker, 'Origins of the Concept of Natural Law', *Essays on Hellenistic Epistemology and Ethics* (Cambridge: Cambridge University Press, 1996), pp. 209–20.
156 *Elementa* and *membra* here – perhaps to be understood as matter and form.
157 Seneca, *Epistles*, XCV.12.
158 In preference to Gummerre's 'embrace the whole of life', in the sense that adherence to doctrines gives one a unified sense of self. Seneca, *Epistles*, XCV.58.
159 Seneca, *Epistles*, XCIV.48.
160 Seneca, *Epistles*, XCV.60.
161 Seneca, *Epistles*, XCIV.25.
162 Seneca, *Epistles*, XCIV.21.
163 Seneca, *Epistles*, XCIV.29.
164 Seneca, *Epistles*, XCIV.33-4.
165 Seneca, *Epistles*, XCIV.41-2.
166 Comparable to Kant's hypothetical imperatives. Seneca, *Epistles*, XCIV.66, 67 and 71.
167 Seneca, *Epistles*, XCIV.47
168 For more on *khreiai*, see Derek Krueger, 'The Bawdy and Society: The Shamelessness of Diogenes in Roman Imperial Culture', in *The Cynics: The Cynic Movement in Antiquity and its Legacy*, ed. R. Bracht Branham and M.-O. Goulet-Cazé (Berkeley: University of California Press, 1996), pp. 223–4.
169 Seneca, *Epistles*, XXXVI.4.
170 David Sedley, drawing from Cicero's *On Ends*, argues that the

pre-Panaetian Stoic ethics was taught without the use of exemplars. David Sedley, 'The Stoic–Platonist Debate on *Kathekonta*', in *Topics in Stoic Philosophy*, ed. Katerina Ierodiakonou (Oxford: Oxford University Press, 1999), pp. 128–52.

171 Seneca, *Epistles*, VI.5.
172 See Michael Frede, 'On the Stoic Conception of the Good', in *Topics in Stoic Philosophy*, ed. Katerina Ierodiakonou (Oxford: Oxford University Press, 1999), pp. 88–9.
173 Seneca, *Benefits*, VII.i.2–3.
174 Cicero, *Ends*, III.xxi.71.
175 The Stoic commitment to truth is not, like Kant's, unconditionally binding.
176 Cicero, *Ends*, III.xxii.73.
177 Seneca, *Epistles*, XXXIII.8.
178 Pindar, *Fragments*, 166f.
179 Plutarch, *The Stoics and the Poets*, *Moralia*,1057d–e.
180 Cicero, *Stoic Paradoxes*, 4.
181 Cicero, *Ends*, IV.xxvii.74.
182 Cicero, *Stoic Paradoxes*, 2.
183 Seneca, *Benefits*, V.xii.3.
184 Cicero objects to the notion that all non-sages are equally vicious. 'Suppose . . . that not one of a number of lyres is strung in such a way that it is in tune. Thus, all are equally out of tune. It is the same with transgressions: Since all are discrepant, all are equally discrepant. So, all are equal. Here we are put off with an equivocation. All the lyres equally are out of tune, but it does not follow that all are equally out of tune . . . It [likewise] does not follow that because we pronounce every case of avarice equally to be avarice, we must therefore pronounce them all to be equal'. Cicero, *Ends*, IV.xxvii.75.
185 Cicero, *Stoic Paradoxes*, 4.
186 Cicero, *Stoic Paradoxes*, 8–9.
187 Cicero, *Stoic Paradoxes*, 19.
188 Cicero, *Stoic Paradoxes*, 20. See also D.L., VII.120
189 Cicero, *Stoic Paradoxes*, 22. See also Seneca, *Epistles*, LXVI.33, LXXI.9; and Cicero, *Ends*, IV.xxvii.74.
190 Cicero, *Stoic Paradoxes*, 34–5. See also Cicero, *Ends*, III.xxii.75 and D.L., VII.121.
191 Cicero, *Stoic Paradoxes*, 47.
192 Cicero, *Stoic Paradoxes*, 51. For other examples, see Seneca, *Epistles*, LXVI.25, 34, LXXXI.11, LXXXV.22, LXXXVII.25, XCVII.14, *Benefits*, II.xxxv.2, VII.xxiii.2–3, *Firmness*, II.1, III.2, *Helvia*, XIII.6; Cicero, *Ends*, III.viii.29, III.xxii.75, III.xxii.75, *Duties*, x.35; Epictetus, *Fragments*, VII; Aurelius, *Meditations*, IX.4; and D.L. VII.122, 123, 124 and 125.
193 Seneca, *Benefits*, VII.xxiii.2–3.
194 D.L., VII.119.
195 Seneca, *Epistles*, CXIII.31.
196 Epictetus, *Discourses*, I.xxvi.15.

197 Cicero, *Ends*, V.xvi.44.
198 Seneca, *Epistles*, XCV.38.
199 Seneca, *Epistles*, LIII.11–12.
200 Aurelius, *Meditations*, XII.4.
201 Seneca, *Epistles*, CXIX.11.
202 Cicero, *Duties*, I.xli.146.
203 Seneca, *Benefits*, VI.xi.3.

CHAPTER 2

THE STOIC PROGRESSOR

'There is a wheel on which the affairs of men revolve and its movement forbids the same man to be always fortunate.'

Herodotus, *Histories*

The first chapter aimed to give readers a general conception of what might be dubbed 'canonical Stoicism' – Stoicism as practised and preached in antiquity roughly from Zeno to Aurelius. Strictly speaking, of course, there is no such thing as canonical Stoicism. Chrysippus' views differed significantly from those of Zeno. The Stoics Panaetius and Posidonius infused Platonic principles into Stoicism. Romanized Stoics focused on ethics.

Moreover, the canonical Stoic view was seen through the eyes of a Stoic sage – an ideal of invincibility that demanded perfection as an ethical ideal. Invincibility as perfection is, I believe, absurdly demanding. Plutarch, in *Progress in Virtue*, points out many of the difficulties of perfectionism, the most perplexing of which is that it casts all persons, other than Stoic sages, into the general category of vice. That puts, for instance, Socrates on a par with his accuser Meletus and just does not seem to accord with observation and common sense. A second difficulty, Plutarch notes, is the 'leap' from progressor to Stoic sage, which is said to occur without the sage's recognition that anything at all has occurred. For Stoics, at some point in the moral development of a sage, a progressor wakes up one morning to find he is a sage. It is as if one could go from woman to man or from beast to deity without recognizing the change, and that, Plutarch says, is absurd.[1] Imagine an athlete, at some point in his career after years of diligent practice and imperfect execution in a sport, who one day finds himself playing his sport faultlessly and continues to do so thereafter.

Stoic moral perfection, seemingly no more plausible than athletic perfection, is much too demanding and, consequently, untenable. Yet rejecting Stoic perfectionism need not involve rejecting Stoic perfectibility – progress toward an ideal that is ultimately unreachable. The remainder of the book, therefore, focuses not on the Stoic sage, but the Stoic apprentice or progressor, who aims at continual progress toward moral perfection. Instead of invincibility as a way of life from the perspective of a Stoic sage, I focus on invincibility as an archetype for life from the perspective of a Stoic progressor.

STOIC COSMOPOLITANISM: STANDING NAKED BEFORE ALL

Book II of Epictetus' *Discourses* compares two styles of living to two people at a fair, where cattle and oxen are bought and sold. One person – concerned with property, slaves and office – lives no differently than the cattle at the fair: He worries about nothing other than his 'fodder'. The other, in contrast, is fond of the spectacle of the fair itself – how, why, by whom and for what purpose it is conducted. The latter is a philosophically-minded person and a true Stoic, who devotes much of his life to leisured contemplation of the cosmos and its myriad events, whether or not he is laughed at and scorned by others around him.[2] In short, a Stoic is predominantly a citizen of the cosmos.

Given the Stoic cosmopolitanist framework, living as a Stoic is a matter of recognizing and contemplating truth within the cosmos. Cosmic unity and harmony are starting points for Stoic ethics, and right-minded participation in the cosmic flow of events is a matter of preserving, not disrupting, that unity and harmony. Aurelius writes:

There is a single harmony [*harmonia*] of all things. Just as the cosmos forms a single body from all bodies, so fate forms a single cause from all causes ... Let us then accept our fate, as we accept the prescriptions of Aesclepius. In fact, in those prescriptions too there are many bitter pills, but we welcome them in hope of health. Take the same view of the accomplishment and consummation of Nature as you do of your health, and thus welcome whatever happens, should it even be somewhat distasteful, as it contributes to the wellbeing and prosperity of Zeus himself. He would not have brought this on humans, if it had not brought welfare to the whole.[3]

The Stoic cosmos comprises two commonwealths – one cosmic, involving gods and men; the other, local, involving communities of men.[4] Aurelius says that his 'city', insofar as he is the particular person he is, is Rome, but, insofar as he is a human being, is the world. Being a part of two cities, his good is what is good in both cities.[5] Epictetus writes that a detached person is no longer a person, just as a detached foot is no longer a foot. A human being is essentially a part of a state.[6]

Epictetus' organic model, drawn from Plato's *Republic*,[7] is not just a local political and ethical ideal as it is for Plato; Epictetus' political and ethical organicism is a universal ideal. Each human being lives in two cities: his own polis and the cosmopolis. How each person stands in his relations to others in those two cities is part of his make-up – his identity.

While living in two cities necessitates a willingness to cooperate as much as possible to facilitate and maintain the order and harmony in both, one must nonetheless recognize that one belongs foremost to the world of gods and humans. That entails a cosmopolitan attitude. Writes Epictetus, 'What other course remains for humans but that which Socrates took when asked to what country he belonged, never to say, "I am an Athenian", or "I am a Corinthian", but "I am a citizen of the world [*cosmios*]".'[8]

How is one to live simultaneously and act rightly in these two cities? Cicero offers a general formula for guiding right-intentioned human activity around conflict, which I name the Principle of Stoic Cosmopolitanism.

Principle of Stoic Cosmopolitanism: Those duties that depend on the social instinct are closer to Nature and more choice-worthy than those that depend merely on knowledge.

Thus grasped, Stoic cosmopolitanism turns Aristotle upside-down, as practical wisdom is dearer to the gods than mere knowing itself.[9] Cicero's Stoic arguments for cosmopolitanism are four. First, no one, overstocked with comforts, would choose to live without the presence of others. Second, as wisdom concerns people's bonds with gods and other men and is acknowledged to be the most important virtue, it demands social activity. Third, study and knowledge of the cosmos would itself be defective without practical benefits. Last, anyone absorbed in study will drop his absorption, if he hears of peril to his country or a loved one.[10]

Stoic cosmopolitanism stands in stark contrast to Epicurean hedonism, which denies that humans have any such social nature and that a social existence is preferred for human fulfilment. Epicureans gathered in small communities principally to learn the words of their master, Epicurus, in order to achieve pleasure through self-sufficiency (*autarkeia*) and freedom from mental disquiet (*ataraxia*). There were in antiquity numerous exchanges between the two schools, which were bitter, but amicable, rivals. Amusingly, Epictetus had this to say about Epicurus' arguments directed against the other-concern of the Stoics:

> Man, why worry about us? Why keep vigil on our account? Why light your lamp? Why stand in revolution? Why write such big books? Is it to keep one or another of us from being deceived in the belief that the gods care for men or is it to keep one or another of us from supposing that the nature of the good is other than pleasure?[11]

The rhetorical force of Epictetus' questions suggests that Epicureans wrote and taught, at least some of the time, out of concern for fellow human beings, which is in effect confirmation of the very thing they essayed to refute – the Stoic belief in the communal nature of humans.

The Stoic philosopher Hierocles explained how Stoic integration in the cosmos occurs through ten concentric circles that bind people locally and globally.

> The first and closest circle is one that a person has drawn as though around a centre – his own mind. That circle encloses the body and anything taken for the sake of the body. It is virtually the smallest circle and it almost touches the centre itself. Next, the second one, further removed from the centre but enclosing the first circle, contains parents, siblings, wife and children. The third one has in it uncles and aunts, grandparents, nephews, nieces and cousins. The next circle (4) includes the other relatives, and that is followed by (5) the circle of local residents, then (6) the circle of fellow-demes-men, next (7) that of fellow-citizens, and then (8) in the same way the circle of people from neighbouring towns, and (9) the circle of fellow-countrymen. The outermost and largest circle (10), which encompasses all the rest, is that of the whole human race.[12]

Of course, appeals to duty, whether local or cosmic, cannot sway everyone. Seneca, perhaps aware that arguments from duty or divine fate might not have their intended effect, gives a very sensible argument for taking the world, instead of any particular city, as the proper sphere for human activity: As virtue is limitless, the world offers a Stoic a larger arena for virtuous activity.[13]

A bedfellow of Stoic cosmopolitanism is Stoic egalitarianism, which was not always a popular feature of Stoicism in antiquity. Egalitarianism bars no one – slave or king – from aiming at the archetype of invincibility. Each person has the same beginning; each has the same end.[14] Each person comes to virtue, as it were, unclothed. Seneca states, 'Virtue shuts out no one. It is open to all, admits all, invites all – the freeborn and the freedman, the slave and the king, and the exile. Neither family nor fortune determines its choice. It is satisfied with a naked human being.'[15]

Stoic egalitarianism has implications for moral action by an apprentice. To those attracted to virtue, a Stoic will act straightforwardly. To those unmoved by virtue, a Stoic will behave with forgiveness, tolerance, gentleness – just as he would to an ignorant child – because 'he knows well the saying of Plato, "Every soul is unwillingly deprived of the truth"'.[16]

Perhaps the most pressing argument for Stoic cosmopolitanism is Stoic pantheism – the notion that the cosmos itself is a living deity and people, as parts, have a duty to act for the sake of the good of the whole. Pantheism is difficult to accept today, if only because there is no compelling reason to believe that the universe is a living deity and economy suggests that it is best not to multiply metaphysical entities beyond necessity. What makes matters worse is Stoic fatalism, which seems to mock reason and responsibility by leaving little room for the former and none for the latter in human activity. Is cosmopolitanism salvageable?

In a modified form, it is. There is nothing untoward and there is even something sensible about the Stoic view that there is a bond that connects each of us as human beings – that each of us is not just a member of a local community, but as Diogenes the Cynic put it, a 'citizen of the world'. At the very least, with the world growing smaller and the community of nations moving towards a global identity of purpose, cosmopolitanism may be practically indispensable today.

Khreia *for 'Stoic Cosmopolitanism'*
- 'Philosophy first promises a sense of community, humanity and unity.'[17]

THE GOOD LIFE

Stoic resignation to fate is neatly illustrated by Seneca's example of the Spartan stand at Thermopylae. With the aid of several thousand Greek auxiliaries, three hundred Spartans, knowing full well of their imminent death, blocked the advance of numerous tens of thousands of Persians, advancing on Athens, in the Thermopylaean pass. After two days of savage fighting in defence of the pass, the Spartan king Leonidas addressed his soldiers on the morning of the third day with the exhortation that they fight well and bravely, for on that night they would dine in Hades. Each Spartan, Seneca relates, ate heartily and anticipated a sumptuous dinner in the underworld, once dead.[18]

Seneca's point in relating the story is that the best sort of life – the greatest good or *summum bonum* – for one aspiring toward virtue is to accept one's fate fully and unquestioningly. Full and unquestioned acceptance is itself complete joy.[19]

Eternal calm cannot come about unless one is the same person in word and in deed: One's actions then ought to accord with one's words. Writes Seneca:

Philosophy teaches us to act, not to speak; it exacts of every man that he should live according to his own standard [*ad legem suam*], that his life should be in harmony with his words, and that his inner life should be of one hue and not out of harmony with all his activities. This, I say, is the greatest duty and the greatest proof of wisdom: Deeds should accord with words and a man everywhere should be equal to himself and the same.[20]

Given that consistency between words and deeds is the best proof of wisdom, proof of lack of wisdom is the continued wavering between a professed love for virtue and the performance of actions consistent with vice.[21]

In the main, virtue exacts a great amount of thought and practice for an apprentice, for he aims at lifelong steadfastness, strength and consistency.[22] Yet because of the contingencies of circumstances, one cannot always wait for complete certainty before acting. Consequently, like the Academic Sceptic, a Stoic will often act on that path, based on a thorough appraisal of impressions, which offers the greatest likelihood of truth and the best chance of securing happiness.[23]

The good life, the invincible life, is a tranquil life through the exercise of good judgment. Consequently, it is a perfectly rational life.[24] Seneca states:

> The good life [*vita beata*] is a life that is in agreement with its own nature and can be attained in only one way. First, one must have a sound mind that is in continual possession of its sanity. Second, one must be courageous and energetic, capable of the noblest fortitude, ready for every emergency, careful of the body and of all that concerns it, and without anxiety. Last, one must be attentive to all the conveniences that adorn life, but without admiration of any of them – a user, not a slave, of the gifts of Fortune.[25]

The good life is filled with joy, one of the 'good' emotions, and joy is exclusive to a Stoic sage. That is so because all other 'joys' may bring with them pleasure or pain.

> Joy [*gaudium*] can be gained only by a sage. For joy is an elation of spirit that trusts in the goodness and truth of it own possessions. The common usage, however, is that we derive great joy from a friend's position as consul, from his marriage, or for the birth of his child. Yet these events, as far from being matters of joy, are more often the beginnings of sorrow to come. No, it is a characteristic of real joy that it never ceases and never changes into its opposite.[26]

To gain a share of joy and preserve it, a progressor must shun wrongdoing and the desire for it. Lack of self-control makes peace of mind impossible. With loss of control, ill deed follows ill deed, and the ever-present pain of regret and fear of having one's vices disclosed follows. Thus, a vicious person is never at ease.[27]

In *The Good Life*, Seneca offers a vivid description of a life, aiming at the greatest good.[28] I summarize his more salient points.

- The greatest good is a mind – made perfect, complete, and whole – which scorns chance and rejoices in virtue.

- The greatest good is invincibility, wisdom from experience and calmness in action.
- A happy person recognizes only a good mind that cherishes honour, is content with virtue, is neither puffed nor crushed by fortune, loves self-sufficiency and finds true pleasure in scorning pleasures.
- A happy person has a life that is free, lofty, fearless and steadfast, because of the gift of reason.[29]

In *On Equanimity*, Seneca describes the Stoic attitude toward the good life:

> What we are seeking, therefore, is how the mind may always pursue a steady and favourable course, may be well disposed towards itself, and may view its conditions with joy and suffer no interruption of this joy, but also how it may tolerate a peaceful state that is never pumped up and never cast down. That is equanimity [*tranquillitas*].[30]

For one who is happy, virtue will shine through in everything he does. 'Virtue, though obscured, is never concealed, but always gives signs of its presence. Whoever is worthy will discover it by its footsteps.'[31]

In *On Ends*, Cicero relates that the Stoic good is typically articulated as a life 'in agreement with Nature' (*secundum naturam*).[32] Zeno says that living in agreement with Nature means 'to live using knowledge of things that naturally come to pass'. Other Stoics say living in agreement with Nature means 'to live performing all or most of one's duties', which seems to include, among those who are happy, the progressor, as it requires an agent to act appropriately most of the time, not perfectly all of the time. Still others say that living in agreement with Nature is 'to live enjoying all or the greatest of those things that are in agreement with Nature', and this seems to require a certain amount of conveniences for a virtuous life.[33]

What can be salvaged from the canonically Stoic notion of the greatest good? Following current trends in the philosophical literature today – the resurgence in interest in ancient authors and in the notion of virtue as the basis or end of a good life – I have been arguing that Stoicism can be studied for more than just historical interest. Stoicism – given certain alterations to their basic tenets, such as rejection of a Stoic perfectionism – offers a surprisingly relevant and rich alternative to contemporary consequentialist, deontological and discourse-based approaches to morality. Thus, the Stoic notion of a life in agreement with Nature may reasonably and simply be interpreted, as Lawrence Becker does, as a commitment to 'follow the facts', wherever they may lead. These facts include one's capacities and the physical and social world in which one lives.[34]

If such modifications are reasonable and acceptable, then the greatest good is graspable as a continued commitment to rationality as a way of life – a life committed to self-discovery and comprehension of the world in which one lives. Thus, the good life for today's Stoic may be the type of invincibility that one may come to have through integrating oneself both with nature – narrowly and broadly construed – and with one's fellow human beings through reason. That is the Stoic conception of freedom.

Khreiai *for 'The Good Life'*

- 'Prosperity does not exalt a Stoic and adversity does not cast him down, for he has always endeavoured to rely wholly on himself and to derive all of his joy from himself.'[35]
- 'No person can be happy if he has been thrust outside the pale of truth.'[36]

THE 'STRONG ODOUR' OF TRUTH

Some 150 years ago, the philosopher Friedrich Nietzsche railed against the 'unconditional will to truth' of philosophers of his day – most notably, Kant.

What *compels* one to this, however, this unconditional will to truth, is the *belief in the ascetic ideal itself*, even if as its unconscious imperative – do not deceive yourself about this, – it is the belief in a *metaphysical* value, a value *in itself of truth* as it is established and guaranteed by that ideal alone (it stands and falls with that ideal). There is, strictly speaking, absolutely no science 'without presuppositions', the thought of such a science is unthinkable, paralogical: a philosophy, a 'belief' must always be there first so that science can derive a direction from it, a meaning, a boundary, a method, a right to existence.[37]

Nietzsche adds that consciousness of the will to truth as a meta-physical problem itself would be the death knell of morality.

> '[*W*]*hat does this will to truth mean*? . . . And here I again touch on my problem . . . what meaning would *our* entire being have if not this, that in us this will to truth has come to a consciousness of itself *as a problem*? . . . It is from the will to truth's becoming conscious of itself that from now on – there is no doubt about it – morality will gradually perish: that great spectacle in a hundred acts that is reserved for Europe's next two centuries, the most terrible, most questionable, and perhaps also most hopeful of all spectacles . . .[38]

Nietzsche's words have been, in some ways, prophetical. To say the least, philosophers today tend to be somewhat squeamish about talking substantively about 'truth' simply as correspondence with reality. For many, Richard Rorty for instance, truth is simply a non-issue that is best not talked about at all.

Though ancient philosophers recognized no 'will to truth', prin-cipally because their notion of 'will' was inchoate, for many ancient schools of thought, truth did have a central ethical role. For Aristotle and the Stoics, for instance, a virtuous life meant living with a soul so undisturbed that it could take in and see impressions of things for what they are. Recall here the Stoic notion of catalep-tic impression – an impression so true to its object that it literally forces the 'voluntary' assent of one's soul.

For Stoics, truth was a vital part of virtuous living. 'The sole func-tion of philosophy', Seneca baldly says, 'is to discover the truth about things divine and things human.'[39] Elsewhere, he adds:

> How does a person reach the state of happiness? He does so, when complete truth has been brought to light; when order, measure, fitness and an inoffensive and kindly will [*voluntas*] – a will intent on reason and never departing from it, intent on love and admira-tion at the same time – have been preserved in the things he does.[40]

Cicero says that virtuous living is principally, though not exclusively, involved with the pursuit of truth:

> In that category that was designated our first division and in which we placed wisdom and prudence belong the search for

truth and its discovery. That is the peculiar province of that virtue. For the more clearly anyone observes the most essential truth in any given case and the more quickly and accurately he can see and explain the reasons for it, the more prudent and wise he is generally esteemed, and rightly so. So, then, it is truth that is . . . the matter with which virtue concerns itself and about which virtue is.[41]

For Stoics, happiness depends fundamentally on truth, which is a matter of forming and assenting to correct and trustworthy judgements of things. Such a life is uncompromising and no one who chooses a different path can be happy, Seneca states. A mind committed to truth, then, is free of every ill. It can escape not only scratches, but also deep wounds, and fortune cannot conquer it.[42]

Whenever rationality fixes one's judgments, reason deliberates on all matters as they pertain to one's wellbeing. It bids him to accept affairs as they happen to be, not as they might have been.[43] Thus, happiness is not only a matter of seeing things as they are, but also of accepting them as they are. Reason, then, has both naturalistic and normative functions: It acts naturally to discern reality and works normatively to reconcile one to it.

In the pursuit of truth, Cicero warns, one must be mindful to avoid two errors. First there is the error of rashness: one must not treat what is unknown like what is known. To avoid rashness, one must use patience and circumspection in seeking the truth. Second there is the error of irrelevance. To avoid irrelevance, one must not spend too much time in the study of recondite, difficult and otiose matters that have little bearing on human affairs.[44]

Truth-telling is a critical part of the pursuit of truth. There is something despicably phony, Aurelius says, about people who say, 'Let me be frank'. He adds:

What does that mean? It should not even need to be said. It will declare itself. It should be written on one's forehead. It should be audible in one's voice and visible in one's eyes, like a lover, who looks into your face and takes in the whole story at a glance. A frank [*haplous*] and good person should be like someone who emits a strong odour: When others are in the same room with him, willy-nilly, they know it. False frankness, however, is like a knife in the back.[45]

Aurelius' point is as relevant now as it was in Greco-Roman antiquity. People today have become so accustomed to deception, lying and dissimulating in public that expressions such as 'let me be frank' are an accepted part of everyday language and do not at all seem queer. They *should*.

Cicero too urges us to be cautious of deceitful speaking. He mentions two sorts of errors people often commit when speaking: speaking forcefully like a lion and speaking cunningly like a fox.

> While injury may be done in either of two ways – that is, by force [*vi*] or by fraud [*fraude*] – fraud seems to belong to the cunning fox, force, to the lion. Each is wholly alien to a human being, but fraud is deemed more contemptible. Yet of all forms of injustice, none is more prominent than that of those who, at the moment they prevaricate the most, make it their business to appear to be good men.[46]

Undeniably, there are circumstances that present difficulties. Unlike Kant, the Stoics do not consider one to be duty-bound to speak the truth at all times. The Stoic Panaetius mentions a debate between two Stoics – Diogenes of Babylon and his disciple Antipater. The debate centres on the supposition of a famine at Rhodes. A man, on a ship filled with grain from Alexandria, sets sail for Rhodes to sell the grain. He knows that several other ships have set sail for Rhodes, though that is unknown to the Rhodians. Ought he to remain quiet about the other ships to maximize his own profit or has he a duty to report them to the Rhodians? Diogenes argues that one has a duty to speak honestly of his grain, but not of the other ships. 'Not revealing is not the same as concealing', he argues in gist. Dissimulation is not dishonesty. Antipater argues that duty compels the man to speak also of the other ships coming to port. 'My interest is identical with that of my fellow countrymen', he argues. Panaetius sides with Antipater: 'It is never expedient to do wrong, as wrong is always immoral, and it is always expedient to be good, as goodness is always moral.'[47] Panaetius' point is that if something is morally wrong, it cannot be morally expedient, as the morally expedient is equivalent to the morally correct. If this is right, it is not necessarily morally wrong to accumulate wealth, so long as one accumulates it through just means.[48] Dissimulation, however, is injustice.

Aurelius states that the injustice of lying has a profoundly disruptive effect: It upsets the cosmic order.

> The liar acts impiously towards the same goddess [i.e. Truth], because 'Nature' means the nature of all things that exist, and all things that exist have an intimate connection with all the things that have ever been. Moreover this Nature is named 'Truth' [*Aletheia*] – and is the primary cause of all that is true. The willing liar then is impious insofar as his deceit is a wrongdoing; and the unwilling liar too, for he is out of tune with the Nature of all things that exist and, fighting with the nature of the Cosmos, he becomes an element of disorder. He is in conflict who allows himself, as far as his conduct goes, to be carried into opposition to what is true.[49]

Aurelius' view, then, seems to make truth-telling a duty.

The commitment to truth-telling and being true to one's word has implication for war also. Promises to an enemy made under stress must be kept. Cicero's example is that of the Roman Regulus, who had been taken prisoner in the First Punic War by the Carthaginians. He was sent back to Rome by the Carthaginians to negotiate an exchange of prisoners. While negotiating with his own people on behalf of the enemy, Regulus himself advised against any such exchange. When negotiations were over, he returned to the Carthaginians only to be rewarded for his integrity by death through torture.[50]

There are difficult cases, however, where fidelity need not be observed. Cicero explains:

> We have laws regulating warfare, and fidelity to an oath must often be observed in dealings with an enemy. An oath sworn with the clear grasp in one's own mind that it should be performed must be kept, but if there is no such understanding, it does not count as perjury if one does not perform the vow.

The explanation suggests that when one entertains the slightest bit of doubt in one's own mind about the rightness of an oath one takes – presumably when one is of sound mind and committed to Stoic principles of morality – then the oath is not morally binding. Cicero illustrates with the example of a pledge made to pirates to give a ransom in return for one's life. Failure to give the ransom, when one is granted one's life, is not a breach of duty, as a pirate is not merely a personal enemy, but is the common foe of the entire world. Such an oath is not binding, for the oath, sworn to a universal enemy of mankind, is falsely sworn.[51]

Moreover, not all promises must be kept, even when there is no doubt in one's mind at the time about the rightness of the promise. Consider a man who has entrusted a substantial sum of money to one of his countrymen and then asks for the money back in order to make war upon their common city. Should the one entrusted with the money now return it? Panaetius maintains that duty to one's city trumps the promise: Right action commands that the money not be returned.[52] Seneca adds that rash promises, in general, ought not to be kept,[53] though rash promise-making is itself clearly a sign of lack of virtue.

Khreiai *for 'The "Strong Odour" of Truth'*

- 'It is the truth that I am after and the truth never harmed anyone. What harms us is persistence in self-deceit and ignorance.'[54]
- 'The person who is unwilling to tell you anything, except in secret, has mostly nothing to say.'[55]

FREEDOM: LEVELLING FORTUNE

The pursuit of truth is at once a declaration of one's freedom, as both comprise magnanimity, for which apprentices strive.[56] The Stoic love of freedom is nicely illustrated in a story by Diogenes Laertius about the Stoic founder, Zeno, and his mentor, Crates the Cynic. One day, Crates found Zeno with another philosopher, Stilpo. Irate, Crates grabbed Zeno's cloak to pull him away from Stilpo. Zeno replied that the correct way to seize a philosopher is by the ears, not by the body, for to seize him by the body is merely to bring along his body, not his mind.[57]

Zeno was making a significant point about Stoic self-sufficiency. It is entirely a rational affair and, as a Stoic, one can be self-sufficient in any set of circumstances so long as one's rational faculty is not impaired by false judgment. Crates' pulling away of Zeno may have been a way of seizing Zeno's body, but it was not a way of seizing Zeno himself. The only way to seize another is through persuasive argument. In other words, true freedom is indifference to everything other than argument and truth.

To get clearer on 'freedom', let us follow a distinction made famous by Isaiah Berlin: freedom from and freedom to.[58] 'Freedom from' is a matter of being free from external constraints, say, by living in a non-oppressive and non-coercive culture. 'Freedom to' is a matter of being free to do what one wants to do, say, by taking control of oneself in such a way as to maximize one's capacities.

The Stoic view of freedom is a strange mix of both, with a mental twist. A Stoic is free from external constraints only insofar as he recognizes fully that he cannot in the least control the arrows of fortune. A Stoic, though not free to do what he wants to do, can take complete control of himself and maximize his capacities just by accepting his fate and giving himself up wholly to fortune. It follows that freedom is wholly a matter of freeing oneself from external constraints and maximizing one's capacities by refusing to allow external affairs to impact one's happiness. Seneca writes, '"What is freedom?" you ask. To be a slave to no circumstance, to no necessity, and to no chance events – to reduce Fortune to level ground.'[59] Thus, as complete indifference to fortune, freedom is not a retreat from worldly affairs. On the contrary, indifference implies acceptance, and acceptance requires full immersion in worldly affairs. Consequently, indifference is not really a measure of ignorance of what will come to pass; it is rather a measure of one's own self-sufficiency and self-mastery.[60]

For Stoics, freedom is living as one wishes to live, and that means living so that external affairs do not mar one's blessedness.[61] How is one to live as one wishes? Epictetus says that knowledge of how to write makes a person free from hindrance, when writing; knowledge of how to play the harp makes a person free from hindrance, when playing the harp; and so too is it with living. One needs knowledge of how to live to be free from hindrance, when living,[62] and such knowledge of how to live requires reconciling one's will to what happens. Says Seneca, 'This is the sacred obligation [*sacramentum*] by which we are bound – to bear mortality and not be perturbed by things that are not within our power to avoid. We are born in a kingdom; to obey deity is freedom.'[63]

Given his complete indifference to circumstances, it should come as no surprise that only a Stoic sage can be wholly free.

> No one is free except a sage. For what is freedom? It is the power to live as one wills. Who then lives as he wills, except one who follows the things that are right, who enjoys doing his duty, who has a well-

considered path of life mapped out before him, who does not obey even the laws because of fear but follows and respects them because he judges them to be most conducive to health, whose every utterance, action and even thought are voluntary and free, and whose enterprises and course of conduct all take their start from himself and likewise have their end in himself, as there is no other thing that has more influence with him than his own will and judgment.[64]

To maximize self-sufficiency, Epictetus maintains, one needs education. He states that the many say wrongly, 'Only the free can be educated', while the philosophers say rightly, 'Only the educated are free'.[65]

Self-sufficiency, through education, necessitates some measure of early training to nurture and guide one's budding rationality. Too much liberty and undeserved praise can breed insolence and temper in a child. Too heavy a hand can crush a child's spirit. Consequently, good guidance, early on, uses both the curb and the spur to steer a child between the two extremes that lead to vice.[66]

To illustrate the Stoic notion of freedom as equanimity, Plutarch mentions a story about Pyrrho, on a perilous voyage during a violent storm. While everyone aboard ship was in a panic, Pyrrho noticed a small pig that contentedly ate some barley, spilled on the deck. The pig's behaviour exhibited the sort of mental equanimity that reason and philosophy should enable a person to attain.[67] Such freedom from externals, then, allows the mind to ascend to higher concerns, such as the contemplation of Nature.[68]

Yet when all paths to freedom seem lost and the possibility of exercising one's virtue seems quashed, there is always for Stoics the path of eternal freedom – suicide. Seneca says:

It is bad to live according to constraint; but no person is constrained to live under constraint . . . On all sides lie many short and easy paths to freedom. Let us give thanks to deity, because no one can be forced to live. It is permitted through suicide to trample on the constraints themselves.[69]

Khreiai for 'Freedom'

- 'Freedom is not acquired by satisfying yourself with what you desire, but by destroying desire.'[70]
- 'The only sure way to secure freedom is to die cheerfully.'[71]

LIFTING THE STONE OF AJAX

Aesop tells a story of a queer hunting partnership, between a lion and an ass, turned sour. After the pair caught a large number of animals to eat, the lion divided the spoils into three lots. He claimed the first lot as holder of the highest rank. He claimed the second lot as an equal partner in the venture. The last lot, to which the ass was entitled, the lion claimed through threat of harm to the ass. The ass, Aesop claimed, was at fault for seeing himself as an equal to the lion and for entering into partnership with one too strong for him.[72]

As Aesop's moral implies, it is critical for a person to know his role in life and for each to perform his role to the best of his ability. That not at all entails that everyone read Chrysippus and philosophize all of each day. Not everyone is cut out for such a role. Epictetus writes, 'So, although we are unable even to fulfil the profession of man, we take on the additional profession of the philosopher – so enormous a burden! It is as though a man who was unable to raise ten pounds wanted to lift the stone of Ajax.'[73]

Few have the capacity to be philosophers and fewer still are born into the role. For some, the role of husbandman is right; for others, builder; for still others, marketer. For each, it is a matter of discovering to the best of one's ability what it is that one does best to help promote and maintain order in the affairs of humans and gods. That is developing fully one's moral character. As Epictetus says, if you are a calf and a lion appears, act like a calf. If you are a bull, charge the lion. Know and be yourself. Otherwise, the consequences will be great.[74]

According to Panaetius, what dictates one's capacity for moral character are these: first, a universal capacity for rational thought; second, certain idiosyncratic capacities that vary considerably from person to person; third, one's unique real-life circumstances; and, fourth, the choices one makes along the way.[75] Yet, even with fully developed rationality and knowledge of one's capacities, fortune is not always compliant.

Overall, each person, according to his capabilities, acts as best he can in the circumstances: A magnanimous person performs magnificent deeds when circumstances allow; at other times he seems quite ordinary. A less competent person, though unable to act spectacularly, acts less ambitiously, but to the best of his ability. In every case, however, appropriate action is determined by the best estimate of circumstances and the best estimate of one's ability to act in such circumstances. Seneca says in *On Tranquillity*: 'We must estimate the matters themselves that we are undertaking, and must compare our strength with the things that we are about to attempt. The doer must always be stronger than his task. Burdens which are too heavy for their bearer necessarily crush him.'[76] Epictetus agrees. 'Do you wish to be a contender in the pentathlon or a wrestler? Look at your arms, your thighs, and see what your loins are like. One man has a natural talent for one thing; another, for another.'[77] Yet he also soberly warns of the danger of a great capacity that is unaware of its nature. Great ability (*megale dynamis*) is dangerous for a novice. Thus, ambition must be accompanied by self-knowledge.[78]

Still, no matter what the circumstances are – whether great or modest – so long as one is committed to virtuous activity, there is always space for virtue to shine. Virtue is sometimes widespread. It may govern kingdoms, cities and provinces. It may create laws, develop friendships and regulate the duties between those related. Virtue is sometimes restricted. Poverty, exile and bereavement may limit its scope. Still, even though virtue may be reduced from proud heights to a private station, from a royal palace to a humble dwelling, or from a broad jurisdiction to a private house, it is not diminished, whenever it acts. Full virtue, wherever it is exercised, is always completely great.[79] It is undiminished even in circumstances that do not allow its fullest display.

It follows that not all Stoics will have the same impact through their deeds. Some will live longer lives; others, shorter. Some will affect others in many places over great distances and time; others will have a more limited influence. Each person is born with certain capacities and into distinct circumstances.[80] Nonetheless, each act of virtue is a full expression of virtue, for the hallmark of invincibility is full integration in human and divine affairs, regardless of circumstances.

The Stoic sage differs markedly from the magnanimous person of Aristotle. For Aristotle, a magnanimous person does astonishing deeds, but does them infrequently, because he is not moved to action by small causes, only by great causes. Aristotle writes:

> The magnanimous person [*ho megalopsychos*] does not face dangers for trifling reasons, and is not a lover of danger, because there are few things he values. Yet he will face danger in a great

cause, and, when he does so, will be ready to sacrifice his life, since he holds that life is not worth living at every price.[81]

The Stoic sage, in contrast, is less of an aristocratic hero and more of a common one, insofar as he prefers what is ordinary to what is great. Says Seneca:

> It is characteristic of a great soul to scorn great things and to prefer what is ordinary rather than what is too great. The one condition is useful and life-giving, but the other does harm just because it is excessive. Similarly, too rich a soil makes the grain fall flat. Branches break down under too heavy a load. Excessive productiveness does not bring fruit to ripeness.[82]

Thus, a Stoic apprentice will relegate himself to the role into which he is cast in life and strive to live to the best of his ability in that role. He strives for invincibility by not overstepping his bounds.

It is worth repeating that successful activity for Stoics is judged entirely by intention, not outcome. As we have seen, Cicero, in *On Ends*, states that appropriate acts, for Stoics, are the means to the primary objects of Nature. Yet, he cautions, that does not mean attaining the primary objects is the proper end of humans.

> If a man were to make it his purpose to take a true aim with a spear or arrow at some mark, his ultimate end, corresponding to the ultimate good as we pronounce it, would be to do all that he could to aim straight. The man in this illustration would have to do everything to aim straight and yet, although he did everything to attain his purpose, his 'ultimate end', as it were, would be what corresponded to what we call the 'greatest good' in the conduct of life, whereas the actual hitting of the mark would be in our phrase 'to be chosen' [*selgendum*], but not 'to be desired' [*expetendum*].[83]

Seneca gets the point across when he says the same act can be shameful or honourable, depending on the intention of the agent doing the action.[84] Outcome is irrelevant to judging an action, because outcome is never within one's full control; fortune always has its say. It is otherwise with intention.[85] Thus, we desire not to hit the mark, but to do all that we can to aim straight. Appropriate action, then, is a matter of right-intentioned effort, not results.

Seneca reiterates the point by contrasting the role of a Stoic to that of a sea pilot. A Stoic does not try to achieve at any cost whatever he tries to do. Instead, he aims at doing all things rightly. In contrast, a pilot aims at bringing his ship into port at any cost and he is measured by the success or failure of his aim. 'The arts are handmaids. They must accomplish what they promise to do. Wisdom, however, is mistress and ruler. The arts are as slaves to life; wisdom issues orders.'[86] Seneca's point is that wisdom demands right intention, not results, whereas craft demands results, irrespective of intention. That is not to say that an apprentice should not expect to hit the mark and hit it often. He should.[87] Thus, 'hitting the mark' is not necessary for virtuous action; right intention is. Right intention means having the best plan possible to achieve success, and one with right intention may certainly expect to hit the mark much more often than one without it.

In summary, we may say that, while there is no one role of life ideally suited for each person aspiring toward virtue, there is a manner of living toward which a Stoic ought to strive: He ought to aim at fulfilling himself as a rational human being, insofar as his capacities allow, in the role in which he is cast.[88]

To fulfil oneself one to one's fullest potential, one ought to labour not only for things that one is capable of doing, but also for things worth doing, even if such actions seem to fall short of magnanimous deeds. Here relentlessness is required, even if one fails in one's objective. Aurelius writes: 'Do not feel nauseous, defeated or despondent, if you do not succeed in acting from right principles [*dogmata orthon*].'[89] Success, one must continually remind oneself, is measured by right-intentioned effort, not results.

Khreiai *for 'Lifting the Stone of Ajax'*

- 'Neither should one's labour be in vain and without result nor should the result be unworthy of one's labour.'[90]
- 'Our own worth is measured by that to which we devote our energy.'[91]

A COMPLETE LIFE AND A GOOD DEATH

In *On the Shortness of Life*, Seneca tells a story, given to us by Herodotus, of how the great Persian King Xerxes wept, when he watched his magnificent army – numbering perhaps as much as 200,000 soldiers – traverse over foreign terrain on its way to raze

Athens and punish the Greeks. What caused him to weep was not overwhelming pride or even concern of imminent danger, but rather the strange thought that 100 years hence not a single soldier of his incomparable army would be alive.[92]

Xerxes' thought was perhaps the one echoed in Euripides' *Hippolytus*, where the chorus says in the final lines of the poem, upon the death of Hippolytus, son of Theseus:

> And each of us will always walk with this sorrow
> That never warns us of its hour – and yet comes.
> There will be weeping, and a sparkle and fall of tears.
> What we have heard is sad and terrible . . .
> It happened to the great, and they are dead.
> That the great should die is greater sorrow.[93]

Aurelius must have had the same sentiments, when he mentioned that Alexander, Pompey and Caesar – each of whom slew thousands of men and razed many cities – succumbed to death; that Hippocrates, who cured many illnesses, himself died of illness; that Heraclitus, saying that the world would end in fire, died smeared with cow-dung; and that, while Democritus was killed by vermin, Socrates was put to death by humans.[94]

For Stoics, life, whether lived long or short, is brief. Moreover, whether it is a young or aged person that dies, each loses the same thing.[95] Thus, it is not the length of life that matters, but the manner in which it is lived.[96] A life lived the right sort of way is a complete life, regardless of its length. States Seneca: 'An expedition will be incomplete, if one stops halfway or anywhere on this side of one's destination, but a life is not incomplete, if it is morally right [*honesta*]. At whatever point you leave off living, provided you leave off living nobly, your life is a whole.'[97]

Being complete, a virtuous life cannot be measured in years, which are variable. Instead, it must be measured by the acquisition of wisdom, which is invariable.[98] We arrive at the Stoic paradox that all virtuous lives, short or long, are equivalent.

Seneca contrasts a virtuous life with a long life without virtue. The latter, he states, is not a long life, but a long existence.

> There is no reason for you to think that any person has lived long, just because he has grey hairs or wrinkles. He has not lived long;

he has existed long. What if you should think that a person who had been caught by a fierce storm as soon as he left harbour – swept here and there by a succession of winds that raged from different quarters and driven in a circle around the same course – has had a long voyage? He did not have much voyaging, but much tossing around.[99]

The suggestion here, spelled out elsewhere, is that a virtuous life and virtuous actions are complete. Virtue and virtuous actions require a true perspective of the cosmos and one's place in it.

In contrast to the virtuous life is the vicious life. Given that a virtuous life is complete, vice, for Stoics, is just a matter of living an incomplete life – seeing life in its parts, not as a whole, and living as if one were a stranger in the cosmos.[100]

Living an incomplete life, vicious people are also often close-fisted with their money and possessions, but prodigal with their time.[101] They live 'without concern for frailty and for how much time has already passed by, as if they were destined to live forever'. Consequently, they live the most unstable of lives: They have the desires of immortals and the fears of mortals.[102] They cling to conveniences and fear death.

In contrast, a Stoic, living a good life, accepts what comes his way, without fear of death. Hence, his life cannot be measured in years, as virtue, being absolute, is not quantifiable. Virtue, Aurelius writes, is characterized by purity, serenity, acceptance and peaceful unity with what must be.[103]

Seneca compares the complete joy of a Stoic to a tapestry that is 'weaved together' (*contexitur*) and indestructible.[104] The suggestion here is that a Stoic's joy, like his life, is unitary, not fragmentary, and that is so because he counts on no other source than one that is internal – reason. Cicero elaborates on the Stoic notion of the unity of one's life.

But the most marked difference between man and beast [*beluam*] is this: The beast, insofar as it is moved by the senses and with very little perception of past or future, adapts itself to what only is present at the moment; while a human being, because he is endowed with reason – by which he comprehends the chain of consequences, perceives the causes of all things, understands the relation of cause to effect and of effect to cause, draws analogies,

93

and connects and associates the present and the future – easily surveys the course of his whole life and makes the necessary preparations for its conduct.[105]

The unity of a Stoic's life comes through consistency of his vision and his actions, in accordance with his vision, over a lifetime. 'Virtue is a consistent character', says Diogenes Laertius, 'that is choice-worthy for its own sake and not from fear or hope or anything external. Happiness consists in virtue, since virtue is a soul that has been formed for consistency in the whole of life.'[106]

We can say more. Cicero says that not only is a Stoic sage's life as a whole perfect, but also every action he performs is complete in every detail (*expletum . . . omnibus suis partibus*) and, thus, cannot be increased or diminished.[107] Seneca adds that the mind of a sage is amply stocked with many arts, precepts and examples of right conduct, taken from many epochs, in such a manner that all things blend harmoniously into one.[108] Once virtuous, even if fortune supplies no grand opportunities for him to exhibit his goodness, his virtue is complete.[109]

Having a virtuous life also exacts that one will have a good death and, in order to have a good death, one must live always with an eye towards death. Seneca tells us that Epicurus was fond of reminding others to think continually about death. In thinking about death, Epicurus was asking them to think about freedom, as freedom comes in freeing oneself by learning how to die. To learn how to die is to be beyond any eternal power.[110]

Yet life itself is just a convenience for Stoics. One must not cling to it needlessly. One must be ready to die, if the time is right.[111] Seneca illustrates with the story of Bassus – an elderly man of weak constitution, whose body through the years had come to resemble a decrepit building, capable of falling at any moment. Yet Bassus, he notes, was young in soul, brave in spirit, and not at all burdened by the nearness of his death.

> A great pilot can sail, even when his canvas is ripped. If his ship is dismantled, he can still put in order what is left of its hull and hold her on course. That is what our friend Bassus is doing. He contemplates his own end with the pluck and stern countenance [*animo vultuque*] that you would regard as undue indifference in a man who so contemplated another's end . . . 'It is just as insane',

Bassus adds, 'for a person to fear what will not happen to him as to fear what he will not feel, if it does happen. Thus, death stands so far beyond all evil that it is beyond all fear of evils.' [112]

It is as foolish to fear death as it is to fear old age, as death follows old age as surely as old age follows youth. A wish to live is at once a wish to die, for one is given life only with the understanding that death must follow. Such terms govern all persons equally. No one is an exception. It is childish to fear death.[113]

Finally, given that suicide is always an option for a Stoic, how long is one to keep on living? The answer is simple: So long as one continues to live joyfully.[114]

Khreiai *for 'Complete Life, Good Death'*

■ 'It matters how well you live, not how long. Often living nobly means not living long.'[115]
■ 'We should strive not to live long, but to live correctly, for to have a long life, you need only Fate, but for right living you need a soul.'[116]

OIKEIOSIS: SECURING ONE'S OWN IN THE FOOT-RACE OF LIFE

Epicureans, we have seen, claimed that humans were animals that sought their own good, which they identified with pleasure. Their communities were loose-knit congregations of people who studied the hedonistic principles of Epicurus to free themselves of mental disquiet. Such principles entailed withdrawal from political activity, debasement of sexual activity, and reinforcement of the notion that the best life is one in which each person strives to maximize his own pleasure through the removal of pain. Fellowship was not needed; it was merely seen as contributing to a more efficient way of maximizing one's own pleasure.

Epicureans, Stoics maintained, were thoroughly confused on human fellowship. A person who cuts off himself from others is like a head, hand or foot severed from a body.[117] The very actions of the Epicureans – the writing down and teaching of their principles – illustrated their confusion. Epictetus exhorts:

Go off to your couch and sleep! Lead the life of a worm, of which you have judged yourself worthy! Eat, drink, copulate, defecate and snore! What do you care how the rest of mankind will think about these matters? What do you care whether their ideas are sound or not? . . . What roused Epicurus from his slumber and forced him to write what he wrote? What else but what is the strongest thing in humans – nature.[118]

The Stoic view was opposite that of the Epicureans. The Stoics thought that Nature brought humans into communities.[119] Thus, Stoic invincibility is not an insular or selfish ideal, but one that is communal or even cosmic. An apprentice will find happiness as he progresses toward virtue by helping others find virtue also. Hence, it is the chief end of each person to make his interest identical to that of every other person.[120]

To achieve this end is to balance self- and other-concern, what the Stoics, in effect, call *oikeiosis*.[121] No one needs to sacrifice completely his own interest to help others. In all actions, one's own interest must be considered too, because one is as much a part of the cosmos as is any other person and one's own interest impacts the interests of others. One must not, however, secure one's own interest to the detriment of another's.

For one person to increase his welfare at the cost of the other person's welfare is more contrary to Nature than death, poverty, pain or any other thing that can happen to one's body or one's external possessions. It destroys human communal living and human society. If we are each about to plunder and carry off another's goods for the sake of our own, that will necessarily destroy what is in fact most according to Nature – namely the social life of human beings.[122]

Chrysippus, Cicero reports, says striking a balance between self- and other-concern does not rule out healthy competition among apprentices, so long as 'competitors' play by the rules.[123]

'When a man enters the foot-race', says Chrysippus with his usual aptness, 'it is his duty to put forth all his strength and strive with all his might to win, but he ought never with his foot to trip or with his hand to foul a competitor. Thus, in the stadium of life, it is not unfair for anyone to seek to obtain what is needful for his own advantage, but he has no right to wrest it from his neighbour.'[124]

Yet the sort of foot-race that best describes the balance a Stoic aims to achieve between self- and other-concern is cooperative competition toward the same goal – virtue – and the prize of virtue can go to more than one victor. Thus, the contest will be better, the more winners the contest produces – a point that Seneca makes: 'Wisdom has this reward, among other things: No one can be vanquished [*vinci*] by another, except when he is ascending. When one has arrived at the top [*ad summum*], however, it is a draw. There is no place for further ascent; the contest is decided.'[125] Hence, mutual succour is ethically desirable in the contest of life.

Overall, the Stoic view is to help as many as one can as often as one can and to do so in such a manner that one's kindnesses are remembered from generation to generation. Cicero says, 'Effort must, therefore, be given to benefit as many as possible with such kindnesses that the memory of such deeds shall be handed down to children and to their children's children so that they too may not be ungrateful.'[126]

In *Letter* XXIX, Seneca considers the view that other-concern should manifest itself by often advising many people so as to sometimes help some of them. Words cost nothing, so such a swamping policy seems to be the most economical way to help others. Yet the effect one will have on those few that one helps will ultimately be minimal. Wisdom is an art and every art must have a definite aim. Therefore, one should choose to help only those who aim to make progress toward virtue, and withdraw from all others – especially those who are hopeless. However, he adds almost parenthetically, one should not abandon those at a critical stage. With them, one should first try drastic remedies. Only if such remedies fail should one judge such persons to be hopeless.[127]

Stoic remedies, of course, are arguments and arguments comprise words. It follows that one must use words with circumspection and due measure, if one is to effect cure.

Words should be scattered like seed. No matter how tiny the seed may be, if it has once found favourable ground, it unfolds its strength and, from an insignificant thing, spreads to its greatest growth. Reason grows in the same way. It is not something large to look at, but increases in size as it does its work. Few words are spoken, but if one's mind has truly caught them, they take root and spring up. Indeed, precepts and seeds have the same quality.

They produce much and yet they are slight things. Only . . . let a favourable mind receive and assimilate them. Thereafter, of itself, the mind, giving back more than it has received, will also produce abundantly in its turn.[128]

Still, there is one great danger in trying to help others: A helper must guard against corruption by those whom he wants to help.

It is from his fellow-man that danger on a daily basis comes to a person. Equip yourself against that. Watch that with a guarded eye. There is no evil more frequent, more persistent and more obscured [*blandius*]. Even the storm, before it gathers, gives a warning. Houses crack before they crash. Smoke is the forerunner of fire. Yet damage from persons is instantaneous and the nearer it comes, the more carefully it is concealed.[129]

The point here is that in attempting to help others, one must be sure to protect oneself. One must be careful not to slide into depravity, while trying to assist another.

How is it best to protect oneself? First, one must try in one's affairs with others to do no harm so that no harm is done to oneself. Rejoice and sympathize with others. The end may not be a life entirely trouble-free, but it will at least be a life that is deceit-free. Second, one must be cautious when entering into friendships. Most importantly, one ought to commit to forming better friendships – those that are productive of virtue and that shield oneself from vice and the fickleness of fortune.[130]

Overall, the aim here is not merely to do one's duty, dictated by reason. Unlike Kant, duty, for the Stoics, is bounded by capabilities, which vary from person to person. Each of us (or nearly so) has a capacity to do certain things, like tell the truth or form genuine friendships, but it is not the case that each of us can do other things, like bail out a friend during financial hardship or help one who is excessively maudlin deal with reality. Thus, it is not because of rationality alone that one is duty-bound to do some action; it is because of rationality *and* a certain set of capabilities that enable one to do that action that one is bound to do it. Remove these capacities and one may no longer be bound to do that action.

Finally, the Stoic view of *oikeiosis* has implications for right and wrong actions in times of war. Cicero expresses the Stoic view on war, a precursor to just-war theory, in *On Duties*. Concerning justice in going to war, he writes: 'No war is just, unless it is entered into after an official demand for satisfaction or warning has been submitted and a formal declaration has been made.'[131] Again: 'The only excuse for going to war is that we may live in peace and unharmed. When victory is won, we should spare those who have not been bloodthirsty and barbarous in their warfare.'[132] Once at war, the objective is simple: 'We should always strive to secure a peace that will not admit of guile.'[133]

In Cicero's day, philosophers, poets, politicians and historians commonly held that one could achieve more through the valour of warfare than one could during peacetime. Hence, the Stoic view in *On Duties* is not only bold, but morally ahead of its time.[134]

Khreiai *for 'Oikeiosis'*

- '"Rational" . . . also implies "civic".'[135]
- 'The branch is cut off by someone else, but people cut themselves off through hatred and rejection and do not realize that they are cutting themselves off from the whole civic enterprise.'[136]

AUTHENTICITY: LIVING WITH ONE'S DOOR OPEN

I begin this section with two stories; only the first is true.

One of the intriguing characters in Greek antiquity was Alcibiades – the great Greek general of the Peloponnesian Wars and renowned pupil of Socrates. He was well born, strikingly handsome, and used to getting his way. Plato immortalized his peculiarities and excesses in *Symposium*. He depicted Alcibiades as a man with a clear recognition of his faults and a great potential for good, who just could not escape his many vices – especially lust and his passion for drink.

Plutarch included him in his *Lives of Eminent Greeks*. He said that Alcibiades' most powerful drives, manifest in his youth, were his desire to compete, his ostentation and his passion for over-indulgence.

As one of the three Athenian generals sent on the critical Sicilian Expedition during the Peloponnesian Wars, Alcibiades was recalled by the Athenians, just after the Athenian ships set sail, on account of certain religious crimes he was said to have committed. Sentenced to death, Alcibiades fled to Sparta and took up the Spartan way of life, as if he had never known another. In Sparta, Alcibiades seduced the wife of King Agis and impregnated her. Eventually the story got out and Alcibiades fled Sparta and took up residence under the satrap Tissaphernes in Persia, where he so won over Tissaphernes that the satrap, no friend to Greeks, named his most beautiful garden 'Alcibiades'. Shortly, Alcibiades too lost Tissaphernes' favour and escaped to join the Athenian fleet along the Ionian coast, where his brilliant generalship soon earned him back the esteem of the Athenians, who had earlier wanted to see him dead. After suffering a key naval setback at Ephesus, perhaps no fault of his own,[137] Alcibiades was again abandoned by the Athenians and forced to live out his life in Phrygia, where he was murdered years later.

In spite of his extraordinary looks and talent, Alcibiades was quite unmanageable and arrogant. While his lack of authenticity and chameleon-like tendencies endeared him to many superficially, it was impossible for those who knew him intimately to love him, without reservation. The attitude of the Athenians toward him was ambivalent and best summed in the words of Aristophanes: 'They miss him and they hate him too [when he is gone], but they cannot live without him.'[138]

There is also the story of Gyges, a Lydian shepherd to the king, which Cicero rehashes in *On Duties* and is taken from Plato's *Republic*. Gyges one day finds a gold ring on the finger of a large corpse in a chasm. He removes the ring, places it on his own finger and goes to an assembly of shepherds. On turning the bezel of the ring toward his palm, he finds that he becomes invisible, though he can still see everyone around him. With the aid of the ring, he eventually seduces the queen of Lydia, kills the king and those loyal to him, and becomes king of Lydia himself. The moral is that all persons, even those professing that the virtuous life is best, would act identically if they could find such a ring.

The Stoic Panaetius, Cicero states, disagrees. 'Now suppose a Stoic had just such a ring. He would not imagine that he was free to do wrong any more than if he did not have it. Good men seek out morally correct actions [*honesta*], not secrecy.'[139]

The story of Gyges, as is the account of Alcibiades, is a story about authenticity – a key virtue in an invincible lifestyle. For the Stoics, one is the same person at all times, in all places and in front of all people, and even by oneself, if one is virtuous. Virtue demands authenticity.

Authenticity, of course, goes against much of today's consequen-tialist thinking, which maintains that actions whose consequences principally impact agents and agents alone are to be judged neither moral nor immoral. That implies a certain amount of social separa-tion in moral activity: One can be one person while alone, so long as one is not the same person while in public.

Social separation has two senses. First, there is the relatively harm-less social separation that guarantees each person some private space for free expression or personal development – what is commonly called negative liberty. Secondly, there is the tendency to wall off the public and private sectors and relegate moral activity to the public sector alone. This view, most recognizable in the work of John Stuart Mill, maintains that morality only concerns the effects of one's inter-actions with others. What one does that impacts only oneself, however seemingly vicious, is not a moral concern.[140] Social separation, then, implies that there cannot be a universalized private morality.

It is otherwise for the Stoics. Seneca states in *On Tranquillity* that it is torturous for anyone, being one person at one time and another person at another time, to be constantly on guard. There is greater simplicity in being one person at all times. He concludes, 'It is better to be scorned by reason of simplicity than tortured by perpetual pre-tence.'[141]

To be authentic is to be able to live, as it were, with one's door open at all times. Seneca says in *Letter* XLIII to Lucillius:

I shall mention a fact by which you may weigh the worth of a man's character: You will scarcely find anyone who can live with his door wide open. It is our conscience, not our pride, which has put doorkeepers at our doors. We live in such a fashion that being suddenly exposed to view is equivalent to being caught in the act. What profit, however, is there in hiding ourselves away? A good conscience welcomes the crowd, but a bad conscience, even in solitude, is disturbed and troubled.[142]

What a person conceals is more to be regarded as his true self than what he readily shows. Seneca gives the analogy of buying a horse or slave. 'When you buy a horse, you order its blanket to be removed. You pull off the garments from slaves that are advertised for sale, so that no bodily flaws may escape your notice. If you judge a man, do you judge him, wrapped in a disguise?'[143]

In *Letter* XXV, Seneca tells us that a good rule of thumb for progress toward virtue is to live as if a Stoic sage were next to oneself at all times.[144] Elsewhere he says that one should act as if all of one's actions were in plain sight of all human beings.[145] Aurelius says that one ought to live as if one were on a mount and in plain view of others.

In short, Stoic authenticity requires each person to act pursuant to his own nature and that demands self-knowledge.

> We must not act to oppose universal Nature, but to follow the bent of our own particular nature [*propriam nostram*], while safeguarding the universal laws. Even if other careers should be better and nobler, we may still regulate our own pursuits by the standard of our own nature. It is pointless to fight against one's nature or to aim at what is impossible to attain.[146]

Cicero adds, 'The more a person's character is his own, the better it suits him.'[147] In consequence, doing what is fitting is nothing more than uniformity of one's life as a whole (*aequabilitatis universae vitae*) through consistency of one's individual actions.[148]

Being in full possession of oneself has implications today for one's choice of career. To live virtuously and increase one's chance of satisfaction in life, one ought to choose a career authentically – that is, in keeping with one's natural talents and inclinations.[149] It follows that it is best to want to do what one can do well instead of wanting to do what one cannot do well.

Authenticity also has implications for how one presents oneself through speech. Seneca writes:

> Speech [*oratio*] is the garb of the soul. If it is trimmed, dyed or treated, it shows that there are defects and a certain amount of flaws in the mind. Elegant speech [*concinnitas*] is not a manly garb. If we should have the privilege of looking into a good man's soul, what a fair, holy, magnificent, gracious and shining expression – radiant on the one side with justice and temperance and on the other with bravery and wisdom – would we see.[150]

Such a beautiful soul does not express itself with honeyed sophistry. Like Socrates, a man of sense and education is content to express his meaning plainly and clearly.[151]

Last, authenticity has implications for thought. For Stoics, one ought not to entertain thoughts one could not share with another. Cicero says, 'To a good man . . . nothing can seem expedient that is not morally right. Thus, such a man will never venture to think or to do anything that he would not dare openly to proclaim.'[152]

Khreiai *for 'Authenticity'*
- 'There is nothing so fitting as in all things to preserve consistency in every act conducted and every plan comprehended.'[153]
- 'The really great person speaks informally and easily. Whatever he says, he speaks with assurance rather than with pains.'[154]

VIRTUE AS PEAK-PERFORMANCE

Aristo of Chios (see Chapter 1) noted what he took to be an inconsistency in Stoic thinking on indifferents. If indifferents have no impact on the happiness of a Stoic sage, there can be no reason for a Stoic to prefer conveniences, like health and wealth, to inconveniences, like illness and poverty.

> Aristo . . . thought all these things utterly worthless, and said, for example, that there was absolutely nothing to choose between the most perfect health and the most grievous sickness; and so people have long ago quite rightly given up arguing against them. In insisting on the uniqueness of virtue in such a sense as to rob it of any power of choice among external things and to deny it any starting-point or basis, the Stoics destroy the very virtue they desired to cherish.[155]

According to Aristo, to say that a Stoic prefers to live with conveniences and without inconveniences can only mean, if it does make sense, that selection of the former and avoidance of the latter have some bearing, even if only minimal, on one's overall happiness. If so, the Stoic view is not substantially different from that of Aristotle, who thought that some measure of external goods was needed for happiness. Is that so?

As Cicero writes, it is certainly uncontested that the Stoic view of selecting conveniences and avoiding inconveniences is a matter of following Nature.[156] The difficulty comes in deciphering just what it means to 'follow Nature'. To do so, however, requires first that we come to grips with what it means for a Stoic sage to act on indifferents,[157] though our emphasis throughout is on the Stoic progressor.

According to one interpretation, what may be called the indifferents-first view, a Stoic sage is thought to use indifferents to maximize virtuous activity. Virtuous action, then, is a matter of calculating, among various possible courses of action involving indifferents, the most virtuous course. Here virtue is a matter of efficiency in using indifferents, presumably to maximize the overall good. A person who continually acts with utmost efficiency on indifferents demonstrates his virtue, so long as we grasp that the efficiency that we describe here is not judged by outcome, but by deliberation on outcomes. The merit of this view is that there is plenty of text consistent with it – especially Cicero's take on Stoicism in *On Ends* III and Seneca's thoughts on suicide.[158]

The chief problem with the indifferents-first view is that it places a premium on deliberation before action, which, I believe, is misguided. It also places a premium on deliberating about indifferents – things inconsequential to human flourishing – and that too seems untoward. Virtue here becomes right thinking about indifferents and that makes the right use of them the cause of goodness and human flourishing.

According to another interpretation, what may be called the virtue-first view, use of indifferents does not determine and is not equivalent to virtue; virtue itself dictates how one uses indifferents. Instead of deliberating on indifferents to maximize virtue, a Stoic sage reflects on his own virtue and that decides which course of action is to be preferred – that is, how indifferents ought to be used.

The virtue-first view makes sense, once one is a sage. Right action then is a matter of deliberating well and correctly from the vantage point of virtue, which implies self-knowledge and flawless judgement. The problem with the virtue-first view is that it does not tell one how to become virtuous in the first place. How does one gain the self-understanding indispensable for sagacity prior to attaining it?

In an effort to overcome the problems of the two views, Tad Brennan considers a different view – what he calls the No-Shoving Model (NSM). It is motivated chiefly by a quote from Chrysippus, which we have already seen.

> When a man enters the foot-race . . . it is his duty to put forth all his strength and strive with all his might to win, but he ought

never with his foot to trip or with his hand to foul a competitor. Thus, in the stadium of life, it is not unfair for anyone to seek to obtain what is needful for his own advantage, but he has no right to wrest it from his neighbour.[159]

NSM has two parts. First, each competitor ought to strive as hard as he can in the competition. Second, each competitor ought to aim for the 'things useful in life' – the Stoic conveniences. Such features of the model are constrained by two Stoic principles of appropriate acts Cicero lists in *On Duties* and in *On Ends*: harm no one and preserve the common utility.[160]

NSM, Brennan believes, avoids many of the pitfalls of the first two models. First, for NSM, a person must go beyond mere consideration of his own virtue, when acting. His own virtue does not play any role in deliberation whatsoever.[161] Second, for NSM, judgements about oneself are also judgements of justice, as they apply to a person's community, country and society.[162]

It is here that the game setting of the NSM is significant. The pursuit of indifferents is likened meaningfully to a game.

> In this context, it is worth pointing out that my deliberations [on indifferents] all take place within the game, and are based on considerations drawn exclusively from within the game. Crossing the finish-line ahead of my competitors is a goal internal to the game of foot-races; tripping and shoving are fouls internal to the game of foot-races (they are permissible in some other games). My piece of bread has value, but only within the game; your property rights have a claim on me, but only within the game. The considerations of virtue and value are all external to this; it is their job to explain why we should have any interest in playing this game, with this set of internal ends, these rules for getting points and these regulations for fouls and penalties.[163]

In the context of a game, virtue has *no* deliberative role; it merely explains to us why we ought to play the game in the first place.[164]

Brennan's NSM is, I think, headed in the right direction, but Brennan, I think, draws too much from the competitive-game analogy and there are good reasons for thinking the analogy to be misleading. The agonistic element of NSM seems wrong-headed. In what follows, I wish to develop a new model, without the agonistic implications, that more sharply delineates progressors from sages.

For progressors, the general and particular principles motivating appropriate acts are fairly well engrained in them, and their will is in the main well harmonized with that of Nature or deity. Because principles motivate behaviour and because their will is not in perfect harmony with Nature, deliberation plays a crucial role in motivating progressive action. Not so for sages, I believe. For sages, the general and particular principles no longer motivate activity; they *underlie* activity. That means that the habitual reference to and reflection on precepts and doctrines that occurs prior to acts of progressors is unneeded for sages. Such principles have been so habitually engrained in them that they are, literally, a part of their character. That is just what it means for something to be done from a settled psychical disposition – to be a right or perfect act. Right acts, then, would seem to be characteristically unreflective or non-deliberative behaviours – at least when it comes to deliberation about principles. So far, that much may seem uncontroversial. What I wish to add, however, is that right acts are also highly unreflective or non-deliberative behaviours, even when it comes to facing everyday-life circumstances. For a sage, there is little deliberating on the value of indifferents and the welfare of others. That applies not only in scenarios that are fairly uncomplicated, but, I believe, even in cases of ample complexity.

We may illustrate the point by the early Stoic Aristo's use of the analogy of javelin-throwing.

When a man has gained a complete understanding of this definition [of the greatest good] and has thoroughly learned it, he can frame for himself a precept, directing what is to be done in a given case. It is just like the student of javelin-throwing. He keeps aiming at a fixed target and thus trains his hand to give direction to the javelin. When, by instruction and practice, he has gained the desired ability, he can then employ it against any target he wishes, as he has learned to strike not any random object, but precisely the object at which he has aimed. Similarly, *he who has equipped himself for the whole of life does not need to be advised concerning each separate item*, because he is now trained to meet his problem as a whole, as he knows not merely how he should live with his wife or his son, but how he should live aright.[165]

What Aristo illustrates, by the use of training at javelin-throwing, is what it means for a Stoic to equip himself for the 'whole of life' – to act rightly in particular situations, to meet problems as a whole and overall to live aright.[166] What Aristo has in mind, I believe, is just what we today would call an athlete 'in the zone'.

It is typical of athletes who have experienced being in the zone to speak of complete immersion in the game, things slowing down, effortless play, freedom from distractions and extreme confidence in their capacities, while competing. It seems reasonable to characterize Stoic sagacity through *homologia* as an application of being in the zone in terms of one's moral activity – what I call the Peak-Performance Model (PPM).

Like athletic activity in the zone, Stoic sagacity would, I think, be similarly unreflective most of the time. Sages do not have to pause and reflect on circumstances, as they immediately 'see' the right course of action. The chief difference would be this. Since sagacity is mostly a permanent state of soul, it would be psychic zoning or ethical peak performance each day. As such, Stoic sagacity as ethical peak performance would not be an episodic phenomenon as is athletic zoning. That is what it means for Stoic sagacity to meet life as a whole – what I take to be the measure of complete cosmic integration.[167] PPM, if correct, explains the Stoic paradox that a sage's change from vice to sagacity occurs not only in a moment, but also often without his awareness.[168]

How does PPM relate to Brennan's No-Shoving Model? We recall that, for Chrysippus, virtue entails that one may compete for the first prize in life, so long as one does not trip or shove competitors along the way. That is, in some sense, the Stoic notion of *oikeiosis*.

Oikeiosis for the Stoics is more than just a matter of respectful competition with others, where 'respect' is cashed out as refusal to harm another while competing. Like NSM, PPM suggests a contest that openly embraces Stoic egalitarianism, other-concern and cosmic culpability. Yet part of other-concern is helping others in their own quest for virtue. For PPM, the contest will be better, the more winners the contest produces.[169] Seneca writes: 'Wisdom has this reward, among other things: No one can be vanquished by another, unless while he is ascending. When you have arrived at the top, it is a draw. There is no place for further ascent; the contest is decided.'[170] So according to the rules, mutual succour is ethically desirable in the contest of life.

Another facet of PPM – one that Brennan does not address – concerns the actions of Stoic sages. Sages, it is acknowledged by Stoics themselves, provide progressors with exemplars for appropriate acts, and such exemplars are needed since ethical rules for right conduct are not categorically binding. Yet such exemplars are of limited use. For a progressor to behave identically to a sage in a situation that is identical is not to act identically, as sages have different psychical dispositions than do progressors. The situation is worse than that, however. It is commonly assumed, due to the perfection and equivalence of each sage's act and the equipotency of each sage, that any sage in a situation identical to another will act identically to that other. That, I believe, is patently false. The Stoics consistently maintain that each person is born with unique capacities and into a unique station in life. Consider again Panaetius' four-*personae* theory, which describes a universal capacity for rational thought; idiosyncratic capacities that vary considerably from person to person; one's unique real-life circumstances; and the choices one makes along the way. What is universal here is only *persona* one. That implies, *ceteris paribus*, an equal capacity for rational thought among human beings. *Personae* two and three strongly suggest real-life idiosyncrasies cannot be washed away once one attains sagacity. *Persona* four, what determines moral worth, differentiates sages from non-sages. Thus, what all sages have in common are an equal capacity for rationality and an equal capacity, through education, for making right choices. That is equipotency and that does not imply sages must make the same choice in the same situation.

Peak performance, then, entails for a Stoic sage or progressor self-understanding – that is, knowledge of what is one's own and not one's own, what is within one's reach and what is outside of it. The right sort of upbringing will help a youth to learn about himself – what he can and cannot do and what desires are worth having. It will also help him to hone his reasoning skills, so that he will know how to adapt himself uniquely to ever-changing circumstances each day. With careful nurture, he will develop a clear grasp of his capacities and his station in life and he will not strive for what is beyond his reach. Epictetus gives a helpful analogy in his *Handbook*. It is meet to behave as if at a banquet. Do not call out or stretch out one's hand for food. Wait for it to come to you and, when it does, take your rightful portion and pass on the food, without delay, to the next person, so that he too may have his rightful share.[171] There is nothing starkly agonistic in Epictetus' analogy, as there seems to be with NSM, and that is how it should be. It is merely doing what one can to the best of one's capacities and allowing sufficient space for others to do the same.

Khreiai *for 'Virtue as Peak-Performance'*

- 'In the sacred games many have won the victory by wearing out the hand of their assailants through stubborn endurance [*obstinata patientia*]. Consider a Stoic in this class of men, who by long and faithful training have attained the strength to endure and tire out any assault of the enemy.'[172]
- 'The excellent person is invincible [*aettetos*]. He enters no contest where he is not superior.' [173]

THE 'INVINCIBLE' APPRENTICE

Does invincibility matter today? One answer is that we live in mad times.

We are mad – not merely privately, but publicly. We prohibit manslaughter and isolated murders, but what of war and the much-vaunted crime of slaughtering whole peoples? There are no limits to our greed and our cruelty . . . [C]ruelties are practised in accordance with acts of Senate and popular assembly and the public is ordered to do what is disallowed the individual. Deeds punished by loss of life when committed in secret are praised by us when uniformed generals have carried them out. Humans, naturally the gentlest class of beings, are not ashamed to revel in the blood of others, to wage war, and to entrust the waging of war to their sons, while the dumb and wild beasts are at peace with each other.[174]

This quote was not taken, as it may seem, from a contemporary source. Instead, it was written some 2,000 years ago by Seneca. The madness about which he speaks is still with us today. It is the reason why we need philosophy and whatever amount of invincibility comes with its cultivation and practice.

'Who is the invincible person [*ho aettetos*]?' Epictetus asks. He is not one who feels no pain with a headache or an earache. The invincible person may even groan from pain, but he will not groan from the centre of his being. He differs not much from an indomitable athlete, who does what he has to do each moment of an event in order to win that event. Whatever one puts in his path – money, sex, reputation, abuse or even praise – he treats, like the indomitable athlete, with indifference. Yet unlike the athlete, the invincible man's confidence comes not from the size of his quadriceps or triceps, but from a doughty stability within.[175]

It is his internal stability that affords a Stoic invincibility of a sort to the arrows of fortune. Following the Socratic dictum that no harm can come to one who is wise, Seneca writes:

> It does not matter how many arrows are hurled against him, because none can pierce [*sit nulli penetrabilis*] him. As the hardness of certain stones is impervious to steel and adamant cannot be cut, hewn or ground, but in turn blunts whatever comes into contact with it; as certain substances cannot be consumed by fire, but, though encompassed by flame, retain their hardness and their shape; as certain cliffs, projecting into the deep, break the force of the sea and, though lashed for countless ages, show no traces of its wrath; in such a manner the spirit of a Stoic is impregnable [*solidus*] and has gathered such a measure of strength as to be no less safe from injury than those things that I have mentioned.[176]

Enjoying perfect happiness, a Stoic sage enjoys a 'happy, perfect, and fortunate life, free from hindrance, interference and want'.[177]

Striving for sagacity, a progressor aims for complete disaffection concerning externals and immunity to the exigencies of fortune. Disaffection does not prevent a Stoic from acting; it merely readies him for any outcome. If right-intended actions should bring favourable results, he is unchanged by them; if they should bring ills, he conquers them.[178] Plutarch mentions a boxing match at the Isthmian Games, where one of the boxers was hit so hard that the crowd groaned. Nonetheless, the recipient of the blow was silent. 'You see what a thing training [*askesis*] is? The man who is hit is silent, while the spectators cry out.'[179]

To strive for invincibility, then, is to strive for oneness in soul and in body. Conveniences, when they come to a progressor, should be like spices to his life that add nothing to his internal stability and goodness.

When a person takes care of his body and his soul, weaving the texture of his good from both, his condition is perfect. He has found the consummation of his prayers, if there is no commotion in his soul or pain in his body. If certain extra conveniences [*blandimenta*] come to him, they add nothing to his greatest good, but, as it were, they season it and add spice to it. For the absolute good of man's nature is satisfied with peace in the body and in the soul.[180]

To be invincible, then, is to be at peace with oneself and peace is entirely an internal affair, indifferent to fortune.

To have internal peace through indifference to fortune is to have one's internal beliefs well ordered and consistent. Thus, an invincible person is one of unshakable conviction. He orders his beliefs in accordance with reality and changes them only when reality dictates that they be so changed. Epictetus speaks of an invincible man as an athletic contestant in life's most important contests. Such an athlete conquers and proves his superiority not through acquiring things, but through letting go of things.

The excellent person [*ho spoudaios*] is invincible [*aettetos*]. He enters no contest where he is not superior. He says, 'If you want my property in the country, take it. Take my servants. Take my office. Take my paltry body. Still you will not make me desire to fail to get what I will. You will not make me fall into what I should avoid.' This is the only contest into which the good person enters – one, namely, that is concerned with the things that belong in the province of the moral purpose. How, then, can he help but be invincible?[181]

Carrying the athletic analogy further, the apprentice should be likened to a pancratiast, not a gladiator. The gladiator lays aside the sword that he uses and takes it up again, but the pancratiast always has his hands and only his hands, and he needs only to clench them and he is ready to compete.[182] Such is his self-sufficiency and freedom from externals.

True invincibility means being untouched by the wickedness of others. Why? Seneca offers several arguments, of which I give two. First, he states that virtue is clearly stronger than wickedness and what is stronger cannot be injured by what is weaker, therefore a virtuous person cannot be harmed by one of lesser virtue.[183] Second and more persuasively, he states that a Stoic is in want of nothing and a wicked person has nothing that a Stoic wants. Thus, a Stoic cannot be benefited or injured by a wicked person.[184]

In addition, true invincibility means suffering no regret. Cicero says: 'It calls for great mental ability, by reflection, to anticipate the future, to discover some time in advance what may happen for good or ill and what must be done in any possible event, and never to be reduced to have to say, "I had not thought of that".'[185]

Thus, a progressor's walk should not be timid and cautious, but sure-footed and measured in order to confront fortune, not retreat from it. He has no reason to fear fortune, as everything that he has – from his most trifling possessions to his family, friends and his very body – is among the things that are given on loan. He lives completely as a renter. Everything that has been given to him on loan will someday be reclaimed.[186]

Finally, there is Seneca's vivid description of an invincible person, a Stoic sage, who sees truth itself.

> A soul, gazing on truth, that is skilled in what should be sought and what should be shunned; that establishes standards of value not according to opinion but Nature; that penetrates the whole world and directs its contemplating gaze on all its phenomena; that pays strict attention to thoughts and actions, equally great and forceful; that is superior alike to hardships and blandishments; that yields itself to neither extreme of fortune; that rises above all blessings and tribulations; that is absolutely beautiful, perfectly equipped with grace as well as with strength, healthy and sinewy, unruffled and undismayed; and that is one which no violence can shatter and one that acts of chance can neither exalt nor depress – a soul like that is virtue itself.[187]

Invincibility here is complete communion with the cosmos. Ultimately, such invincibility means that one can die with the same freedom and peace of mind one had at birth.

Is invincibility, as perfection, a manifestly unreachable end? Is it too ethically demanding? Epictetus says, 'Is it possible to be free from fault altogether? No, that cannot be achieved, but it is possible always to be intent on avoiding faults. We must be satisfied if we succeed in escaping at least a few faults by never relaxing our attention.'[188] Seneca too, in his letters and moral essays, often wavers on the possibility of Stoic perfectionism. Most often, he gears his advice toward the lifelong progressor. Why, then, ought one to aim at perfection, if it is an ideal that seems in principle unattainable, even for Stoic philosophers?

This much can be said to answer the question. First, perfection for Stoics was likely put forth as an ideal that was *not* in principle unattainable. Even though there has likely never actually been a real sage in human history, the possibility of there being one had to be real, given the high regard that Stoics had for reason – something humans shared with gods. Consequently, perfectionism was not an unassailable ideal, but rather an extraordinarily demanding ideal. Second, to the objection that perfectionism is too demanding to be ethically serviceable, the Stoics would say, in avoiding vice, each person certainly moves closer to self-sufficiency and invincibility. How much closer, one might ask, and will the end be worth the effort? Invincibility is desirable, because psychic stability, in any amount, is desirable. We may call this the 'Progressivist Principle':

Progressivist Principle: The proper end for a Stoic initiate is to live a life that approximates as much as possible a life of freedom from emotion and full awareness of what is and what is not one's own.

Khreiai *for 'The "Invincible" Apprentice'*

- 'For the invincible person, every action of the whole of life is regulated by consideration of what is morally right and morally wrong.'[189]
- 'Philosophy can settle this problem for you and give you, to my thinking, the greatest gift that exists – lack of regret for your own actions.'[190]

INVINCIBILITY AS COSMIC INTEGRATION

The sixteenth-century poet Robert Southwell, in these lines of his poem, 'Content and Rich', nicely captures Stoic cosmopolitanism.

I have no hopes but one,
Which is of heavenly reign;
Effects attained, or not desired,
All lower hopes refrain.

I feel no care of coin;
Well-doing is my wealth;
My mind to me an empire is,
While grace affordeth health.

I clip high-climbing thoughts,
The wings of swelling pride;
Their fall is worst, that from the height
Of greatest honour slide . . .

No change of Fortune's calms
Can cast my comforts down;
When Fortune smiles, I smile to think
How quickly she will frown.

And when in forward mood
She proves an angry foe,
Small gain I found to let her come,
Less loss to let her go.

By today's philosophical standards, it is no exaggeration to say that the Stoic good life is one of hyper-rationality. Epictetus says that rationality provides the foundation of philosophy. 'This, then, is a starting point [*arkhe*] in philosophy – a perception of the state of one's own governing principle [*hegemonikou*]; for when once a man realizes that it is weak, he will no longer wish to employ it upon great matters.'[191] He adds that rationality also helps people to recognize and resolve conflicts among human beings. Epictetus goes so far as to say that it is by virtue of rationality that humans are not at all inferior to the gods.[192] Seneca expresses a similar sentiment. 'Reason is nothing else than a portion of the divine spirit set in a human body.'[193]

Stoic hyper-rationality takes cosmic form in Zeus, with humans as rational parts. 'This whole universe [*totum*] that encompasses us is one and it is deity. We are associates [*socii*] and members of deity.'[194]

Cosmological unity has local, ethical implications. To commit harm to another person is at once to commit harm to the whole and, thus, to oneself. Cicero says: 'To injure one's country is a crime. Therefore, to injure a fellow citizen is a crime, for he is a part of the country and, if we revere the whole, the parts are sacred. Thus, to injure any man is a crime, for he is a fellow citizen in the greater commonwealth.'[195] Aurelius gives a similar argument:

> What happens to an individual is a cause of the wellbeing, fulfilment and even existence of what directs the world. The whole is damaged, if you cut away anything at all from its coherence and continued existence. Not only are its parts damaged, but its purposes are also. This is what you are doing, when you complain: You are hacking and destroying.[196]

Cosmic belonging implies cosmic responsibility, which is a matter of aiming, through use of reason, at what is possible and rejecting what is impossible. Epictetus states that only fools and slaves reach for what is impossible. Thereby they act as strangers in the cosmos, who fight against deity with false judgments.[197] To know what is possible, cosmic belonging is strictly a matter of keeping one's eyes opened to the truths of Nature. Seneca writes:

> First of all, truth and Nature exist. A Stoic does not follow Nature as do the other animals – with their eyes too dull to perceive the divine in it. In the second place, there is the law of life and a Stoic's life is made to conform to universal principles [universa]. The law of life has taught us not merely to know the gods, but to follow them and to welcome the gifts of chance, precisely as if they were imperatives [imperata]. The law of life has forbidden us to give heed to false opinions and has weighted the value of each thing by a true standard of appraisal. The law of life has condemned those pleasures with which remorse is intermingled and has praised those goods that will always satisfy. The law of life has published the truth abroad that he is most happy who has no need of happiness and that he is most powerful who has power over himself.[198]

In seeking and grasping truth, the mind, unbounded by space, participates in divinity and tolerates only those limits that Zeus has established.[199] To such a person, time has no meaning. A short life and a long life afford the same pleasure. Death, whenever it may come, is always welcome.

> If death comes near with its summons, even though it is untimely in its arrival, though it cut one off in one's prime, a person has had

a taste of all that the longest life can give. Such a person has in great measure come to understand the universe. He knows that morally correct things do not depend on time for their growth, but that any life must seem short to those who measure its length by pleasures that are empty and, for that reason, without limit.[200]

Posidonius succinctly and beautifully expresses the sentiment: 'A single day among the learned lasts longer than the longest life of the ignorant.'[201] The notion of cosmic belonging through participation in the divine has its roots in human aesthetic sensibility.[202]

Khreiai *for 'Invincibility as Cosmic Integration'*

- 'We should . . . in our dealings with people show . . . reverence toward all men, not only toward the men who are best, but toward others as well.'[203]
- 'And yet what reason is there for a sage to need a living? If it is to support life, then life itself is after all something indifferent. If it is for pleasure, pleasure too is something indifferent. Yet, if it is for virtue, virtue itself is sufficient for happiness.'[204]

NOTES

1 Plutarch, *Progress in Virtue*, 75e–76b.
2 Epictetus, *Discourses*, II.xiv.23–9.
3 Aurelius, *Meditations*, V.8.
4 See Dirk Obbink, 'The Stoic Sage in the Cosmic City', in *Topics in Stoic Philosophy*, ed. Katerina Ierodiakonou (Oxford: Oxford University Press, 1999), pp. 178–95.
5 Aurelius, *Meditations*, VI.44.
6 Epictetus, *Discourses* II.vi.26. See also II.x.4.
7 Plato, *Republic*, 462a.
8 Epictetus, *Discourses*, I.ix.1.
9 Aristotle, *Nicomachean Ethics*, X.6–8.
10 Cicero, *Duties*, I.xliii.153–4, 160.
11 Epictetus, *Discourses*, II.xx.8–11.
12 *ISA*, Hierocles, IV.671.7–673.11.
13 Seneca, *Equanimity*, IV.4.
14 Seneca, *Benefits*, III.xxviii.1.
15 Seneca, *Benefits*, III.xviii.2.
16 Epictetus, *Discourses*, II.xxii.34–6.
17 Seneca, *Epistles*, V, 20–1.
18 Seneca, *Epistles*, LXXXII.20–1.
19 Seneca, *Epistles*, LIX.16.

20 Seneca, *Epistles*, XX.2.
21 Seneca, *Epistles*, CXX.20.
22 Cicero, *Ends*, III.xv.50.
23 Seneca, *Benefits*, IV.xxxiii.1–3.
24 Seneca, *Epistles*, XCII.2.
25 Seneca, *Good Life*, III.3.
26 Seneca, *Epistles*, LIX.2.
27 Seneca, *Epistles*, CV.7.
28 Seneca, *Good Life*, IV.2–V.1.
29 Seneca, *Good Life*, IX.3.
30 Seneca, *Equanimity*, II.3–4.
31 Seneca, *Equanimity*, III.6.
32 Diogenes Laertius says that Zeno, Cleanthes, Posidonius and Hecato followed this definition. D.L., VII.87.
33 Cicero, *Ends*, IV.vi.14–15.
34 Lawrence Becker, *A New Stoicism* (Princeton, NJ: Princeton University Press, 1998), chapter 5.
35 Seneca, *Helvia*, V.1.
36 Seneca, *Good Life*, V.3.
37 Friedrich Nietzsche, *On the Genealogy of Morality*, trans. M. Clark and Alan Swensen (Indianapolis: Hackett Publishing Company, Inc., 1998), pp. 109–10.
38 Nietzsche, *Genealogy of Morality*, p. 117.
39 Seneca, *Epistles*, XC.3.
40 Seneca, *Epistles*, XCII.3.
41 Cicero, *Duties*, I.v.15–16.
42 Seneca, *Good Life*, V.3.
43 Seneca, *Good Life*, VI.1–2.
44 Cicero, *Duties*, I.vi.13, 18–19.
45 Aurelius, *Meditations*, XI.15.
46 Cicero, *Duties*, I.xiii.41.
47 Cicero, *Duties*, III.xii.50–7.
48 Cf. Robert Nozick, *Anarchy, State, and Utopia* (New York: Basic Books, Inc., 1974).
49 Aurelius, *Meditations*, IX.1.
50 Cicero, *Duties*, I.xiii.39.
51 Cicero, *Duties*, III.xxix.107.
52 Cicero, *Duties*, III.xxv.95.
53 Seneca, *Benefits*, IV.xxxvi.3.
54 Aurelius, *Meditations*, VI.21.
55 Seneca, *Anger*, II.xxix.4.
56 Cicero, *Duties*, I.iv.13.
57 D.L., VII.26.
58 Isaiah Berlin, 'Two Concepts of Liberty', *Four Essays on Liberty* (Oxford: Oxford University Press, 1969).
59 Seneca, *Epistles*, LI.9.
60 Cicero, *Stoic Paradoxes*, 33.
61 Epictetus, *Discourses*, IV.iv.30–2.

62 Epictetus, *Discourses*, IV.i.62–3.
63 Seneca, *Good Life*, XV.7.
64 Cicero, *Stoic Paradoxes*, 34.
65 Epictetus, *Discourses*, II.i.21–3.
66 Seneca, *Anger*, II.xxi.3.
67 Plutarch, *Progress in Virtue*, 82f.
68 Seneca, *Epistles*, XCII.6.
69 Seneca, *Epistles*, XII.10.
70 Epictetus, *Discourses*, IV.i.175.
71 Epictetus, *Discourses*, IV.i.30.
72 Aesop, *Fables*, XXI.
73 The reference is to *Iliad*, VII.264. Epictetus, *Discourses*, II.9.xxii.
74 Epictetus, *Discourses*, III.xxii.6–7.
75 Cicero, *Duties*, I.xxx.107–17.
76 Seneca, *Tranquillity*, VI.3 and *Anger*, III.vi.3.
77 Epictetus, *Handbook* 5.
78 Epictetus, *Discourses*, III.xiii.20.
79 Seneca, *Epistles*, LXXIV.27–9.
80 Seneca, *Epistles*, LXXXV.22.
81 Irwin translation. Aristotle, *Nicomachean Ethics*, IV.3 (1124b6–9).
82 Seneca, *Epistles*, XXXIX.4.
83 Cicero, *Ends*, III.vi.22–vii.23.
84 Seneca, *Epistles*, XCV.43.
85 Seneca, *Epistles*, XIV.16.
86 Seneca, *Epistles*, LXXXV.33.
87 Seneca, *Epistles*, XXIX.3.
88 Seneca, *Good Life*, XX.2. In keeping with the Kantian maxim to develop one's natural capacities to their fullest potential. Immanuel Kant, *Groundwork for a Metaphysics of Morals*, #423.
89 Aurelius, *Meditations*, V.9.
90 Seneca, *Equanimity*, XII.1.
91 Aurelius, *Meditations*, VII.3.
92 Seneca, *Shortness of Life*, XVII.1. See Herodotus, *Histories*, VII.45–6.
93 Euripides, *Hippolytus*, trans. Kenneth Cavander (New York: Dell Publishing Co., Inc., 1965).
94 Aurelius, *Meditations*, III.3.
95 Aurelius, *Meditations*, II.14.
96 Seneca, *Epistles*, LXXIV.27–8 and *Benefits*, V.xvii.5–7.
97 Seneca, *Epistles*, LXXVII.4.
98 Seneca, *Epistles*, XCIII.8.
99 Seneca, *Shortness of Life*, VII.8.
100 Seneca, *Epistles*, LXXI.2–3.
101 Seneca, *Shortness of Life*, III.1.
102 Seneca, *Shortness of Life*, III.4.
103 Following Hays' translation here. Aurelius, *Meditations* III.16.
104 Seneca, *Epistles*, LXXII.4.
105 Cicero, *Duties*, I.iv.11.
106 D.L., VIII.89.

107 Cicero, *Ends*, III.ix.32 and xiv.45–6.
108 Seneca, *Epistles*, LXXXIV.10.
109 Seneca, *Benefits*, IV.xxi.4.
110 Seneca, *Epistles*, XXVI.10.
111 Seneca, *Epistles*, XXVI.10.
112 Seneca, *Epistles*, XXX.3–6.
113 Seneca, *Epistles*, XXX.10–11.
114 Seneca, *Epistles*, XCIII.9.
115 Seneca, *Epistles*, CI.15.
116 Seneca, *Epistles*, XCIII.2.
117 Aurelius, *Meditations*, VIII.32.
118 Epictetus, *Discourses*, II.xx.10–16.
119 Cicero says, however, that the chief reason for the establishment of con-
     stitutional states was for the securing of property rights. *Duties*,
     II.xxi.73.
120 Cicero, *Duties*, III.vi.26.
121 Literally, the process by which things are rendered familiar to oneself
     or one's own. When I refer to *oikeiosis* here, I am referring to what is
     most rightly one's own as a fully rational, adult human being.
122 Cicero, *Duties*, III.v.21.
123 Brennan takes this as the model for Stoic right action, which he calls
     the No-Shoving Model. See Tad Brennan, *The Stoic Life: Emotions,
     Duty, and Fate* (Oxford: Clarendon Press, 2005), chapter 13.
124 Cicero, *Duties*, III.x.42.
125 Following Gummere's translation here.
126 Cicero, *Duties*, II.sviii.62–3.
127 Seneca, *Epistles*, XXIX.3.
128 Seneca, *Epistles*, XXXVIII.2.
129 Seneca, *Epistles*, CIII.1–3.
130 Seneca, *Epistles*, CIV.22.
131 Cicero, *Duties*, I.xi.36.
132 Cicero, *Duties*, I.xi.35.
133 Cicero, *Duties*, I.xi.35.
134 Cicero, *Duties*, I.xxii.74.
135 Aurelius, *Meditations*, X.2.
136 Aurelius, *Meditations*, XI.8.
137 Because of the foolishness of Antiochus, whom Alcibiades left in
     charge of the fleet during a brief fund-raising campaign in Caria.
138 Aristophanes, *Frogs*, 1424.
139 Cicero, *Duties*, III.ix.38.
140 John Stuart Mill, *On Liberty.*
141 Seneca, *Tranquillity*, XVII.2.
142 Seneca, *Epistles*, XLIII.4–5.
143 Seneca, *Epistles*, LXXX.9.
144 Seneca, *Epistles*, XXV.5.
145 Seneca, *Epistles*, LXXXIII.1.
146 Cicero, *Duties*, I.xxxi.110.
147 Cicero, *Duties*, I.xxxi.113.

148 Cicero, *Duties*, I.xxxi.111.
149 Cicero, *Duties*, I.xxxiii.120.
150 Seneca, *Epistles*, CXV.2–3.
151 Cicero, *Ends*, III.v.19.
152 Cicero, *Duties*, III.xix.77. See also Seneca, *Epistles*, LXXXIII.1.
153 Cicero, *Duties*, I.xxxiv.125.
154 Seneca, *Epistles*, CXV.2.
155 Cicero, *Ends*, II.xii.43.
156 E.g., Cicero, *Ends*, III.iv.12 and D.L., VII. 87–8.
157 Following Brennan's analysis here. Brennan, *The Stoic Life*, pp. 194–8.
158 Especially *Epistles*, LXX.
159 Cicero, *Duties*, III.x.42.
160 Cicero, *Duties*, I.20–1 and *Ends*, III.67.
161 Brennan, *The Stoic Life*, p. 222.
162 Brennan, *The Stoic Life*, p. 224.
163 Brennan, *The Stoic Life*, pp. 223–4. Gisela Striker makes a similar point. See 'Following Nature: A Study in Stoic Ethics', *Essays on Hellenistic Epistemology and Ethics* (Cambridge: Cambridge University Press, 1996), p. 31.
164 Brennan, *The Stoic Life*, pp. 222–3.
165 Seneca, *Epistles*, XCIV.3.
166 See too Aurelius, *Meditations*, V.6 and Cicero, *Tusculan Disputations*, IV.12.
167 See M. Andrew Holowchak, 'Carrying One's Goods from City to City: Seneca on Friendship, Self-Sufficiency, and the Disdain of Fortune', *Ancient Philosophy*, XXVI.1 (2006):.
168 Plutarch, *Common Conceptions*, 1062B.
169 Within reason, that is. As Aurelius often notes, there cannot be good without evil. Aurelius, *Meditations*, VI.42, VIII.15 and IX.42.
170 Following Gummere's translation here.
171 Epictetus, *Handbook*, 15. See also *Discourses*, IV.iv.31.
172 Seneca, *Firmness*, IX.5.
173 Epictetus, *Discourses*, III.vi.5–7.
174 Seneca, *Letters*, XCV.30–2.
175 Epictetus, *Discourses*, I.xviii.19–23.
176 Seneca, *Firmness*, III.5.
177 Cicero, *Ends*, III.vi.26.
178 Seneca, *Epistles*, LXXXV.38.
179 Plutarch, *Progress in Virtue*, 79e.
180 Seneca, *Epistles*, LXVI.46.
181 Epictetus, *Discourses*, III.vi.5–7.
182 Aurelius, *Meditations*, XII.9.
183 Seneca, *Firmness*, VII.2.
184 Seneca, *Firmness*, VIII.2.
185 Cicero, *Duties*, I.xxiv.83.
186 Seneca, *Equanimity*, XI.1–2.
187 Seneca, *Epistles*, LXVI.6.
188 Epictetus, *Discourses* IV.xii.19–21.

189 Seneca, *Epistles*, LXXVI.
190 Seneca, *Epistles*, CXC.18.
191 Epictetus, *Discourses*, I.xxvi.15.
192 Epictetus, *Discourses*, I.xii.26.
193 Seneca, *Epistles*, LXVI.12.
194 Seneca, *Epistles*, XCII.30.
195 Cicero, *Anger*, II.xxxi.7.
196 Aurelius, *Meditations*, V.8.
197 Epictetus, *Discourses*, III.xxiv.21.
198 Seneca, *Epistles*, XC.34.
199 Seneca, *Epistles*, CII.21–2.
200 Seneca, *Epistles*, LXXVIII.27.
201 Seneca, *Epistles*, LXXVIII.28.
202 Cicero, *Duties*, I.iv.14.
203 Cicero, *Duties*, I.xxviii.99.
204 D.L., VII.189.

CHAPTER 3

EQUANIMITY IN ADVERSITY

'We must heal our misfortunes by the grateful recollection of what has been and by the recognition that it is impossible to make undone what has been done'.

Epicurus

'Life has its wisdom,' writes Maxim Gorky in *Red*, 'its name is accident. Sometimes it rewards us, but more often it takes revenge on us, and just as the sun endows each object with a shadow, so the wisdom of life prepares retribution for man's every act.'

Hegesias of Cyrene, Cicero says in his *Tusculan Disputations*, preached that life was merely one gross misfortune after another. The best one could do to escape this disheartening series of calamities was to commit suicide. He was presumably forced to stop lecturing, Cicero tells us, because his disciples were following his advice.[1]

Unhappiness is commonplace in everyday human living, writes Sigmund Freud in *Civilization and Its Discontents*. Suffering assails us from three directions: from our own body, from the external world, and, most frustratingly, from our relationships with other humans. None of the remedies humans have routinely adopted have proven successful in removing their suffering. Even science with its vaunted technical advances has given us nothing more than the 'cheap enjoyment' of 'putting a bare leg from under the bedclothes on a cold winter night and drawing it in again'.[2]

'All living is battling',[3] writes the Stoic philosopher Seneca, in agreement with Gorky, Hegesias and Freud. Yet, for Stoics, the situation is not inescapably dire; the battle can be won. Stoicism offers itself as a curious sort of remedy for human suffering. It promises not to remove suffering, but rather to help one bear suffering through fundamentally changing one's attitude toward it. Pain is real, but one can overcome it through accepting and enduring it. Moreover, the best life must have some adversity in it, as virtue withers without an adversary.[4] The sentiment expressed here and less economically in numerous other places is that virtue can best be cultivated and preserved by adversity. Adversity is the best test of virtue and the invincibility that comes with it.

'INCONVENIENCES': STORM-CLOUDS AT SEA

For an apprentice, adversity is a matter of turning one's attitudes of distress and fear – the attitudes of avoiding present and future things deemed ill – to attitudes of acceptance and indifference.

Yet many things seem unendurable and it is easy to give in to them and pass on the blame for one's surrender to them to others.

> Forgetting what a torment it is to many men to abstain from wine or to be roused from their beds at the break of day, we regard those things, about which we are all by disposition infirm, as difficult and beyond endurance. Those things are not difficult by nature; rather we are limp and weak. We must pass judgment on great matters with magnanimity; otherwise, what is really our fault will seem to be another's.[5]

Many, who surrender, find pleasure in their many vices. Unlike other crafts, where error brings shame to good craftsmen, the errors of life are an undeniable source of pleasure to those inclined toward vice.[6] Thus, it is easy, if unprepared or under-prepared, for one to lose the battle.

Those few who are prepared become suitable contestants in the greatest of all contests – life.[7] In life, a Stoic overcomes and conquers adversity through endurance. Seneca elaborates:

> I show myself like some solitary rock in the sea, which the waves never cease to beat on from every quarter from which they come, yet for all that they cannot move it from its base and cannot wear it away by their ceaseless attack through countless ages. Leap upon me, Fortune; make your assault! I shall conquer you by enduring [*ferendo vos vincam*]. Whatever strikes against things

that are firm and unconquerable [*inexsuperabilia*] expends its power to its own detriment. Thus, seek some soft and yielding object in which to stick your arrows![8]

Given the Stoic view that virtue is knowledge and vice is ignorance, the means of attaining equanimity in adversity is to avoid foolish or rash judgments of impressions about things outside of *prohairesis* – our faculty for judging aright – and to make correct judgements about things within the moral compass. Those who form judgements about things lying outside of moral purpose or form false judgments about things lying within moral purpose, fall into vice.[9]

Why is it that people fail to form the right sorts of judgements and fall into vice? Seneca states that outward appearances seduce the soul and pull it away from knowledge.[10] Once seduced, these wrong opinions bring about wickedness and corruption in the soul. In the main, a soul that goes astray has not been properly conditioned to see things as they are; it is not a vessel for virtue.

How can one avoid wickedness? First, one ought not to allow emotions to enter into the soul at all. It is much easier to disallow them in the first place than to allow them in and try to control them. Emotions are not readily controlled and are of such a nature as to contaminate all things around them. Moreover, if reason is allowed to mingle with the emotions, it is easy for it to become contaminated and enslaved by them. Seneca gives the extreme example of someone hurled off a precipice. Once hurled off, he has lost all control and it no longer makes sense to reconsider, repent or try to keep himself from his unavoidable destiny. To act thus is to be under the spell of anger, love or any of the other emotions.[11] Second, one must refrain from judging whatever has happened to oneself to be something good or bad. Emotions are not immediate responses to events; they occur only with the assent of the mind. For instance, desire for revenge, through unbridled anger, is desire based on the impressions both that one has been wronged and that it is right for one to seek revenge. Both are false judgments.[12]

To strive for invincibility, one must come to see adversity not as disaster, but as mere inconvenience.[13] Virtue, when fully cultivated, will ultimately prevail.

Vexation, pain and other inconveniences [*incommodi*] are of no consequence, as they are overcome by virtue. Just as the brightness of the sun dims all lesser lights, so virtue, by its own great-ness, shatters and overwhelms all pains, annoyances, and wrongs. Wherever its radiance reaches, all lights that shine without the help of virtue are extinguished. Inconveniences, when they come in contact with virtue, play no more important a role than does a storm-cloud at sea.[14]

So radiant and overpowering is virtue that it is its existence and not its dwelling place that matters. It is equally praiseworthy when in a healthy and free body as it is when in a sickly and bound body. So great is it that it dwarfs its dwelling place and makes the very state of this dwelling place to be a matter of indifference.[15] To think other-wise is to be confused about goods.

The things people tend to call 'goods' – victory, health, and the welfare of one's country – are things in agreement with Nature and, thus, things desirable and primarily so. It is the same with things like torture or ill health, which are called 'ills'. These things are contrary to Nature and cannot be states reasonably desired by any sane person. Seneca writes to Lucilius:

You ask me whether every good is desirable. You say that if it is a good to be brave under torture, to go to the stake with a stout heart and to endure illness with resignation, it follows that these things are desirable. Yet I see none of them as worth praying for. Anyways, I have yet to know a man who has paid a vow for being cut up by the whip, twisted out of shape by gout or made taller by the rack.[16]

Undesirable states – such as being wounded, being burnt by fire and being afflicted with ill health – are indeed states contrary to Nature and so they are truly not desirable. What is in agreement with Nature is not the foul state itself, but a mind that can tolerate such a foul state and remain unperturbed. In short, the 'material' with which a good is concerned may be contrary to Nature; what is good itself – an attitude of acceptance – cannot be, for good requires reason and reason is always in agreement with Nature.[17]

What that shows is that, while certain bodily states – for instance, being tortured or ill – are contrary to Nature, certain dispositions of soul – for instance, resignation and equanimity while ill or being tor-tured – are in agreement with Nature. Overall, no inconveniences are to be wished for, but some may be in one's future and, consequently, ought not to be despised. Consequently, to be invincible, one must be suitably prepared for all things. 'The conclusion is not that inconveniences are desirable, but that virtue, which enables us patiently to endure inconveniences, is desirable', and virtue is best tested by hardship.

Yet virtue is not just a matter of endurance through hardships, for this could presumably come about through a non-volitional conditioning over time; virtue is a matter of brave (*fortiter*) endurance.[18] It is a feature of one's mental state, not one's actions, and that is what Seneca means when he states: 'What is significant is not what you endure, but how you endure.'[19]

Khreiai *for 'Bearing Life's "Inconveniences"'*

- 'Constant misfortune brings this one blessing: Those whom it always assails, it eventually fortifies.'[20]
- 'The mind without passions is a fortress. A person has no place that is more impregnable, in which to find refuge and be forever safe. Whoever does not see this is ignorant. Whoever sees it but does not take refuge is unfortunate.'[21]

TELA FORTUNAE AND LIFE ON THE 'DEAD SEA'

Hemingway's *The Old Man and the Sea* is a classic heroic tale of Stoic proportion about an old Cuban fisherman, his very young friend and a three-day battle with a giant marlin. The old man, Santiago, is an outcast from his village. He has failed to catch fish for very many days and is deemed unlucky. The young boy, who has found a close friend in the old man, refuses to leave his unlucky friend and accompanies the old man on fishing trips for 40 unsuccessful days, against the wishes of his parents. After 40 days of fishless fishing, the boy's parents refuse to let him accompany the old man anymore. Santiago continues to fish on his own and goes 44 more days without success.

An uncommon friendship develops between the two. When together and not speaking about fishing, the old man teaches the boy about baseball, especially the New York Yankees and the great DiMaggio (baseball's symbol of endurance, with his record 56-game hitting streak).

On the forty-fifth day of fishing without the boy, Santiago is not so unlucky. He hooks a gigantic marlin. The enormous fish jumps into the air soon after it is caught. 'I wonder why he jumped,' thought Santiago. 'He jumped almost as though to show me how big he was . . . I wish I could show him what sort of man I am.' There begins a brutal three-day battle between Santiago and the giant fish.

Santiago's perseverance with fishing, after such an unthinkable drought, and his fight with the marlin are a microcosm of his life, which is about overcoming through enduring. In famine, he overcomes adversity; in fame, he does not let his pride swell. Throughout it all, he never loses faith in himself. Soon after he catches the marlin, he says to himself: 'Christ, I did not know he was so big. I'll kill him though . . . in all his greatness and his glory.' Yet that very thought seems to him unjust. He continues to himself, 'But I will show him what a man can do and what a man endures.' He then wonders whether the great DiMaggio, who has hit successfully in 56 straight games, would have had the staying power he knows he will have with this fish.

While fighting the marlin, he draws upon memories of past successes in his life for sustenance. He recalls an arm-wrestling victory at Casablanca over a strong, gritty negro – the strongest man on the dock – that lasted one complete day. After beating the negro, he was no longer 'Santiago', but 'Santiago the Champion'. He also recalls a favourite dream, where he sees lions prancing playfully on a peaceful, long, and yellow shore.

When he eventually subdues the beautiful giant marlin, he has to fight off a shark in a battle that is not about flesh, but morality. The shark, before Santiago kills it, takes 40 pounds of the marlin's flesh, his harpoon, and all of his rope. 'But a man is not made for defeat. . .. A man can be destroyed but not defeated', Santiago says. More sharks eventually come. Soon there is no flesh on the once giant marlin. The old man then returns with what is left of the marlin to his village, where he collapses into a sound sleep to gather his strength until such time as he fishes on the sea again – this time, with the help of the boy.

In *Consolation of Marcia*, Seneca says, 'Life is full and beset with various tragedies, from which there is a lengthy respite for no one – scarcely a truce.'[22] Seneca often speaks of invincibility as imperviousness to the 'arrows of Fortune' (*tela fortunae*). Those arrows vanquish most people, but they not at all impact a Stoic; they bounce off him just like great hail that rattles on the roof of a house and then melts away, without harming anyone within the house.[23]

We find safe harbour in the preparation for misfortune through indifference to fortune's arrows. 'The only safe harbour from the seething storms of this life is scorn of the future, a firm stand in the present, and readiness to receive Fortune's arrows, full in the breast, without skulking or turning one's back.'[24]

Seneca often speaks as if a life untroubled by ill fate is a life unworthy of a Stoic. People of common abilities can be successful, but they cannot be invincible. They cannot overcome great terrors and calamities. To overcome them, it takes an uncommon, heroic person. Thus, to pass through life without tragedy is to have lived without experience of one half of what Nature has to offer.[25]

Along such lines, Seneca is fond of comparing an easy life, without fear of misfortune, to a trip on a calm sea, and a hard life, fraught with misfortune, to a trip on a stormy sea. Consider the following two passages:

> Our friend Demetrius . . . calls an easy existence, untroubled by the attacks of Fortune, a 'Dead Sea' [*mare mortuum*]. If you have nothing to stir you up and rouse you to action, if you have nothing that will test your resolution by its threats and hostilities, and if you recline in unshaken comfort, it is not tranquillity. It is merely calm at sea [*malacia*].[26]

> Disaster is virtue's opportunity. One may rightly call those miserable, who are numbed by excess of good fortune and who are idle and, as it were, detained on a lazy sea [*in mari lento*]. Whatever happens to them will come as a change.[27]

Consequently, the path toward excellence and invincibility is not smooth and straight. It is steep and difficult. One who is invincible must steer his craft through stormy waters. In doing so, he will be wave-tossed and sea-tested. Yet if he is true to virtue, he will stay his course, though the journey will be rough and difficult. In contrast, not to be sea-tested – that is, life on a 'Dead Sea' – is clearly a fate unworthy of a virtuous person.

Khreiai *for* 'Tela Fortunae'

- 'Never pity a good man, for I can call him 'miserable', but he cannot be miserable.'[28]
- 'If a man is to know himself, he must be tested. No one finds out what he can do, except through effort.'[29]

THE TROUBLED SLEEP OF THE FEARFUL

The pure men of old days, the ancient Taoist philosopher Zhuangzi writes in Stoic fashion, were without fear and anxiety. They slept without dreams and woke worriless. They ate without concern for flavour. They drew sure, deep breaths from their heels. The vulgar today, he adds, draw breaths from their throat and spew up words like vomit. Their attachment to things is deep, while they have few divine endowments.

> The pure men of old did not know what it was to love life or hate death. They did not rejoice in birth or strive to put off dissolution. Unconcerned they came and unconcerned they went. That was all. They did not forget whence it was they had sprung; neither did they seek to inquire their return thither. Waiting patiently for their restoration, they accepted life cheerfully. This is what is called not to allow the mind to lead one astray from Tao and not to supplement the natural by human means. Such a one may be called a pure man.[30]

Zhuangzi's description of a fearless Taoist sage seems to apply equally as well to a Stoic sage.

Fear, as one of the four main emotions, is a desire to avoid some anticipated ill. There are three kinds of fear for Seneca. We fear poverty, death and whatever happens to us through the power of those who are stronger.[31] Yet none of those 'ills', whether unde-served or deserved, are worth fearing. Wickedness alone, because of its concomitant fear, is its own deterrent.

> Whoever expects punishment, receives it, but whoever deserves it, expects it. Where there is a wicked conscience, something may bring shelter, but nothing can bring security. For a man imagines that, even if he is not under arrest, he may soon be arrested. His sleep is troubled. When he speaks of another's crime, he reflects on his own, which seems to him not sufficiently blotted out or hidden from view. A wrongdoer [*nocens*] sometimes has the luck to escape notice, but never the assurance of it.[32]

Proof of the undesirability of vicious actions comes in the form of a test of sorts – captured by what may be called the Principle of

Impunity. Cicero asks: 'Who is or ever was there of greed so consuming and appetite so unbridled that, even though willing to commit any crime to achieve his end with absolute impunity, would not a hundred times rather attain the same object by honest rather than blameworthy means?'[33] We may sum the Principle of Impunity as follows:

> **Principle of Impunity:** Anyone who has committed (or is about to commit) a crime in order to gain something would prefer to have gained (or gain) that thing through innocent rather than vicious means.

The Principle of Impunity, I believe, the Stoics would hold to be true of any person whomsoever – even the most depraved, at some point on his slide to vice.

Fear is also often used as a political 'motivator'. It is a tyrant's preferred means for securing authority, yet a poor way for a ruler to preserve lasting power.[34] Cicero states:

> Of all motives, none is better adapted to secure and hold assistance than love; nothing is more foreign to that end than fear . . . No amount of power can withstand the hatred of the many. The death of this tyrant [Julius Caesar], whose yoke the state endured under the constraint of armed force and whom it still obeyed more humbly than ever though he is dead, illustrates the deadly effects of popular hatred. The same lesson is taught by the similar fate of all other tyrants, almost none of whom has ever escaped death. Fear is a poor safeguard of lasting power; while goodwill [*benevolentia*] may be trusted to keep it safe forever.[35]

The best way to expunge fear from one's life is to live a life that is free from mental disquiet, a philosophical lifestyle, insofar as that is possible. That is what the Greeks call *ataraxia* – freedom from mental disturbance.

How is *ataraxia* achieved? For Stoics, there are certain emotions that cannot be eliminated, as they are in accordance with Nature. As we have seen, some are desirable, *eupatheia*; others, first motions, are merely outside of our immediate control. Of the latter, Seneca says:

> There are certain emotions . . . that virtue cannot avoid. Nature reminds virtue how perishable a thing it is. Thus, a Stoic will

contract his brow, when the prospect is forbidding, will shudder at sudden apparitions, and will become dizzy, when he stands at the edge of a high precipice and looks down. That is not fear; it is a natural feeling [*naturalis adfectio*] that reason cannot expunge.[36]

I return to the first motions in the section on anger (p. 136).

To expunge all undesirable types of fear, an apprentice needs to cultivate courage (*fortitudo*) – 'the virtue that champions the cause of moral right'.[37] Courage is characterized by indifference to outward circumstances and the taking up of deeds that are great, maximally useful, extraordinarily difficult and laborious, and extremely dangerous.[38]

Yet courage is not a matter of needlessly exposing oneself to dangers in order to test one's mettle. That is rashness, perhaps even hubris. Courage is a matter of having the right disposition – one that is rational and accepting – toward those circumstances in which one finds oneself. Cicero writes:

> In encountering danger, we should do as doctors do in their practice. In light cases of illness, they give mild treatment. In cases of dangerous sickness, they are compelled to apply risky and even desperate remedies. It is, therefore, only a madman [*demens*] who would pray for a storm, when it is calm. Thus, the way of a Stoic is, when the storm does come, to withstand it with all the means at his disposal – especially if the advantages gained by carrying the matter through are greater than the disadvantages that may occur in the struggle.[39]

Fear, then, is a reactive, irrational disposition to a future situation that ought not to evoke anxiety. The invincibility of a Stoic progressor, however, is cognitively proactive: He anticipates and is ready for all possible circumstances. There is no place left for fear.

Khreiai *for 'The Troubled Sleep of the Fearful'*

- 'Life is not worth living and there is no limit to our sorrows, if we indulge our fears to the greatest possible extent.'[40]
- 'Shame does not consist in not having anything to eat, but in not having reason sufficient to ward off fear and anxiety.'[41]

BRAVERY IN BEDCLOTHES

Health, we have seen for the Stoics, is nothing good, though it is something each person would prefer to have, were it up to him. Yet while some of us are by disposition healthier than others and others are healthier because of attention to their physical health, no one is guaranteed good health over a lifetime. No matter how much attention one pay's to one's health, one's state of health is never fully under one's control. Everyone who lives long enough at some point undergoes illness. That is why Stoics believe health and other such 'goods' are external matters – mere conveniences.

Illness is one of the most dastardly and debilitating arrows of fortune, as it strikes a person, so it seems, from nowhere and presumably for no good reason. It disregards neither the vicious nor the virtuous, neither the penurious nor the wealthy. It even takes hold of the physician, who treats the ill.

Epictetus writes that if a Stoic falls ill, he will bear illness well. Deity and friends will be his nurses. He will take any convenient bed and house for convalescence and will take in simple food. In short, he will bear his illness with courage. Knowing that death is the ultimate end of any illness, he also realizes that death will be a release from suffering and that the only real illness is fear of death.[42] Ridding oneself of the fear of death is to be free and psychically healthy.

When one is ill, there is an inescapable closing in of one's sphere of concern. That is in keeping with Stoicism, which demands social participation for the fullest possible life, but acknowledges that self-preservation is what is to be expected during times of illness. That is in keeping with Nature's most primitive impulse. Seneca elaborates:

> Do you believe that you achieve nothing, if you are ill with self-control? You will show that a disease can be overcome or, at any rate, endured. There is, I assure you, a place for virtue even upon a bed of sickness. It is not only the sword and the battle-line that prove a soul alert and unconquered [alacris animi indomitique] by fear. A person can display bravery even when wrapped in his bed-clothes.[43]

One can always make the fight with the illness a noble one and thereby, at least, set a signal example of fortitude for others. More than that, a noble fight through enduring illness is a sign of one's indifference to the outcome as being something good or bad.

The greatest exhibition of courage in the face of adversity that I have ever witnessed is that of a former student, while I was a lecturer at Marygrove College in Detroit many years ago. This young lady had missed a number of classes and it came to my attention that she was in the hospital and very ill. She had not told me, or anyone, that she was suffering from sickle-cell anaemia, a particularly debilitating and deadly blood-cell disease for which there is no known cure. I went to the hospital to visit her. She was surprised to see me. While I visited, she did not talk much about her sickness. Instead, she talked about how lucky she was to have a mother and friends, who came to see her so often, in contrast to many other friends of hers in the same hospital with sickle-cell, who had few visitors. She talked as well about her 'poor mother', who was spending too much time at the hospital and worrying too much. She talked about herself only insofar as she mentioned that she would like to become a doctor to research sickle-cell and help find a cure for the disease. It was the most moving experience in my life. Never did I expect to find such heroism, courage and selflessness in one so young. That young lady, having cultivated courage perhaps more than anyone else I have ever known, embodied Stoic invincibility. Writes Seneca:

> Teach me not whether courage [*fortitudo*] is a living thing, but show me that no living thing is happy without courage, unless it has grown strong to oppose obstacles and has overcome every impact of chance, by rehearsing and anticipating their attack. What is courage? It is the impregnable fortress for our mortal weakness. When a person has surrounded himself with that, he can hold out free from anxiety during life's siege, as he is using his own strength and his own arrows.[44]

Khreiai *for 'Illness and Bedridden Heroism'*

- 'If you try to avoid disease, death or poverty, you will experience misfortune. Hence, withdraw your aversion from all matters not under your control and transfer it to what is unnatural of the matters that are.'[45]
- 'Just as physicians always keep their lancets and instruments at hand for emergency operations, so too keep your doctrines

[*dogmata*] ready both for the diagnosis of divine and human affairs and for being able to perform every action, even the least, with the fullest consciousness of the mutual ties between the two.'

PAIN: WIPING A RUNNY NOSE

The difference between Stoics and Epicureans is that Epicureans feel no pain, insofar as they shun pain altogether, while Stoics feel it, but make little of it. For Epicureans, pain is the sole ill and pleasure is the sole good. For Stoics, neither pain nor pleasure is good or ill; what is bad is the perception that pain is something ill and that pleasure is something good.[46] Seneca sums the Stoic view, 'Do not of your own doing make your troubles heavier to bear and burden yourself with complaining. Pain is slight, if opinion has added nothing to it.'[47]

Stoic invincibility comes not with trying to escape pain, but through enduring it.

'I am unfortunate that this trouble has happened to me!' No. 'It is fortunate that this trouble has happened to me and I am still unharmed, neither crushed by the present nor frightened of the future.' Some such thing could have happened to anyone. Yet not everyone could have remained unharmed by it ... Do not forget the future, when anything would lead you to feel pain, and take your stand on this doctrine: This trouble is not misfortune, but to bear it nobly is good fortune.[48]

Thus, only one aspiring to wisdom has the courage to endure pain.

For Stoics, pain is a part of life and a Stoic will see that it is for the best and make light of it. Writes Epictetus:

Still some unpleasant and hard things happen in life. Do they not happen at Olympia? Do you not swelter while there? Are you not cramped and crowded while there? Do you not bathe with discomfort while there? Are you not drenched while there, whenever it rains? Do you not have your fill of tumult and shouting and other annoyances while there? Yet I fancy that you tolerate and endure all of those annoyances by balancing them off against the memorable character of the spectacle.[49]

Like a spectator at the Olympic festival, one prepared for pain can endure it readily. Cicero considers men who voluntarily undergo pain for the sake of their country. Such men endure great pain with little complaining. Moreover, they seem to suffer less than they do when they commit to a lesser cause that requires less effort. That shows that there is nothing intrinsically wicked about pain; its wickedness depends rather on the mind of the sufferer.[50]

Some pains are just part of the normal course of everyday living. One has only to consider hunger and thirst. No one, not even a Stoic sage, can escape these 'annoyances'. Yet even these not at all trouble a Stoic, as his aim is to fill oneself, when one is empty, and filling what is empty does not take extraordinary effort. Stuffing oneself does.

> Hunger is not ambitious. It is quite satisfied to come to an end. It does not care very much what food brings it to an end. Such things are only the tools of an unhappy luxury. This luxury seeks how it can prolong hunger even after repletion, how to stuff the stomach and not to fill it, and how to rekindle a thirst that has been slaked with the first drink.[51]

Escaping the pain of hunger or thirst is easy for one who enjoys the simplest food and drink. In *Letter* CXIX, Seneca relates that the simplest, most immediate foods for hunger are best, since a starving man despises nothing. 'Nature does not care whether the bread is of the coarse kind or of the finest wheat. She does not want the stomach to be entertained [*delectari*[52]], but to be filled.' It is the same with thirst. 'Nature orders that my thirst be quenched. It does not matter whether I drink from a golden, crystal, or a myrrh-coloured goblet, a cup from Tibur,[53] or a cupped hand.'[54]

Epictetus humorously mentions a person who complains of a runny nose. He states, quite sensibly and tersely, that it would be much easier to wipe one's nose than to complain. Such sorts of 'pains' are shameful. What would Hercules have amounted to, he adds, without the labours of the lion, boar, hydra and stag? He could have rolled himself up in a blanket and slept, yet that would have been a colossal waste of strength, courage, resolve and nobility.[55] To one whose home is the whole world, like Hercules, even the pain of exile is endurable.[56]

Stoics acknowledge that it is not so easy to endure some pains. Dionysius the Renegade, for instance, turned from Stoicism to

---

Cynicism because of severe and unendurable eye pain. He could not consider such pain something indifferent to his happiness.[57] Still, the Stoics could reply, it makes little sense to complain. Complaining does not remove the pain; it amplifies it, by drawing one's attention to it. Aurelius argues sharply: Whatever happens is either endurable or it is not. If it is endurable, then merely endure it and stop complaining. If it is not, then death will put an end to it at some point. Either way, it is best not to complain.[58]

Aurelius also offers this advice to one suffering pain:

> Whenever you are in pain, have this at hand: Pain is nothing shameful. It cannot make the mind that is at the helm worse. It cannot impair the mind, insofar as it is rational or social ... Recollect too that many of our everyday discomforts – such as drowsiness, high temperature, and lack of appetite – are really pain in disguise. And so when you are annoyed at any of these, tell yourself: I am giving in to pain.[59]

In short, pain does not diminish the equanimity of an invincible person. Thus, it causes him no harm. Because of that, it can be called 'bad', but it cannot be bad.[60]

Khreiai *for 'Pain'*

- 'Pain has this most excellent quality: If prolonged it cannot be severe, and if severe it cannot be prolonged. We should bravely accept whatever the inevitable laws of the universe command us to do.'[61]
- 'A person has learned wisdom, if he can die as free from care as he was at birth.'[62]

ANGER AND THE BAYING OF SMALL DOGS

One of the strongest arguments for extirpating the emotions completely is given in the Stoic view of anger.[63] As Seneca's *On Anger* is the largest and most complete Stoic work on the subject, it will be the focus of this section.

Anger is, Seneca says baldly, 'temporary insanity' that is devoid of self-control, decency, reason and discernment. It is excited by trifles and driven to finish what it starts.[64] It is the most bestial and frenzied of the emotions.

The other emotions have in them some element of peace and calm, while this one is wholly violent [*concitatus*] and has resentment in its brutal onrush [*impetu*]. It rages with a most inhuman lust for weapons, blood, and punishment. It does not think about itself, if it can hurt another. It hurls itself upon the very point of the dagger and is eager for revenge, though it may drag down the avenger along with it.[65]

Often anger arises from insignificant sources, but, relying on its own power, it quickly grows to a frightfully large size. It is the most arrogant of the emotions, when successful in its rage, and the most insane, when unsuccessful. If the object of anger is accidentally removed, it may even turn its rage on its possessor.[66]

Seneca's depiction of one under the spell of anger is stirring.

For as the marks of a madman are unmistakable – a bold and threatening mien, a gloomy brow, a fierce expression, a hurried step, restless hands, an altered colour, and quick and more violent breathing. The marks of the angry man are the same: His eyes blaze and sparkle, his whole face is crimson with the blood that surges from the lowest depths of the heart, his lips quiver, his teeth are clenched, his hair bristles and stands on end, his breathing is forced and harsh, his joints crack from writhing, he groans and bellows, bursts out into speech with scarcely intelligible words, strikes his hands together continually, and stamps the ground with his feet. His whole body is excited and performs great angry threats. It is an ugly and horrible picture of distorted and swollen frenzy. You cannot tell whether this vice is more execrable or more hideous.[67]

Anger is driven by the perception that one has received an injury and received it unjustly.[68] Yet for Stoics, since no one can bring harm to a person except the person himself, anger is always a misperception that does its greatest harm to the soul of the angry person and not to the recipient of one's anger.

Given that anger is judgment that is false, it follows that of all beasts, only humans can be subject to anger. Wild beasts have impulses, madness, fierceness and aggressiveness, but cannot be angry any more than they can wallow from luxury. Even athletes, who spend most of their time cultivating the basest part of their soul, Seneca says, avoid anger in order to subdue their opponents most effectively. 'Pyrrhus, the most famous trainer for gymnastic contests, made it a rule, it is said, to warn those, whom he was training, against getting angry, as anger confounds art and looks only for a chance to injure.'[69]

Epictetus too argues that anger is futile. He has us consider the issue of putting to death one who has committed wrongdoing through thievery or adultery.

> Ought not this person to be put to death, who is in a state of error and delusion about the greatest matters and is in a state of blindness, not, indeed, in the vision that distinguishes between white and black, but in the judgment [*diakritiken*] that distinguishes between good and evil? If you put it that way, you will realize how inhuman a sentiment it is that you are uttering and that it is just for you to say, 'Ought not this blind man, then, or this deaf man be put to death?' If the loss of the greatest things is the greatest harm that can befall a person, while the greatest thing in each person is right judgment [*prohairesis*], and if a person is deprived of this very thing, what ground is left for you to be angry with him?[70]

What is his advice to those who fear the thief or adulterer? Stop admiring 'possessions' such as your wife's beauty, he says simply. Otherwise, you behave like one who parades a cake in front of gluttons.[71] The implication here is that one who parades around his wife's beauty is just as guilty as another man who lusts after it. Both are guilty of gluttony.

Seneca's arguments against anger in *On Anger* are numerous and generally given in syllogisms. I list several. First, humans are naturally gregarious animals, but anger works toward mutual destruction. Therefore, anger is against Nature.[72] Second, punishment is an ill, since punishment injures the one punished and all injury is an ill. Likewise anger is an ill, since anger essays to injure through punishment.[73] Third, if something is good (e.g., justice or courage), then the more of it that one has, the better off one is, and the less of it one has, the worse off one is. Yet no one would say that a surfeit of anger is something good, as all admit it is something ill. Thus, a small amount of anger is a small amount of something ill, not something good. Therefore, any amount of anger is undesirable.[74] Fourth, though anger seems to make men fearless in war, so too do drunkenness and lunacy. Seneca sums, 'No person is ever made braver through anger, except the one who would never have been brave without it. Anger comes, then, not as an aid to virtue, but as a substitute for it.'[75] Finally, because no one is angry with one who stumbles in the dark, with those who do not hear because they are deaf, with forgetful children, or with the old and weary, so too should no one be angry at the mistakes of men, since mistakes are due to ignorance.[76]

The Stoic view is in stark contrast with that of Aristotle, who argues that anger, in some small measure, is just one of many emotions that are needed for virtuous activity. Aristotle's view accords with common sense, as people are inclined to praise those who feel angry at the right person, at the right time, for the right reason and in the right manner, and to consider as fools those who do not.[77] It follows that anger, for Aristotle, is conformable to the dictates of reason, not against it. Seneca, of course, disagrees. On the one hand, if anger is submissive to reason and willingly follows it, it is no longer anger, for stubbornness (*contumacia*), not compliance, is the chief characteristic of anger. On the other hand, if anger is not submissive to reason, but carried away by its own fury, it will be useless to reason through its disobedience. Either way, anger cannot be serviceable for virtue.[78]

Seneca's intuitions may seem correct, but is it humanly possible to subdue or eliminate anger completely? What does one say about times where one is unduly insulted? Would not it, as Aristotle says, be foolish to be made foolish by another? Seneca counters in Socratic fashion, 'Indeed the success [*fructus*] of an insult depends on the sensitiveness and the indignation of the victim.'[79] One who is aims at invincibility will be unmoved by even the most slanderous words. He will recognize that such words harm only the slanderer, not the one at whom the slander is aimed.

What ought one to do with those who have physically injured others or those who have broken the law? What ought one to do with the incurably vicious person, who makes harming others a way of life? Seneca illustrates incurable vice with the story of the Persian king Cambyses and his friend Praexaspes. One day, observing Cambyses begin to drink heavily, as was his wont, Praexaspes advised the king not to drink so much, as drunkenness was not befitting kingly status. Cambyses took offence and began to drink gluttonously. He then ordered Praexaspes' son to be brought into the room. Standing some distance away from the youth, he drew his bow and shot the lad straight through the heart, his aforementioned target. Thereupon, he cut open the boy to show the arrow had pierced the heart. Praexaspes, fearing another shot by the king, flattered the king by saying that Apollo himself could not have shot straighter. Seneca's point here is not that Praexaspes was right to flatter the king, but that it is possible to suppress anger even in the most demanding of all possible circumstances.[80]

Revenge or retaliation against wicked people is itself vicious to a right-minded person. '"Revenge" [*receptum*] is an inhuman word and yet one accepted as legitimate and "retaliation" [*talio*] is not much different, except in rank. The man who returns a pain commits merely a more pardonable ill', but an ill, all the same.[81] If revenge were the object, the most humiliating kind of revenge would be to have it appear that the perpetrator was not worth revenging. 'He is great and noble, who acts like a great wild beast that plainly hears the baying of small dogs without concern.'[82] When laws are broken, criminals must be prosecuted out of concern for order and justice, not revenge.[83]

Always, the Stoic aim is to rehabilitate, not punish. The best course of action is to help one who has lost his way to find it again.

> In every case of punishment, a Stoic will keep before him the knowledge that one form is designed to make the wicked better; the other, to remove them. In either case, he will look to the future, not to the past. For as Plato says, 'A sensible person does not punish a man, because he has committed a crime, but in order to keep him from committing a crime. While the past cannot be recalled, the future may be forestalled.'[84]

In hopeless cases, a criminal may have to be exterminated. 'Let them be removed from human society, if they are bound to spoil all that they touch, and let them cease to be wicked, in the only remaining possible way, but let this be done without hatred.'[85] Thus, putting an incurably vicious person to death is not something to be undertaken with relish, but with a sense that that is the only reasonable, humane thing left to do – the only 'remedy' left for such incurable vice. Seneca sums aptly, 'Sometimes killing is the truest form of pity.'[86] The psychological awareness and sensitivity here is greatly ahead of its time.

The remedy for anger is reason. To each case of anger we must oppose, not align, reason. The appropriate virtue here is justice.

> Reason grants a hearing to both sides and then seeks to postpone action, even its own, so that it may gain time to sift out the truth; anger is precipitate. Reason wishes the decision that it gives to be just; anger wishes to have the decision it has given to seem the just decision. Reason considers nothing except the question at issue; anger is moved by trifling things that lie outside the case.[87]

Cicero speaks of two offices of justice in *On Duties*: one concerns harm done to others, the other concerns ownership of property. To secure justice, one must not appropriate things that are not one's own, through retribution. One must instead contribute to the general welfare by using skill, industry and talent in benefaction.[88]

When and how does reason take hold and oppose anger? Seneca appeals, as it is customary today, both to nurture and nature. First, he argues that one must habituate people, while young, to avoid anger. It is easiest to educate the young to avoid bouts of anger, for their minds are still tender and malleable, while adults have vices that are resilient to corrective measures.[89] Second, though each person has his own natural constitution – e.g., some are fiery by nature; others, cool and lethargic – and though it is difficult to alter what is fixed by birth, one can channel or shape what is constitutionally fixed. For instance, fiery constitutions can be kept from wine and excesses of food. They can be exposed to moderate exercise and games to relax and balance the mind.[90]

Physical disposition and nurture, however, are not complete determinants of our actions. Reason stands above them. Seneca says, 'Nature and nurture apply to our children. In our case, however, our lot at birth and our education give us no excuse for our faults or our precepts. It is their consequences that we must regulate'[91] and reason is the regulator.

How precisely can reason regulate anger? In specific situations, the first prompting (*motus*) of anger, as is the case with first promptings of other emotions, is involuntary and cannot be controlled. Yet this first motion, with proper training, can readily be subdued by reason so that it leads to no further motions, since the internal bodily motion that is born by reason is completely within the control of one who is invincible.

We can no more avoid by the use of reason that first shock [*ictum*] that the mind experiences than we can avoid those effects, mentioned before, which the body experiences – the temptation to yawn, when another yawns, and the temptation to blink, when fingers are suddenly pointed toward one's eyes. Reason cannot conquer such things, though perhaps practice [*consuetudo*] and continual vigilance will weaken them. The other motion [*motus*], which is born by judgment, is cast away by judgment.[92]

In short, one can subdue anger through practice by not allowing the first motion to be coupled with any act of judgement. In such a manner, reason nips anger before it buds. That, of course, takes practice and time, but anger is conquerable. One must merely be continually aware that anger comprises two judgements: that one has been wronged by another and that revenge is the appropriate action to right the perceived wrong. Both judgements are false.

Khreiai *for 'Anger and the Baying of Small Dogs'*
- 'The best corrective of anger is delay.'[93]
- 'The best way of defusing the anger of another is kindness.'[94]

GRIEF AND THE BROKEN CRYSTAL GOBLET

Seneca, in *Letter* IX to Lucilius, reports the tale of the philosopher Stilbo, who lost his children, wife and city to Demetrius, called 'City-Sacker'. Upon losing everything, Stilbo was asked scornfully by Demetrius whether he had lost anything. The stouthearted philosopher replied to Demetrius' astonishment, 'I have all my goods with me.' It was, Seneca relates, as if the city-sacker had been sacked himself.[95]

The story of Stilbo is one of many illustrations of unsurpassed courage that Seneca relates in his letters and essays. Though Stilbo was no Stoic, Seneca uses him to demonstrate the type of radical invincibility that Stoic ethical thinking, if fully assimilated, can give a person in a lifetime. In light of the many arrows of fortune, the benefits of Stoic invincibility are incalculable.

Was Stilbo so extraordinary a person that he was completely unmoved by the loss of children, wife and city? Even if that were so, one still might wonder why such things would seem to mean so little to him. In the main, there seems to be something morally objectionable about a person who is not, at least for a short time, devastated by such losses.

It is not the case that children, wife and city meant little to Stilbo and that he was completely unmoved. For a Stoic, invincibility does not mean invulnerability and detachment from life. As I have been arguing, a Stoic is invincible because he acknowledges his vulnerability, but does not let it affect his goodness, and because of his radical attachment to all things. Such attachment, however, is not emotional; it is rational.

Seneca gives the example of the Roman emperor Augustus. Having lost his children and grandchildren, his sister and her son, and his sons-in-law, Augustus could have wallowed in grief. Yet he refused to do so. Instead, having no legitimate heirs, he merely adopted a child.[96]

Seneca gives the examples of Stilbo and Augustus to show not that a Stoic is unaffected by pain, for like any other person he will feel the pain of loss. The difference, however, is that the pain will not linger for long and never cower or consume a Stoic. Seneca writes in *Consolation of Marcia*:

> You say, 'Still, grieving for our loved ones is natural.' Who denies it, so long as grief is tempered? Not only the loss of those who are dearest to us, but a mere parting brings an inevitable pang and depresses the stoutest souls. Yet belief [*opinio*] adds more to our grief than Nature bids.[97]

Moreover, he adds, grief is diminished with time, which shows that grief is not natural, as whatever is in agreement with Nature is not diminished in time.[98] Finally, all things – such as children, honours, wealth, spacious halls, numerous clients, fame and even a beautiful wife – are each lent to us by fortune and must be returned at the appropriate time. We do not grieve when it comes time for a loan to be repaid, so too we ought not to grieve when all other things that are lent to us are taken away from us.[99]

Seneca gives many other arguments against grieving in *Consolation of Polybius*. First, either the deceased person for whom one grieves does not wish for one to suffer or he does not know that one suffers. If he continues to exist in some measure, he will not want the mourner to suffer; if not, the mourner's grief is in vain. Either way, grieving is pointless.[100] Second, one ought to cast out one's sorrow entirely or hide it within. In doing so, one becomes an example for others to emulate. In failing to do so, one indulges his sorrows.[101] Third, one either grieves because of oneself or because of the departed. If one grieves because of oneself, one strays from what is honourable and moves toward personal gain. If one grieves because of the departed, one grieves either for someone who no longer exists and is incapable of knowing one's grief or for someone who has escaped human existence for divine existence. Either way, grieving is pointless.[102] Fourth, Nature gives each person life and Nature ultimately takes back what she has given. Since Nature gives each person life freely, she may take back what she has given, whenever she best sees fit. In consequence, grieving is against Nature.[103] Fifth, all of life is merely a sure-footed journey towards death. Therefore, no one should be surprised at another's death, for to be surprised at another's death is to be surprised that what is inevitable has come to pass, and that is unreasonable.[104] Finally, one can, Seneca advises, always memorialize one's loved one through writings. That is a more fruitful use of energy and time than grieving is.[105]

Overall, no one can lose what is not his to lose, whether it is one's wife, children or even one's life.[106] All that he really possesses is completely within him. The point is brought home most forcefully and dramatically by Epictetus.

> When you grow attached to something, do not act as if it were something that cannot be taken away. Act as though it were something like a jar or a crystal goblet, so that, when it breaks, you will remember what it was like and not be troubled. It is the same in life. If you kiss your child, your brother or your friend, never give free rein to your imagination and do not let your exuberance go as far as it would like. Hold it back, stop it . . . In such fashion remind yourself that the object of your love is mortal; it is not one of your own possessions. It has been given to you for the present, not inseparably or forever, but like a fig or a cluster of grapes, at a fixed season of the year, and that if you hanker for it in the winter, you are a fool.[107]

When one grieves because the loss is great, it is perhaps natural and impossible not to hold back tears, but the tears must not flow to excess. One must check them. 'We may weep, but we must not wail.'[108] One must bear in mind that everyone awaits the same fate.

Death has levelled a loved one; it will eventually level each of us. 'Whoever complains about the death of anyone is complaining that he is a man. Everyone is bound by the same terms. Whoever is privileged to be born is destined to die. Periods of time separate us, but death levels us.'[109]

Even if the loss is great, it is vain to mourn excessively. Instead, one should find another loved one or friend to replace the one lost. Seneca compares one who mourns excessively to one who has had a cloak stolen and continually bewails his condition, instead of looking for another cloak or some other way to beat the cold. If you have buried a loved one, then look for another to love. Weeping for a friend does not bring him back. Replacing him gives you another to love.[110] Grief carried too far makes one a fool.

The Stoic view of the foolishness of grief sounds quite hard-hearted and inhumane. Not to grieve or to grieve too little, say, for an intimate friend seems to be a thankless way of expressing oneself for all that one has received from the friendship over the years. It seems to be burying the friendship with the friend. Yet the friendship and the friend are never completely buried. Seneca says laconically, 'Though chance has removed their person, a great part of them, whom we have loved, still abides with us.'[111] Thus, the character of a magnanimous person lives on in those numerous people whom he has touched.

Khreiai *for 'Grief and the Broken Crystal Goblet'*

- 'How many a Chrysippus, how many a Socrates, and how many an Epictetus have time already devoured! Apply this same thought to every man and thing.'[112]
- 'For a Stoic, some tears fall by consent; others fall by their own force.'[113]

FOULEST DEATH VS FAIREST SERVITUDE

The poet Matthew Arnold expresses eloquently the dismay and injustice many feel, when a youth passes away, before he has been given a chance to live, in a passage from 'Early Death and Fame'.

But, when immature death
Beckons too early the guest
From the half-tried banquet of life,

Young, in the bloom of his days;
Leaves no leisure to press,
Slow and surely, the sweets
Of a tranquil life in the shade;
Fuller for him be the hours!
Give him emotion, though pain!
Let him live, let him feel: *I have lived!*
Heap up his moments with life,
Triple his pulses with fame!

One person dies young; another, old; and a third, in infancy. One dies while dining; another, while asleep; another, through dissipation; still another, through disease. One person dies by the sword; another, by snakebite; another, crushed by falling ruins; still another, by torture. We regard some deaths as better than or, at least, preferable to others. Yet the dying is equivalent in each case. 'Death has no degrees of greater or lesser, as it has the same limit [*modum*] in all instances – the cessation of life.'[114]

While no fear is more absurd than fear of death, due to the inevitability of death, no fear is so nearly universal as fear of death. People fear death, because it is against their natural inclination toward self-love and self-preservation and because it relates to the future, about which they are ignorant.[115]

The Stoic remedy for the fear of death is Stoic cognitive therapy directed against fear. Writes Aurelius: 'A trite but effective tactic against the fear of death is to think of the list of people who had to be pried away from life. What did they gain by dying old? In the end, they all sleep six feet under ... They had buried their contemporaries and were buried in turn.'[116] For Stoics, death is not to be dreaded, but only the fear of death. Seneca states that death is nothing to fear, as he has already experienced it.

> I myself have for a long time tested death. You ask, 'When?' I tested it before I was born. Death is non-existence and I know already what that means. What was before me will happen again after me. If there is any suffering in that state, there must have been suffering also in the past, before we entered the light of day. Actually, we felt no discomfort then ... [W]e go astray in thinking that death only follows us, when in reality it has both preceded us and will in turn follow us.[117]

Elsewhere, Seneca sums the Stoic attitude to death bluntly. Death annihilates one or it strips one bare. If it strips one bare, the better part – the soul – remains after one has been released from the burden of the body. If it annihilates one, good and ill are removed. Nothing is left. Either way, it is foolish to fear death.[118]

More than changing one's thinking about death, Seneca argues that one must learn just how to live one's life rightly and that, in some sense, is a lifelong commitment. It takes the whole of one's life to learn how to live[119] and death means nothing to those who have learned how to live. It is frightful only to those who lose everything in losing life.[120]

Like Seneca, Epictetus argues that people did not come into being when they wanted, but when the universe had need of them. Thus, coming into being was not up to them and causes them no anxiety. Similarly, passing away is not up to them. So, too, they should not fear passing away.[121]

Epictetus also gives a clever argument from selfishness. When the Olympic Games are over, certain spectators linger with the vain hope of still seeing athletes compete. It is the same with life. Many hold on to life, when the time for them to depart has come.

> Make room for others. Others still must be born, just as you were born. Once born, they must have land, houses and provisions. If the first-dwellers [*hoi protoi*] do not move along, what is left for those who follow? Why are you insatiate? Why are you unsatisfied? Why do you crowd the cosmos?[122]

The most controversial issue regarding the Stoic view of death concerns suicide. Seneca tackles this issue directly in *Letter* LXX.

Seneca argues that it is not mere living, but living well that is good. Thus, a Stoic will live as long as he must, not as long as he can. To that end, a Stoic must, in some measure, deliberate on the opportunities for good living – that is, for the exercise of virtue – before taking his life. When circumstances disturb him so that his tranquillity is hampered and he becomes defenceless against fortune, he frees himself from the difficulties of living. 'It is not a matter of dying earlier or later, but of dying well or ill, and dying well means escaping [*effugere*] from the danger of living ill.'[123] Elsewhere Seneca says:

> It makes a great deal of difference whether a man is lengthening his life or his death. If the body is useless for service [*ministeriis*],

why should one not free the burdened soul? Perhaps one ought to do that a little before the debt is due, otherwise when it is due, he may be unable to perform the act. Since the danger of living in wretchedness is greater than the danger of dying soon, a fool refuses to stake a little time and win the risk of great gain.[124]

The Ukrainian poet Taras Shevchenko echoes Seneca's sentiments in his poem 'From Day to Day'.

> Wretched is the fettered captive,
> Dying, and a slave;
> But more wretched he that, living,
> Sleeps, as in a grave,
> Till he falls asleep for ever,
> Leaving not a sign
> That there faded into darkness
> Something once divine.[125]

Seneca considers the case of a certain Telesphorus of Rhodes, who was encaged and treated bestially by the tyrant Lysimachus. When someone advised Telesphorus to end his life through fasting, Telesphorus replied: 'A man may hope for anything, while he is alive.' Seneca's reply is that such a life as that 'purchased' by Telesphorus comes at too high a price – shameful confession and weakness. Telesphorus here is not self-sufficient, but at the mercy of fortune. One who knows how to live and when to die has control over fortune. Socrates, Seneca relates, spent 30 days in prison before his death. He spent that time not spent in hope of some reprieve or change of fate, but rather in obedience to the laws. His life and his very death, having conformed to the laws of Athens, served to edify the people of Athens.[126]

Moreover, a change of fate, like that hoped for by Telesphorus, may bring along with it longer life, yet a longer life does not guarantee a better life. However, a longer death is certainly worse. One must not cheat or humour death by living a false life through extending life, when the time is right to die.[127] Seneca states, 'The foulest [spurcissimam] death is preferable to the fairest [mundissimae] servitude',[128] and 'the worst ill is to leave the number of the living before you die'.[129] He adds, 'I shall not kill myself because of pain, for death under such circumstances is defeat. Yet if I find out that the pain must always be endured, I shall depart, not because of the pain, but because it will hinder me in all things for which I live.'[130] The sentiment here and elsewhere is that suicide is a sensible option, when the opportunities for virtuous activity are severely diminished or quashed. Here, as I have argued elsewhere, Seneca is expressing the sentiments of the Stoic progressor, not the sage, as the opportunities for the complete exercise of virtue for a sage are seldom diminished in 'inconvenient' circumstances.[131]

Cicero argues similarly that the Stoic position on suicide may be dictated by indifferents.

> Since these neutral things form the basis for all appropriate acts, there is good ground to say that all our deliberations, including the will to live and the will to quit this life, deal with these things. When a person's circumstances contain a preponderance of things in accordance with Nature, it is appropriate for him to remain alive. When he possesses or sees the prospect of a majority of contrary things, it is appropriate for him to depart from life. This makes it plain that it is occasionally appropriate for a sage to quit life, although he is happy, and also for a foolish person to remain alive, although he is miserable ... Hence, reasons for remaining alive and departing from life are measured wholly by the primary things of Nature.[132]

Thus, Cicero goes on to say, a Stoic may justifiably quit life, when he is sublimely happy, if the opportunity exists for a timely exit.

The columnist Art Buchwald, who was born in 1925 and died on 18 January 2007, was a fine example of someone preparing for a timely exit. During the last years of his life, Buchwald had been suffering from vascular problems that forced the amputation of his right leg. He had rejected kidney dialysis, which would have hooked him up to a machine three times a week for five hours at a time. 'I just decided "to hell with it". I haven't been afraid to die. I'd had a wonderful life. I'm 80 years old, so I'm not afraid.'[133]

What of the sorrow that one brings to others by suicide? Is not such an escape catering to one's selfishness? Epictetus writes:

> 'But if I leave, I shall cause these women sorrow?' You cause them sorrow? Not at all, but it will be the same thing that causes you sorrow – opinion [dogma]. And so, what can you do? You can get

rid of that opinion, and if the women do well, they will get rid of their opinions. Yet if they do not, they will lament because of themselves.[134]

Buchwald too had to deal with the issue of disappointing loved ones and friends. In Stoic-like fashion, he merely noted that the decision was entirely his own.

> Your loved ones don't like the idea. Your friends don't like the idea. No one likes the idea, but once I made it, everyone knew it was my choice. They've gone along with it. It was purely a decision about 'Did I want to stay or did I want to go?' It's one of the few things where you have choice.[135]

For Stoics, it may seem queer that life and death themselves should be considered indifferents. They argue thus. First, death cannot be a good or an ill, as it is a nothing – and a nothing that reduces all things to nothingness. Only a something can be good or ill.[136] Furthermore, it is not every life, but the virtuous life, that is worth living. More than that, life and death are outside of the things within one's moral choosing. Each person comes into the world not according to his own volition, but according to the dictates of deity.[137]

> All things that Fortune looks upon become productive and pleasant, if he who possesses them is in possession also of himself and is not controlled by what belongs to him. People err . . . if they hold that anything good or evil is given to us by Fortune. It is simply the raw material of goods and ills that she gives to us – the sources of things that, in our keeping, will develop into good or ill. The soul is more powerful than any sort of Fortune. By its own agency, it guides its affairs in either direction and, of its own power, it can produce a good life or a wretched one.[138]

When and how should one commit suicide? What sort of principle ought one to follow? The 'how' is easy enough. Having lived the right sort of life, one will choose the right sort of death.

> The fatted bodies of bulls fall from a paltry wound and creatures of mighty strength are felled by one stroke of a man's hand. A tiny blade will sever the sutures of the neck and when that joint,

which binds together head and neck, is cut, the body's mighty mass crumples in a heap. No deep retreat conceals the soul. You need no knife at all to root it out. You need no deeply driven wound to find the vital parts. Death lies near at hand. For these mortal strokes, I have seen no definite spot. The way is open, anywhere you wish.[139]

Overall, there is no general principle that dictates the 'when'. That is entirely up to one's own choosing. In the end, like Buchwald, a Stoic will know when the time is right.

Khreiai *for 'Foulest Death vs Fairest Servitude'*

■ 'He who fears death will never do anything worthy of a man who is alive.'[140]
■ 'Everyone ought to make his life acceptable to all others, but his death to himself. It is the best death that pleases us.'[141]

BUGBEARS: REMOVING THE MASK OF IGNORANCE

The Stoic conception of the good life is a matter of having the right disposition toward conveniences and inconveniences – choosing the former and shunning the latter, while desiring neither. In desiring neither, one eliminates one's affective disposition toward indifferents in selecting and avoiding them. All such things – wealth and poverty, health and illness, and even life and death – are, as Socrates called them 'bugbears' (G., *mormolukeia*, L., *formidines*). To behave affectively toward them is to adopt a childlike disposition toward them – that is, to behave ignorantly, as a child does, when he fears a mask and is relieved to find that, behind it, is the face of someone friendly. Yet when one eliminates a child's ignorance, one eliminates a child's fear as well.[142] So acts one who is invincible.

Nonetheless, what of considerable twists and turns of fortune, like the loss of one's job or the death of a loved one, which come unexpectedly? Such events seem to be more than just bugbears. These too can be endured with the right frame of mind.[143] A progressor is seldom taken aback by the unexpected, for few things are unexpected to one who aims at virtue. A Stoic is moved by reversals of fortune, but his uncertainty is immediately settled by a correct judgment that the impression is neither something good nor bad. In *Letter* LXXXV, Seneca writes:

'Will a Stoic brave man expose himself to dangers?' Not in the least. He will not fear them, though he will avoid them. It is proper for him to be careful, not to be fearful. 'What then? Does he not fear death, imprisonment, burning, and all the other arrows of Fortune?' Not at all, for he knows that those things are not bad, but seem to be bad. He considers all those things to be the bugbears [*formidines*] of human existence . . . Those things are only to be feared by the fearful.[144]

Nothing and no one can harm one who is in full possession of himself. Socrates, Epictetus states, blamed no one for his death – not deity, the attendant who gave him the hemlock, or even those who charged him with crimes. 'Anytus and Meletus can kill me,' he is said to have stated, 'but they cannot harm me.'[145]

Even exile Seneca treats as a bugbear. In *Consolation of Helvia*, he states that exile is a mere change of place, accompanied by inconveniences (*incommoda*). Exile is completely tolerable, as 'wherever we take ourselves, two most admirable things go with us: Universal Nature and our own virtue'. Moreover, he adds, a Stoic should be welcome everywhere, as every place is his city. 'The mind can never suffer exile, as it is free, kindred to the gods, and at home in every world and every age. Its thought ranges over all heaven and projects itself into all past and future times.'[146]

Khreiai *for 'Bugbears'*

- 'Apply this rule: If the community is not injured by any action I might find personally offensive, neither am I.'[147]
- 'Virtue is enfeebled without an adversary.'[148]

NOTES

1 Cicero, *Tusculan Disputations*, I.83.
2 Sigmund Freud, *Civilization and Its Discontents*, trans. James Strachey (New York: W. W. Norton & Company, 1989), pp. 26, 40.
3 Seneca, *Epistles*, XCVI.5.
4 Seneca, *Providence*, II.4.
5 Seneca, *Epistles*, LXXI.23–4.
6 Seneca, *Epistles*, XCVII.10.
7 Aurelius, *Meditations*, III.4.
8 Seneca, *Good Life*, XXVII.3.
9 Epictetus, *Discourses*, IV.xi.7–8.
10 Seneca, *Epistles*, XCIV.13.

11 Seneca, *Anger*, I.vii.2–4.
12 Seneca, *Anger*, II.i.4–5.
13 Plato in *Republic* gives four arguments against being carried away by adversity. First, things may yet turn out for the better in the long run. Second, anguish does not change the future. Third, human affairs are not so significant. Fourth, anguish prevents healing. The right attitude toward adversity is acceptance, as one accepts the outcome of a roll of the dice (604b–c).
14 Seneca, *Epistles*, LXVI.20.
15 Seneca, *Epistles*, LXVI.23.
16 Seneca, *Epistles*, LXVII.3.
17 Seneca, *Epistles*, LXVI.38–9.
18 Seneca, *Epistles*, LXVII.3–4.
19 Seneca, *Providence*, II.5.
20 Seneca, *Helvia*, II.3.
21 Aurelius, *Meditations* VIII.48.
22 Seneca, *Marcia*, XVI.5.
23 Seneca, *Epistles*, XLV.9.
24 Seneca, *Epistles*, CIV.22.
25 Seneca, *Providence*, IV.1.
26 Seneca, *Epistles*, LXVII.14. *Malacus* means 'calm', 'delicate' and 'effeminate'.
27 Seneca, *Providence*, IV.6.
28 Seneca.
29 Seneca, *Providence*, IV.3.
30 *Inner Chapters*, II.4. Quoted in Lin Yutang, *The Wisdom of Laotse* (New York: The Modern Library, 1976), p. 107.
31 Seneca, *Epistles*, XIV.3.
32 Seneca, *Epistles*, CV.8.
33 Cicero, *Ends*, III.xi.36.
34 Plato gives one of the most vivid sketches of a tyrant's degradation in Books VIII and IX of *Republic*.
35 Cicero, *Duties*, II.vii.23.
36 Seneca, *Epistles*, LVII.4–5.
37 Cicero, *Duties*, I.xix.62.
38 Cicero, *Duties*, I.xx.66.
39 Cicero, *Duties*, I.xxiv.83.
40 Seneca, *Epistles*, XIII.12.
41 Epictetus, *Discourses*, III.xxiv.117.
42 Epictetus, *Discourses*, III.xxvi.37–9.
43 Seneca, *Epistles*, LXXVIII.21.
44 Seneca, *Epistles*, CXIII.27.
45 Epictetus, *Handbook*, 2.
46 Seneca, *Epistles*, IX.2–3.
47 Seneca, *Epistles*, LXXVIII.13.
48 Aurelius, *Meditations*, IV.49.
49 Epictetus, *Discourses*, I.6.xxvi–xxviii.
50 Cicero, *Ends*, III.xiii.42.

51 Seneca, *Epistles*, CXIX.14.
52 Implying some sort of diversion from the most natural state of affairs.
53 I.e., made of common earthenware.
54 The cupped hand is likely a reference to Diogenes the Cynic. Seneca, *Epistles*, CXIX.3.
55 Epictetus, *Discourses*, I.6.xxx–xxxvi.
56 Cicero, *Stoic Paradoxes*, 18.
57 D.L. VII, 166.
58 Aurelius, *Meditations*, X.3.
59 Aurelius, *Meditations*, VII.64.
60 Seneca, *Epistles*, LXXXV.30.
61 Seneca, *Epistles*, XCIV.7.
62 Seneca, *Epistles*, XXII.16.
63 One must, of course, exercise caution here. To show that one emotion is strong and wicked is not to show that all emotions are worth stamping out, as Seneca suggests in *Anger*.
64 Seneca, *Anger*, I.i.2.
65 Seneca, *Anger*, I.i.1.
66 Seneca, *Anger*, III.i.5.
67 Seneca, *Anger*, I.i.3–5.
68 Seneca, *Anger*, II.xxxi.1.
69 Seneca, *Anger*, II.xiv.2–3.
70 Epictetus, *Discourses* I.xviii.5–8.
71 See also *Discourses*, I.xviii.11–12.
72 Seneca, *Anger*, I.v.2–3.
73 Seneca, *Anger*, I.vi.5.
74 Seneca, *Anger*, I.xiii.1–2.
75 Seneca, *Anger*, I.xiv.5.
76 Seneca, *Anger*, II.x.1.
77 Aristotle, *Nicomachean Ethics*, IV.5.
78 Seneca, *Anger*, I.viii.2–3 and III.i.1.
79 Seneca, *Firmness*, XVII.4.
80 Seneca, *Anger*, III.xiv.1–4.
81 Seneca, *Anger*, II.xxxii.1.
82 Seneca, *Anger*, II.xxxii.3.
83 Cicero, *Duties*, II.xiv.51.
84 Seneca, *Anger*, I.xix.7.
85 Seneca, *Anger*, I.xv.1.
86 Seneca, *Anger*, I.xvi.3.
87 Seneca, *Anger*, I.xviii.1–2.
88 Cicero, *Duties*, I.vii.20–2.
89 Seneca, *Anger*, II.xviii1–2.
90 Seneca, *Anger*, II.xx.1–4.
91 Seneca, *Anger*, II.xxii.1–2.
92 Seneca, *Anger*, II.iv.2.
93 Seneca, *Anger*, II.xxix.1. Plutarch bids one to remind oneself that delay can only help oneself to see events clearly. A guilty person is still guilty a day after having committed a wrongdoing, and no harm is done in

punishing late. However, there may be great harm in punishing hastily. *Control of Anger*, 459f.

94 Seneca, *Anger*, II.xxxiv.5.
95 Seneca, *Epistles*, IX, and *Tranquillity,* V.6–7.
96 Seneca, *Marcia*, XV.2 and *Polybius*, XV.3.
97 Seneca, *Marcia*, VII.1. Called *praesumpta opinio* at VII.4.
98 Seneca, *Marcia*, VIII.1.
99 Seneca, *Marcia*, X.1–2.
100 Seneca, *Polybius*, V.1.
101 Seneca, *Polybius*, V.4–5.
102 Seneca, *Polybius*, IX.1–4.
103 Seneca, *Polybius*, X.5.
104 Seneca, *Polybius*, XI.2.
105 Seneca, *Polybius*, XVIII.2 and *Epistles*, XCIX.6.
106 Aurelius, *Meditations* III.14.
107 Epictetus, *Discourses* III.xxiv.84–7. See also IV.x.31–6.
108 Seneca, *Epistles*, LXII.3.
109 Seneca, *Epistles*, XCIX.8.
110 Seneca, *Epistles*, LXII.11–12.
111 Seneca, *Epistles*, XCIX.4.
112 Aurelius, *Meditations*, VII.19.
113 Seneca, *Epistles*, XCIX.18.
114 Seneca, *Epistles*, LXVI.42–3.
115 Seneca, *Epistles*, LXXXII.15–16.
116 Aurelius, *Meditations* IV.50
117 Seneca, *Epistles*, LIV.4–5.
118 Seneca, *Epistles*, XXIV.18. In *Consolation of Marcia*, Seneca offers an indirect, Hegesias-like argument for not fearing death: Death is preferable to life. Seneca, *Marcia*, XXII.3.
119 Seneca, *Shortness of Life*, VII.3.
120 Cicero, *Stoic Paradoxes*, 18.
121 Epictetus, *Discourses*, III.xxiv.94.
122 Epictetus, *Discourses*, IV.i.106.
123 Seneca, *Epistles*, LXX.4–5.
124 Seneca, *Epistles*, LVIII.34.
125 Taras Shevchenko, 'From Day to Day', *Poems* (Munich: Molode Zyttia Press, 1961), p. 59.
126 Seneca, *Epistles*, LXX.6–9.
127 Seneca, *Epistles*, LXX.12. See also *Epistles*, LXXVII.
128 Literally, 'filthiest death' and 'cleanest servitude'.
129 Seneca, *Equanimity*, V.5.
130 Seneca, *Epistles*, LVIII.36.
131 See M. Andrew Holowchak, 'Carrying One's Goods from City to City: Seneca on Friendship, Self-Sufficiency, and the Disdain of Fortune', *Ancient Philosophy*, XXVI.1 (2006): [?].
132 Cicero, *Ends*, III.xviii.60–1.
133 Darlene Superville, 'Fabled Columnist Enjoys his Long Goodbye', *The Morning Call*, Allentown, PA, 9 April 2006, E1, E9.

134 Epictetus, *Discourses*, II.xvi.40.
135 Superville, 'Fabled Columnist Enjoys his Long Goodbye', E9.
136 Seneca, *Marcia*, XIX.5.
137 Epictetus, *Discourses*, III.xxiv.95.
138 Seneca, *Epistles*, XCVIII.2.
139 Seneca, *Providence*, VI.8–9.
140 Seneca, *Equanimity*, XI.6.
141 Seneca, *Epistles*, LXX.11–13.
142 Epictetus, *Discourses*, II.i.14–15.
143 Seneca, *Providence*, II.4.
144 Seneca, *Epistles*, LXXXV.26–7.
145 Epictetus, *Discourses*, I.xxix.18, I.xxx.64–6.
146 Seneca, *Helvia*, VI.1, VIII.2, IX.7, XI.7.
147 Aurelius, *Meditations*, V.21.
148 Seneca, *Providence*, II.4.

CHAPTER 4

EQUANIMITY IN PROSPERITY

'A person's dignity may be enhanced by the house he lives in, but not wholly secured by it. The owner should bring honour to his house, not the house to its owner.'

Cicero, *Duties*, I.xxxix.139

Mack W. Metcalf and Virginia G. Merida, his estranged second wife, split a $34 million lottery jackpot in 2000. Metcalf – who prior to this windfall had difficulty keeping a job, due to problems with alcohol, and even once lived in an abandoned bus – bought a huge estate in Kentucky along with vintage cars and several horses. Merida, who prior to the windfall worked wherever she could just to make ends meet, purchased a mansion overlooking the Ohio River as well as a Mercedes-Benz.

Three years after winning, Metcalf died from alcoholism at the age of 45. Merida suffered a similar fate. Her partly decomposed body was found in her bed, prior to Thanksgiving of 2005. A drug overdose was suspected to be the cause of her death. She was 51.[1]

What that sad story shows is that good fortune overwhelms some people, as ill fortune overwhelms many. Strangely, the Stoics believe there is more to say than that. They maintain that relatively few people are able handle the vagaries of good fortune. Seneca says, 'Those who are most prosperous and wealthy are beset with the most trouble, and the more property they have to cause them turmoil, the less they find themselves.'[2] Most people, I suspect, would find Seneca's claim paradoxical, if not manifestly absurd. For who, if things could be so, would not want to be in a position to test the hypothesis by having a run of great good fortune?

Is the Stoic position absurd or is it just paradoxical? Before passing judgment, let us consider the following. A 1997 article in the *New York Post* reported that about one-third of all lottery winners file for bankruptcy.[3] The article shows that many such instant millionaires are poorly suited to be millionaires. Moreover, winning the lottery does little to slake people's thirst for further wealth. A Duke University study shows that lottery jackpot winners, after winning, substantially increase the amount of money they had previously spent on tickets.[4] Having more than one needs, it seems, creates a desire for having even more than more than one needs.

For the Stoics, good fortune is not so different from, and may even be worse than, ill fortune.

> While all excesses are in a way hurtful, the most dangerous is unlimited good fortune [*felicitates intemperantia*]. It excites the brain. It evokes empty fancies in the mind. It clouds in a deep fog the boundary between falsehood and truth. Would it not be better to summon up virtue's help and to endure everlasting misfortune [*perpetuam infelicitatem*] than to be bursting with unlimited and immoderate feelings? Death from starvation comes very gently, but from gorging, men explode.[5]

The proper Stoic attitude toward ill fortune is not distress and desire – related to present and future attitudes of avoidance – but indifference. Similarly, the proper Stoic attitude toward good fortune is not pleasure and desire – related to present and future attitudes of attraction – but indifference. Good fortune is choice-worthy only insofar as its 'goods' are embellishments of, though not needed for, a good life. It is the opposite with ill fortune.

> No one can doubt that a Stoic finds in riches, not in poverty, ampler material for displaying his powers, because in poverty there is room for only one kind of virtue – not to be bowed down and crushed by it – while in riches moderation, liberality, diligence, orderliness and grandeur each have a wide field . . . For certain things, even if they are trifles [*parva*] in comparison with the whole and can be withdrawn without destroying the essential good, still contribute something to the perpetual joy [*perpetuam laetitiam*] that springs from virtue.[6]

What I wish to show in this chapter is that good fortune, if we are not ready for it, can mar character every bit as much as and perhaps even more than ill fortune. It is for this reason that one ought to adopt an attitude of indifference toward good fortune and ill fortune alike: Such things are not up to us.

GAIN AND THE GOLD-LEAF LIFE

The Stoics are fond of claiming that a philosopher, indifferent to the arrows of fortune, has a better claim to the title of 'king' than a king himself.[7] Seneca illustrates the point with a story of how Diogenes the Cynic, a disdainer of possessions, marched naked through the midst of the treasures of the Macedonian king, Alexander. In doing so, the philosopher seemed to tower above the king, who had command of the world. 'Far more powerful and richer was Diogenes than Alexander, who then was master of the whole world', Seneca said, 'since what Diogenes refused to receive was even more than what Alexander was able to give.'[8]

Such stories have a certain amount of charm, if only because they illustrate plainly the absurdity of a life of boundless ambition. Yet one might still not be convinced that an attitude of complete indifference to material things is preferable to one that countenances, say, moderation in their acquisition. The Stoics have a lot of convincing yet to do.

Aristotle notes that the good life requires the greatest amount of contemplative activity, directed not at all at practical concerns, and contemplative activity, of course, imposes certain demands on one aspiring to virtue – for instance, leisure and wealth enough to enable one to be self-sufficient.

For Stoics, it is otherwise. Leisure and wealth are not considered goods in themselves; rather, they have the status of conveniences. As is the case with any convenience, one has to be careful that they do not impede one's quest for happiness.

Of all Stoics, Seneca most of all often writes as if conveniences are impediments to virtue. In *Letter* XVII, Seneca talks of the problems frequently occasioned by wealth. He begins by exhorting Lucilius: 'Cast away all things of that sort [i.e. riches], if you are wise – instead, so that you may be wise.' All in all, poverty is preferable to an abundance of wealth. Riches do more to keep one from philosophy, while poverty provides one with unburdened leisure. Poverty attends to pressing needs; luxury, to artificial ones.

'The acquisition of wealth has been for many men, not an end, but a change of troubles', Epicurus writes. I am not astonished. The fault is not in the wealth, but in the mind itself. What has made poverty a burden to us has made wealth also a burden. Just as it matters little whether you lay a sick man on a wooden or a golden bed, for wherever he is moved he will carry his illness with him, so one need not care whether a diseased mind is given riches or poverty. His malady [*malum*] follows him.[9]

Elsewhere Seneca states that no one finds contentment in prosperity, even if the prosperity is unexpected, because everyone always prefers to have not what they have, but what they do not have.[10] Moreover, prosperity is greedy. It smites people with a greater craving for itself. When one possesses more, one wants still more, and one who cannot be satisfied cannot satisfy others.[11] In *On Equanimity*, Seneca goes so far as to say that wealth is the greatest source of human sorrow.[12]

It is not that wealth is itself wicked, but it turns men to wickedness by giving them an inflated sense of self-significance.

> Wealth puffs up the soul and begets haughtiness. It brings on unpopularity and unsettles the mind to such an extent that the mere reputation of having wealth, though it is bound to harm us, affords pleasure ... Those things that are goods produce trust, but wealth produces arrogance. The things that are goods give us magnanimity, but wealth gives us insolence and insolence is none other than a false show of greatness.[13]

Epictetus compares a rich, desirous person to a feverous, thirsty person. Unlike a healthy person, one feverous drinks and obtains only a momentary slaking of his thirst. He gets nauseous, transforms the water to bile, throws up and suffers bowel pain and an even greater thirst than before.[14]

In *Letter* CX, Seneca states that at a certain elaborate entertainment he once saw a display of luxurious objects (*divitiae*) that rivalled the wealth of an entire city. There were numerous gold and silver items on parade as well as coloured tapestries and beautiful slave-boys and slave-women. The event stirred up feelings of passion and despicability in him, and though slow-moving it was, it seemed to be over all too quickly. Overall, the parade of riches seemed to be more ostentatious than substantive. 'Such things are displayed, not possessed. They please, but they pass away.' The free person, he goes on to say, is not one whom fortune slightly affects, but the one whom fortune does not affect. Freedom comes in emulation of Jupiter, who craves nothing.[15]

Constantly wanting conveniences – things the Stoics repeatedly tell us that are not up to us – brings about 'gold-leaf happiness' (*bratteata felicitas*).[16] To have enduring happiness, one must renounce all false goods and embrace virtue, and that is impossible to do if one's mind is continually distracted by the thought of possessing anything other than oneself. Hence, an apprentice will strive to live simply.[17]

To illustrate, Seneca tells the story of the Cynic Diogenes, whose slave Manes had run away. Instead of worrying about getting him back, Diogenes is reputed to have said: 'It would be a shame, if Diogenes could not live without Manes, when Manes can live without Diogenes.' Manes' freedom, then, was his own.[18]

Ought one who desires invincibility to consign oneself to a life of poverty? Riches, as conveniences, do have some inherent value, Seneca maintains. Yet it is a matter of knowing when one has had one's fill and then not desiring more. A Stoic prefers having enough to having much, for one who has much does not have what one who has enough has – a limit.[19] Conveniences, then, need not to be spurned, as they have selective value; but, being at the whim of fortune and not being goods, they ought not to be sought.

What is one to do, for instance, if one is born into wealth? It is not so much the having of property with which Stoics find fault. Unlike the Cynics, Stoics do not actively seek to simplify their lives as much as possible by casting away the things that they happen to possess beyond what they need for mere survival. For Stoics, it is not having things that makes one unhappy; it is longing for things that makes one unhappy. To have things without longing for them – without being concerned about losing them – is to be unencumbered by them.[20] Overall, an abundance of material conveniences ties one down and makes self-sufficiency difficult.

The Stoic Panaetius reminds us that accumulation of property is not objectionable; unjust accumulation of it is.

Fine furnishings and the comforts of life in elegance and abundance also give one pleasure, and the desire to secure it gives rise to an insatiable thirst for wealth. Still, I do not mean to find fault with the accumulation of property [*rei familiaris amplificatio*], provided that it hurts no one, yet the unjust acquisition of it is always to be avoided.[21]

Cicero illustrates with a hypothetical example of a debate between the Stoic Diogenes and his pupil Antipater. Suppose one is selling his house and conceals from a potential buyer certain facts about the house – that it is unsanitary, that it has vermin and that it is constructed with unstable timber. Is it the vendor's duty to disclose these facts, even when he is not asked, as Antipater believes, or does the vendor have no duty to speak of such things, as Diogenes maintains, unless the potential buyer asks? Concealment here seems to be in the interest of the seller, though not in the interest of the buyer. True concealment, Panaetius argues, is not just a matter of holding one's tongue, but doing so for one's own profit at the expense of another.[22] Antipater's argument ultimately wins the day and rightly so.

Khreiai for 'Gain and the Gold-Leaf Life'

- 'Wealth is not to be greedy; income is not to love to buy things. Indeed, contentment with one's own possessions is itself a very large and perfectly secure fortune.'[23]
- 'It is in the power of any person to despise all things, but in the power of no person to possess all things. The shortest path to wealth is to despise wealth.'[24]

BENEFACTION: THE CORNERSTONE OF JUSTICE

Once, when Socrates' pupils were giving their teacher gifts, each according to his means, Aeschines, a man of little means, said he would give Socrates everything and the only thing he possessed – himself. Socrates, seeing the character of Aeschines, acknowledged the greatness of the gift and pledged to return it back to its owner in better shape than it was received.[25]

As a general rule of thumb, for Stoics, benefaction – the proper giving and receiving of gifts – ought to be undertaken with great circumspection. 'Whoever thinks that giving is an easy matter makes a mistake', Seneca writes. 'It is a matter of very great difficulty, provided that gifts are made with wisdom and not scattered haphazardly and by caprice.'[26] The Stoic view on benefaction is most elaborately expressed in the seven books of Seneca's *On Benefits*.

A benefit (*beneficium*) Seneca defines as a substantial act of giving, done voluntarily and with the aim to spread joy, to one in need by one who has more than he needs.[27] For benefaction, as with all activities, it is the state of the giver's mind and not the benefit that determines the benefit's worth. It is not the size of the gift, but the spirit in which it is given that counts.[28] The measure of a benefit is the goodwill of the one giving it.

Overall, Seneca's attitude toward benefaction illustrates neatly that virtue is not practised for personal gain – that giving is not undertaken with the aim of a return. A good deed is itself its own reward.[29] 'A good person gives a benefit', Seneca says, 'not because he does what he ought to do, but because it is not possible for him not to do what he ought to do.'[30] Virtue cannot fail to act in the most effective ways.

Benefits are of three kinds. First, there are necessary benefits (*necessaria*): those things without which one cannot live, such as being freed from the wrath of an enemy or tyrant;[31] those things we ought not to live without, such as liberty, chastity and good conscience; and those things we are not willing to live without, such as children, a wife and household goods.[32] Second, there are useful benefits (*utilia*). These include material, social and political conveniences such as money, awards of public office, grants of citizenship and gifts of land.[33] Last, there are pleasant benefits (*iucunda*), which include books, hunting nets and wine.[34] Of pleasant benefits, the best are those things that endure.[35]

Cicero, in *On Duties*, gives three needed conditions for a benefaction to be given properly to another.

> We must, first, see to it that our act of kindness will not injure the beneficiary or any others. Second, we must see to it that it will not be beyond our means. Finally, we must see to it that it will be given in proportion to the worth of the recipient. Those make up the cornerstone of justice [*iustitiae fundamentum*], by which all acts of kindness must be measured.[36]

He later adds that one must help others not only in proportion to their worth, but also commensurate with their individual needs and the closeness of one's relationship with them.[37]

Seneca too lists rules for giving. One confers a benefit rightly, if he considers all relevant circumstances: not only what he has given, but when, in what manner, and to whom he has given it.[38]

First, the giving must be prompt, not hesitant or delayed.

> In sickness, food at the right moment promotes health, and water given at the proper time serves as a remedy, so a benefit, no matter how trivial and commonplace it may be, if it has been given promptly and without wasting even an hour, gains greatly in force and is more welcome than any costly present that is slow in coming and long considered.[39]

To hold a gift in one's hand and debate over giving it, through reluctance, is not to give. Hesitation is nearly refusal.[40] To promise a gift and then to delay in giving it is also wrong, but to keep back a gift that was rashly promised is right. It is also right to demand back what was wrongly given.[41]

Second, as the character of the giver is the true measure of the gift, it is critical to be in the right state of mind when giving. The right state of mind entails that the giving is voluntary,[42] that the giving is not made when one's mind is uneasy or when one's will is ill[43] and that the giving is done altruistically.[44]

Finally, benefits must also be given to the right people. First, they ought not to be given arbitrarily.[45] Second, they ought to be given proportionate to the character of the one benefiting.[46] To the virtuous, only honour is appropriate.

> This is the duty we owe to the virtuous – to honour them, not only when they are present with us, but even when they have been taken from our sight. They have made it their aim, not to confine their services to one age alone, but to leave behind their benefits even after they themselves have passed away, so let us not confine our gratitude to one age alone.[47]

Third, gifts ought to be given to humanity in general before individuals, as the duty each owes to humanity is greater than the duty each owes to any one person.[48]

How is one to repay a benefit? In general, what applies to the giving of benefits applies as well to their reception. The receiver must be in the right state of soul on receiving the benefit. He must also consider from whom and at what time the gift has come.

First, being in the right state of soul on the receiving of benefits returns us to the issue of gratitude, which can be shown in many ways.

I list two. To begin, a benefit is adequately repaid with the correct measure of gratitude, upon its reception, and the correct measure is ascertained in proportion to the gift.[49] To be overly grateful is to be insincere. To be insufficiently grateful is to be ungrateful.[50] Complete ingratitude is generally a sign of a recipient's greed for receiving other gifts.[51] Next, benefactors may also express gratitude through the right amount of publicity, which is itself a munificent way of praising a giver's generosity. 'As the giver should add to his gift only that measure of publicity that will please the one to whom he gives it, so the recipient should invite the whole city to witness it.'[52]

Second, from whom should one be willing to receive a benefit? The receiver must be just as chary as the giver here. One need not receive a benefit from everyone, Seneca states, but only from those to whom one could have given one.[53]

Finally, benefits must be returned at the right time. The right time to return a benefit is dependent upon the character of the benefactor. 'To a good man I shall make a return, when it is convenient; to a bad man, when he asks for it.'[54]

Overall, how is one to evaluate benefaction? Here Seneca assumes a third-party perspective:

> Compare the characters of the two concerned in a benefaction and weigh the gift itself against them so as to determine whether, in the case of the giver, it will be either too generous or too small, and whether, in the case of the receiver, it will be disdained or found to be too large.[55]

Such an evaluative scheme is needed because, for Stoics as with Aristotle, virtue is a mean state, and excess and defect in giving and receiving are equally in error.[56]

Khreiai *for 'Benefaction'*

- 'He who does not return a benefit errs more; he who does not give one errs earlier.'[57]
- 'Whatever I have given, that I still have.'[58]

BACCHANALIAN REVELRY: BIRDS OF THE NIGHT

Tennessee Williams' play *The Night of the Iguana* is set mostly at a Mexican seaside resort during World War II. It is the story of a defrocked Episcopal minister, Rev. Lawrence Shannon, and his perpetual fight with alcohol and with his inner erotic impulses.

Working as a travel guide, Shannon accompanies a busload of female American tourists to a Mexican resort. At his wit's end, he deliberately leads them astray, and arrives at another resort – that of an old friend, whose help he desperately needs. Leaving the tourists in the bus, he rushes up to the hilltop resort and is greeted by his friend's wife, Maxine, who relates that her husband is no longer alive. Desperate, he convinces Maxine, a woman of great sexual passion, to put up him and his captive tourists to give him time to wrestle with his inner demons. Maxine, whose attraction to Shannon is obvious, is delighted to have Shannon stay.

There soon arrives at the resort a penniless, wandering artist, Hannah Jelkes, and her aged grandfather, Jonathan Coffin, a Romantic poet, 98 years young. They pay their way, as they travel together, by her art and an occasional reading by the aged poet. Maxine allows the two to stay for a while. As Maxine prepares dinner for the tourists, Hannah offers Maxine help in setting the table for dinner and the two exchange words.

> MAXINE: You're completely broke, are you?
> HANNAH: Yes, we are – completely.
> MAXINE: You say that like you're proud of it.
> HANNAH: I'm not proud of it or ashamed of it either. It just happens to be what's happened to us, which has never happened before in all our travels.

To Maxine's dismay, late in the day, Shannon finds a confidant in Hannah, who helps him pass a most troublesome night, as he panics inwardly about his love of booze and his lust for women. Hannah tells him not to worry: He seems to enjoy his panic too much too die from it. Shannon snaps back angrily and Hannah replies: 'That wasn't meant as an insult, just an observation. I don't judge people, I draw them. That's all I do, just draw them, but in order to draw them I have to observe them, don't I?'

Hannah adds with plain frankness that Shannon's problem is not alcohol, but his inner demons. She knows, because she too has struggled with demons of her own, but she has learned how to manage them successfully and pledges to help him too.

HANNAH: Yes. I can help you because I've been through what you are going through now. I had something like your spook – I just had a different name for him. I called him the blue devil, and . . . oh . . . we had quite a battle, quite a contest between us.

SHANNON: Which you obviously won.

HANNAH: I couldn't afford to lose.

SHANNON: How'd you beat your blue devil?

HANNAH: I showed him that I could endure him and I made him respect my endurance.

SHANNON: How?

HANNAH: By just, by just . . . enduring. Endurance is something that spooks and blue devils respect. And they respect all the tricks that panicky people use to outlast and outwit their panic.

Hannah's reply, as in her exchange with Maxine, is Stoic-like and has its effect on Shannon. Overall, he survives his nocturnal crisis (and mutiny by the tourists) and accepts an offer by Maxine to stay with her and help her run the resort. Hannah, whose grandfather dies that night, leaves the resort to work by herself in the town.

Seneca's *Letter* CXXII to Lucilius describes men like the Rev. Lawrence Shannon, who sleep away most of the day and live for the pleasures of the night. As the night approaches, they wake, after much effort, and their eyes are swollen and heavy with the debauch of the previous night.

> Do you think that these men, who do not know when to live, know how to live? Do these men fear death, if they have buried themselves alive? They are as unfortunate as birds of the night. Although they pass their hours of darkness amid wine and perfumes and spend all of their unnatural waking hours in eating dinners – and those too cooked separately to make up many courses. They are not really banqueting. They are conducting their own funeral services. The dead at least have their banquets by daylight.[59]

Abstaining from alcohol – at least, refraining from habitual or heavy consumption – is also an important feature of living a virtuous, invincible life. It is not that drunkards are unreliable confidants, but rather that inebriation makes virtuous activity difficult, if not impossible. How often do people act, while drunk, and regret their actions, once sober. Recall the wickedness to Praexaspes of the Persian king Cambyses, while drunk. Moreover, drunkenness usually paves the way for continued cruelty. Continued drunkenness over time bestializes the soul, so that when the liquor is gone, the bestiality still remains.[60]

Overall, 'birds of the night' – in choosing softness to hardness, excess to sufficiency, and lethargy to activity – are like those birds fattened up in preparation for a banquet, who are purposely kept from the light of day.

Similarly, if people vegetate without physical activity, engorgement overtakes their listless body and, in magnificent leisure [*superba*[61] *umbra*], a numbing fat [*iners sagina*[62]] swells. Moreover, the bodies of those who have sworn allegiance to the dark hours have a loathsome appearance. Their complexion is more alarming than that of anaemic invalids. Pale, they are sluggish and deteriorating. Though alive, their flesh is dead. Yet those, to my thinking, are the least of their ills. How much more darkness is in their souls! Such a person is inwardly dazed [*se stupet*]. His vision is darkened. He envies the blind. What person ever had eyes for seeing in the dark?[63]

Khreia for 'Bacchanalian Revelry'

■ 'Drunkenness is nothing but a condition of voluntary insanity.'[64]

GORMANDIZING AND THE SOFT LIFE

Today, unlike any other time, there are culinary options to accommodate pernickety persons. For instance, on a simple trip to the local grocery 40 years ago, one could choose from a small sample of condiments for a burger or sandwich – perhaps, mustard, ketchup and mayonnaise. Today there are numerous sorts of spices and flavourings added to these condiments, and many other sorts of condiments from which to choose. Grocers also carry numerous sorts of prepared and semi-prepared foods, from simple to gourmet, so that one could completely avoid one's kitchen, should one so choose. One could grow dizzy just trying to select among the myriad foodstuffs at larger food stores.

Similar to those who live for the night are those who live from meal to meal. They preoccupy themselves, upon waking each day, with what they will eat in the morning and later that day and night, as if there is nothing else worthwhile about which to deliberate.

Of course, a gluttonous lifestyle cannot be virtuous. Virtue requires moderation. Seneca's arguments for enjoying simple fare and refraining from delicacies are neatly expressed in *Letter* CVIII. His own dietary frugality was passed on to him by his mentor, Attalus – a poor and simple philosopher, who fashioned himself, on account of his few desires, a king. Of his own simple preferences, Seneca states:

> That is why I have forsaken oysters and mushrooms forever, as they are not really food, but are relishes to bully the full stomach into further eating – the habit of gourmands and those who stuff themselves beyond their powers of digestion. Down with it quickly and up with it quickly! That is why I have also avoided perfumes throughout my life, as the best scent for a person is no scent at all. That is why my stomach is unacquainted with wine. That is why throughout my life I have shunned the bath and have believed that to emaciate the body and sweat it into thinness is at once unprofitable and effeminate [*delicatum*].[65]

Desire for extravagant foods and other such luxuries brings about idleness and softness. Seneca tells the story of Mindyrides of Sybaris. Mindyrides presumably complained that the swinging of a mattock[66] by a worker was making him dizzy and ordered the man to work elsewhere, out of his sight. He also complained that the rose leaves upon which he was lying while the man was swinging his mattock were crumpled and disturbing his rest.

> Why is it that we are thrown into a rage by somebody's cough or sneeze, by negligence in chasing a fly away, by a dog's hanging around, or by the dropping of a key that has slipped from the hands of a careless servant? Will the poor wretch whose ears are hurt by the grating of a bench dragged across the floor be able to bear with equanimity the strife of public life and the abuse rained down on him in the assembly or the senate-house? ... Nothing, then, is more conducive to anger than the intemperance and the intolerance that comes from soft living. A mind must be strengthened by hardship, so that it feels nothing but a grave blow.[67]

In his *Letter* LXXXII, Seneca asks Lucilius to consider what one means by 'He lives luxuriously'. It can mean no other, he states baldly, than 'He is softened by luxury'. He adds, 'The soul is made effeminate by degrees and is weakened until it matches the ease and laziness in which it lies.' Thus, there is little difference between such a soul, softened by idleness, and one that lies buried. 'He who lies on a perfumed couch is no less dead than he who is carried off by an executioner's hook.'[68]

Epictetus in his *Discourses* says:

> You fear hunger, as you believe. Yet it is not hunger that you fear, but you fear that you will not have professional cooks. You fear that you will not have another servant to buy you delicacies, another to put on your shoes for you, another to dress you, others to give you your massage, and others to follow at your heels, so that when you have undressed in a bath and stretched yourself out like men who have been crucified, you may be massaged on this side and the other . . . And then, when you have left the bath and gone home, you may shout out, 'Is no one bringing me something to eat?' . . . What you fear is this: You may not be able to live the life of an invalid [*arrostou bion*] . . . You have only to learn the life of healthy men – how the slaves, the workmen, the genuine philosophers live; how Socrates, with a wife and children, lived; how Diogenes lived; how Cleanthes, who combined going to school and pumping water, lived.[69]

Food is used not as a measure of softness, but as a measure of appetite, in the film director Marco Ferreri's black 'comedy' *La Grande Bouffe*. Four successful mid-aged men – Ugo, a master chef, Michel, a television executive, Marcello, a pilot, and Philippe, a judge – meet at Philippe's remote villa with the aim of eating themselves to death. Food, here, is likely a metaphor for indulgence in life's pleasures, and it seems that it is their everyday-life lust for indulgence that has exhausted them to such a point that they want to quit life. As they arrive at the villa, truckloads of food arrive to meet them, and the men set themselves up for a few days of suicidal, gastronomical indulgence.

On the second day of alimentary indulgence, Marcello, tired of food without sex, convinces the others to invite a few prostitutes to join them. A schoolteacher, Andrea, also joins them. One by one and quite paradoxically, the prostitutes, sickened by the over-indulgence, leave. Only Andrea remains. One by one, the men die through over-indulgence until only Andrea and Ugo remain. Andrea stays with Ugo until he too dies. Ferreri makes one general point ring true: Over-indulgence in life's pleasures forces one to quit life itself, if not through death, then through estrangement.

In contrast to the soft and over-indulgent life is the simple life. How frequently the Stoics, having roots in Cynicism, use the Cynic Diogenes to illustrate simplicity of living.

> Diogenes says, 'To be naked is better than any scarlet robe and to sleep on the bare ground is the softest couch.' He offers as a proof of each statement his own courage, equanimity, freedom, and finally his body, radiant with health and hardened. 'There is no enemy near,' he says. 'All is peaceful.' How is that so, Diogenes? 'Look', he says, 'I have not been struck by any arrow, have I? I have not been wounded, have I? I have not fled from anyone, have I?'[70]

In *Letter* XC, Seneca reports that Diogenes, upon seeing a young boy scoop up water from the hollow of his own hand, took his cup from his wallet, broke it to pieces and said, 'I am a fool to have been carrying useless baggage [*supervacuas sarcinas*] all this time!' Seneca sums, 'The things that are necessary require no elaborate pains for their acquisition. It is only luxuries that call for labour.'[71]

Finally, the Stoic admiration for simple living is no more evident than in Seneca's vivid description, in a letter to Lucillius, of the simple country villa of the great Roman general Scipio Africanus – so simple it was redolent of Scipio's heroism.[72]

Khreiai *for 'Gormandizing and the Soft Life'*

- 'You must reflect carefully beforehand with whom you are to eat and drink, rather than what you are to eat and drink. For a dinner of meats without the company of a friend is like the life of a lion or a wolf.'[73]
- 'Practise at some time the lifestyle of an invalid [*arrostos*], so that at another time you may live like a healthy man. Take no food, drink only water, refrain sometimes from desire altogether, so that at other times you may exercise desire and then with good reason.'[74]

IN THE FOOTSTEPS OF HERCULES

Plutarch, in his *Lives of Eminent Greeks*, relates a story about the fearless Greek general Pyrrhus (319–272 BC), who reigned as king of the Molossian tribes for 25 years until his death, while fighting in Argos. Through his campaigns, Pyrrhus befriended a certain wise Thessalian by the name of Cineas. Cineas asked Pyrrhus one day about his upcoming Italian campaign. If you should be fortunate enough to take Italy, Cineas asked, what then? Pyrrhus said that he would have proven himself a match for any country or tribe of men. Asked what he would do after having taken Italy, Pyrrhus replied that he would move on Sicily. Cineas pressed on, and Pyrrhus stated that Libya or Carthage would be next and then perhaps Macedonia and all of Greece itself. Again, Cineas pressed on. If you should secure those, Cineas asked, what would you then do? Not seeing the point of such questions, Pyrrhus smiled and said that he would then reap the benefits of such hard-fought victories by reclining, with drink, and engaging in polite conversation with friends. Cineas replied smartly:

> What stands in our way now, if we want to drink and while away the time with one another? Surely the privilege is ours already, and we have at hand, without taking any trouble, those things to which we hope to attain by bloodshed, great toils, and perils, after we do much harm to others and suffer much ourselves.

Cineas' reply profoundly troubled Pyrrhus. Pyrrhus saw plainly that his great ambition was costing him great happiness, yet he failed to take Cineas' advice to shackle his desires.[75]

The best example of boundless ambition in antiquity was Alexander of Macedon. After the death of his father Philip in 336 BC, Alexander inherited the most formidable army of his day and began his invasion of Persia in 334 BC. After defeating the Persians and gaining control of their vast empire, Alexander continued the carnage with a senseless and brutal campaign into India in 329 BC and only stopped when his troops, having had enough, threatened mutiny at the Hyphasis River in 326 BC. Writes Seneca of Alexander's ambition, turned madness:

> Alexander was driven to misfortune and dispatched to unknown countries by a mad desire to lay waste to other men's lands . . .

Not content with the ruin of all the states that Philip had either conquered or bribed into bondage, Alexander overthrew various commonwealths in various places and carried his weapons all over the world. Though his cruelty, like a wild beast that tears to pieces more than its hunger demands, was overextended, it never stopped. Though he had joined many kingdoms into one, had made the Greeks and Persians fear the same lord, and had yoked many of Darius' free nations to the yoke, he still desired to pass beyond the Ocean and the Sun. Deeming it a shame that he should shift his course of victory from the paths that Heracles and Bacchus had made, he threatened violence to Nature herself. He did not wish to go, but he could not stay. He was like a weight that fell headlong – its course having ended only when it has lain motionless.[76]

To Seneca, the Macedonian general was a poor, pathetic figure, though he conquered much of the known world and gained the vast treasures of the mighty Persian Empire, because he sought more than what Nature had in store for him.[77] What is worse, he conquered and sought to govern others, when he could not govern himself. 'Whom will you more admire than the man who governs himself, who has himself under control? It is easier to rule savage nations, impatient as they are of the authority of others, than to restrain one's own spirit and submit to self-control.'[78] A king of nations, Alexander was a slave to his own unbridled ambition.

Alexander's illimitable ambition is perhaps even better illustrated in a story Plutarch relates. Upon hearing of the philosopher Anaxachus' discourse about an infinite number of worlds, Alexander presumably wept and said, 'Is it not worth tears, if the number of worlds is infinite and we have not yet become lords of one of them?'[79]

In *Letter* LXXIII, Seneca makes some general points about ambition (*ambitio*). First, the cravings of ambition in no time grow disproportionately to their satisfaction. When satisfied, they seek new and greater satisfactions, and the cycle continually repeats itself until ambition is the governor of the governing faculty itself – reason. Second, ambition is never backward-looking. No one takes heed of those he has surpassed, but everyone looks only to those he has yet to catch, and the few ahead of him are a greater cause of psychical disquiet than the many behind him.[80]

One of the driving forces of ambition is glory (*gloria*). Glory, Seneca says, wears a thin garment and is fickle. It even seeks the praise and approbation of inferior persons. 'Why do you take pleasure in being praised by men whom you yourself cannot praise?' Seneca asks.[81] Cicero, elaborating on Stoic doctrine, says, 'True and wise magnanimity is that moral character that follows Nature maximally. It consists in deeds, not in fame, and prefers to be first in reality rather than in name.'[82] Later he adds, 'True glory shoots out deep roots and spreads its branches wide, but all pretences [*ficta*] quickly fall to the ground like underdeveloped flowers, since nothing fake [*simulatum*] can be lasting.'[83]

Similar to ambition and glory is renown. Renown (*claritas*), Seneca tells us, is not the same thing as glory. It is adequately satisfied by the judgement of one good person, which follows from the Stoic claim that all good persons judge identically.

> Yet the position of the many is different from that of the one. Why? If a good person thinks well of me, it is the same as my being thought well of by all good persons, as they will all think the same, if they know me. Their judgment is alike and identical. The effect of truth on judgment is equal. Good people cannot disagree ... With a good person, truth causes belief and truth has only one force and one face, while among inferior people, the ideas on which they agree are unsound.[84]

Renown, then, is the praise of the good by the good; glory depends on the judgements of the many.[85]

In addition to the glory-seeking ambition of the conqueror, there is the glory-seeking ambition of the scholar.

> What need is there to compose something that will last for centuries? Will you not give up striving to keep posterity from being silent about you? You were born for death. A quiet burial [*tacitum funus*] is less troublesome. Thus, to pass the time, write something in simple style, for your own use, not for publication.[86]

Khreiai *for 'In the Footsteps of Hercules'*
- 'A contest with an equal is uncertain, with a superior is mad and with an inferior is degrading.'[87]

- 'Many have removed the boundary lines of another person's lands; no one has set limits to his own.'[88]

BOOKS AND SCHOLARLY SELF-INDULGENCE

Like many others, I too enjoy books and consider myself fortunate to possess and have read many of them. Some of the most pleasant experiences I have experienced are associated with books – Aristotle's *Politics*, Freud's *Beyond the Pleasure Principle*, Goncharov's *Oblomov*, Plato's *Symposium* and Laotzu's *Tao Te Ching* – each of which has moved me remarkably on one occasion.

I suspect that few people, of those who have discovered the joy of reading, would regard the reading or possession of books as an injurious habit. The Stoics, however, were not ordinary thinkers and, to them, books had a status no different from health and wealth. It is nice to have them, but not necessary.

Epictetus states that reading is a boon only insofar as it may lead to a life of serenity.

> What difference does it make to say, 'I am bad off; I have nothing to do, but am tied to my books as though I were a corpse' or to say, 'I'm bad off; I have no leisure to read'? Just as salutations and office-holding are among things external and things that lie outside moral choice, so also is a book. For what purpose do you wish to read? Tell me. If you turn to reading merely for entertainment or for learning something, you are futile and lazy. Yet if you refer reading to what you ought to refer it to, what else is this but a life of serenity [*euroia*[89]]? However, if reading does not secure for you a life of serenity, what good is it?[90]

Overall, reading for Stoics is only useful as preparation for living. One lives, not through reading about life, but through living it. To illustrate, Epictetus gives two analogies: that of an athlete, on the day of a competition, and that of an ordinary person, whose mind is flooded with sensory impressions of various sorts on a given day. Consider how absurd it would be for the athlete, at the time of entering the stadium en route to competing, to complain that he is no longer exercising outside of the stadium in preparation for the event in which he is about to compete. He has trained in order to compete. Now it is time to compete, not time to train. Consider too how absurd it would be for someone, flooded by clear and unclear sensory impressions, to prefer at that moment to reread a treatise on judging sensory impressions rather than clearing away the confusion through the act of judging between the impressions. Thus, as an end in itself, reading has the function of cheap and frivolous entertainment – a diversion from life.[91]

In several of his works, Seneca rails against the acquisition of books. First, in his second letter to Lucilius, he states that possession of too many books is not only extravagance, it is also a symptom of lack of equanimity.

> Nothing is so useful that it can be of any service in the mere passing. A multitude of books only gets in one's way. So it is, if you are unable to read all the books in your possession. You have enough when you have all the books you are able to read. If you say, 'But I feel like opening different books at different times', my answer will be this: 'Tasting one dish after another is the sign of a fussy stomach. Where the foods are dissimilar and diverse in range, they lead to contamination of the system, not nutrition.'

For proper nutrition, one principally chooses foods that have proven their nutritional value. Thus it is with books. One ought to read and reread authors, whose books have proven their ethical value. Just as the right foods are few, so too are the right authors.[92]

In *On Equanimity*, Seneca states that many collectors of books get more pleasure from their outside appearance, rather than what they have in them.[93] The library at Alexandria was one such superfluous and needless display.

> Forty thousand books were burned in the library at Alexandria. Let someone else – like Titus Livius, who says that it was the most distinguished achievement of the good taste and devotion of kings – praise that library as the most notable monument of kingly wealth. That was not good taste or devotion, but scholarly self-indulgence [*studiosa luxuria*] – in fact, not even scholarly, since they had collected the books not for learning, but for display. In the same way, you will find that many people, who lack even elementary culture, keep books not as tools of learning, but as decoration for their dining-room. Therefore, let us acquire enough books for our use, none for display.[94]

While the reading of books Seneca holds to be an important vehicle for moral progress, as reading nourishes and refreshes the mind, continual reading is inadvisable. It is best to combine reading with writing, for the two complement each other, while each by itself dissolves and dilutes one's strength. Reading gives one material for writing; writing gives one an outlet for what one has read.[95] Yet, one must not forget to live.

Khreia *for 'Books and Scholarly Self-Indulgence'*

■ 'In writing and reading, you should not instruct, before you have been instructed. What pertains to reading and writing is much truer of life.'[96]

FRIENDSHIP AND SELF-SUFFICIENCY

Jean Anouilh's *Becket* is a story, set in 12th-century England, of the lives of two unlikely friends: King Henry II of England, a Norman, and Thomas Becket, a Saxon. Becket, though a Saxon and a servant of the king, is also a companion to the king, and his most trusted counsellor. By day, he assists and advises the king as his servant in his kingly duties; by night, the two get drunk and whore around together as friends. Becket teaches the king everything from how to bathe and eat properly to how to think. Yet Becket is also a man who seeks his honour, which he admittedly 'improvises' so long as he serves the king.

King Henry, taking Becket by surprise one day, elevates his servant to the post of Chancellor of England. Becket accepts the post gratefully, but knows that he shall not find his honour in serving mother England. Yet he does find a sense of duty and direction in his new office. There is something aesthetic in doing what he has to do and doing it well. Henry finds in Becket, as chancellor, not only a friend four-square, but also a formidable ally against the powerful church, which is continually challenging the king's authority, and a capable advisor on military affairs.

Upon the death of the Archbishop of Canterbury, Henry once again takes Becket by surprise by telling him that he wants to have him elected to the office of Archbishop. Becket responds with ghastly horror: 'Don't do this . . . If I become Archbishop, I can no longer be your friend . . . I could not serve both God and you.' King Henry is unperturbed and Becket, against his own wishes, is ordained Archbishop. Becket now discovers that he belongs to God first and England second. In serving God, he finds his honour, though in doing so he must renounce his friendship with Henry – at least, that is how the king sees things. Henry now takes Becket to be his bitter enemy. The play ends with the killing of Becket, inside of a cathedral, on Henry's orders.

The view of friendship in Anouilh's play illustrates a key feature of the Stoic view of friendship. Becket's life and death have meaning, because he subordinates friendship to duty. The king, on the other hand, can find no meaning in his life without Becket's love. In Stoic terms, Henry's happiness, having an external source, is completely controlled by fate and is lost as soon as Becket turns to God. On the other hand, Becket's happiness comes from a sense of duty and, thus, is entirely up to him. As Cicero states, friendship (*amicitia*) for Stoics must always be subordinated to duty or appropriate action, though it does seem to have a privileged place among conveniences.

> In the case of friendships, however, a person's duties are most confused, for it is a breach of duty either to fail to do for a friend what one rightly can do or to do for him what is not right. Yet for our guidance in all such cases, we have a precept that is short and easy to master: Apparent advantages – political preferment, riches, sensual pleasures and such things – should never be preferred to the obligations of friendship. Still an upright man will never for a friend's sake do anything in violation of his country's interests, his oath or his sacred honour, not even if he sits as judge in a friend's case. He lays aside the role of friend, when he assumes that of judge.[97]

Seneca's *Letter* IX is our best direct source of the Stoic view of friendship. Here Seneca tries to show why a Stoic, who is completely self-sufficient through virtue, will still wish to have friends. He gives several arguments throughout.

First, Seneca states, 'A Stoic, although he is self-sufficient, still desires to have a friend – if only for the purpose of exercising friendship so that such a great excellence [*magna virtus*] does not lie idle.'[98] Friendship, though called *magna virtus* here, is certainly not a virtue for Seneca and so it ought to have no more inherent value than does money or health to a Stoic. Why is it then that a Stoic will feel compelled to exercise friendship?

For Stoics, friendship has the status of a convenience. A life with friends is not at all needed for a good life; it is merely convenient and preferable to live with friends. Seneca says:

As much as a Stoic is self-sufficient, he has need of friends. He wants to have as many as possible[99] – not so that he may live happily, since he will still live happily without friends. The greatest good does not require tools outside of itself. It is cultivated at home; it is complete in itself. If it seeks in whatever manner a part of itself from without, then it begins to be subject to fortune.[100]

Cicero in *On Ends* adds that even though friendship is a convenience, it is still not sought (principally) for its utility, though it is among things beneficial. Some Stoics profess that a friend's interests will be as dear as one's own. Others maintain that one's own interests must always take pride of place. Cicero adds:

Yet the school I am discussing [the Stoics] emphatically rejects the view that we adopt or approve of justice or friendship for their utility. If it were so, the same claims of utility could undermine and overthrow them. In fact, the existence of both justice and friendship would be impossible, if they were not desired for their own sake.[101]

Thus, to say that friendship is a convenience is not to say that it deserves no rational consideration in the life of a Stoic and that it has no intrinsic merit, which is not to concede that it is a good.

Seneca's final argument for friendship comes just after he considers a particularly thorny problem for a Stoic. He considers the forlorn existence of one imprisoned, exiled in a foreign country, delayed on a voyage or cast on to some empty shore. Such a life – lonesome, friendless and seemingly despondent – might not be worth living. Nonetheless, a Stoic, if in full possession of his judgement, could still retire into himself and find happiness therein. Does not Jupiter himself do the same with the dissolution of the physical universe, when all gods merge into one and there is nothing for him to do other than self-reflect?[102] After all, a Stoic, like Jupiter, is self-sufficient.

Still Seneca denies that such a life, though self-sufficient and under full rational control, would be choice-worthy without some hope of a future return to friends and companions. Seneca states flatly, 'though he is self-sufficient, he would not live, if he had to live without friends'.[103] For, notwithstanding his self-sufficiency, a Stoic would prefer suicide to an existence without the company of other humans, especially friends. The argument runs:

1 A natural inclination (*natura inritatio*) draws each person into friend-ships and makes each person repulsed by continual solitude.
2 An alienated or estranged, though self-sufficient, person is living a life against his natural inclination.
3 One ought to live in accordance with Nature.
4 So, the self-sufficient Stoic will cultivate friendship and may justifiably prefer suicide to a life without the prospect of future friends.

Overall, the argument seems to presuppose that virtue is a matter of acting on indifferents as efficiently as possible and friends are such an important convenience that a life without them often makes vir-tuous activity impossible.

It is obvious that friends, when they are around one, can improve one, yet Seneca maintains that friends can even improve one when they are not around, but merely brought to mind. 'Happy is he who improves others not only by his presence but also when he is brought to mind. Happy is he who can so revere someone in order to compose and regulate himself by calling him to mind. Who can so revere someone will soon be revered himself.'[104]

Overall, none of these arguments, however, seem compelling in light of the Stoic ideal of self-sufficiency, for self-sufficiency requires nothing but equanimity through indifference to the arrows of fortune. Why, then, will a Stoic pursue friends?

The most straightforward answer is that humans are, by nature and because of their reason, communal, even cosmopolitan, animals. Thus, living outside of the community of fellow beings, though not needed for virtue, would be queer behaviour for one, were it chosen in preference to community. For one to live outside of a community of people would be for him to live at odds with his own nature and cosmic Nature.

Friendship produces between us a partnership [*consortium*] in all our interests. There is no such thing as good or bad fortune for the individual. We live in common. No one can live happily who has regard for himself alone and transforms everything into a question of his own utility. You must live for your neighbour, if you live for yourself. This fellowship [*societas*] – maintained with scrupulous care, making us mingle as humans with our fellow-humans and holding that the human race has certain rights in common – is also of great help in cherishing the more intimate fellowship that is based on friendship . . .. He who has much in common with a fellow-human will have all things in common with a friend.[105]

Furthermore, to show that friendship is a strange sort of convenience, Cicero tells us that friendship for Stoics is to be cultivated 'almost equally' among the virtuous and the non-virtuous.[106] For the virtuous, friendship is an opportunity to share virtue with others of like disposition. For the non-virtuous – at least, those who aspire to invincibility – friendship with another, who is nearer to virtue, is an opportunity to progress morally.[107]

Khreiai *for 'Friendship and Self-Sufficiency'*

■ 'As the sum total of friendship consists in making a friend equal to ourselves, consideration must be given at the same time to the interests of both.'[108]
■ 'When friendship is settled, you must trust; before friendship is formed, you must pass judgment.'[109]

REST AND RESTLESSNESS: *ADDAMUS CALCAR!*

On 14 February 2001, Gary Hatter, completing a 14,594.5-mile drive, entered Daytona Beach, Florida. The drive, as lengthy as it was, had an even more incredible feature: It was taken on a lawnmower. Hatter began in Portland, Maine, on 31 May 2000 and took 260 days to finish the drive. During the trip, he passed through all 48 contiguous states as well as Canada and Mexico. He landed in the *Guinness Book of World Records* for his effort.

Why would anyone want to take such a trip – especially on a lawnmower? One seemingly reasonable answer is that it is something to do that no one else has hitherto done. Another is that 'it passes the time', as my dear Aunt Anna used to say, when we got together to play pinochle.

For the Stoics, such answers are unthinkable. Invincibility is never a matter of doing things just because no one else has done them or because one wants to pass the time. They believe that some activities – motivated by escape from boredom – are simply valueless, vain and a sign of moral weakness.

> Would you call those people at leisure, who while away many hours at a barber shop, so as to be stripped of whatever grew out the night before, while a solemn debate is held over each separate hair, and disarranged locks are restored to their proper place, while thinning locks are drawn from each side toward the fore-head?[110]

Invincibility is always a matter of spending one's time in virtuous activity as efficiently as circumstances allow. Continually passing one's time in trivial pursuits is a clear indication of one's lack of virtue due to self-discontent.

Self-discontent may often take the form of restfulness. Lolling and yawning, restful people never change their lives. Through a sort of inertia based on laziness, not equanimity, they live as they did when they had begun their life.[111] To return to the realm of modern-day fiction, one may consider Ivan Goncharov's brilliant novel, *Oblomov*. Oblomov is a Russian civil servant in his early thirties, retired because of the stress of his occupation's responsibilities, and for whom life's most profound question each day is, 'Should I get out of bed?'

Self-discontent may often also take the form of restlessness, which deserves greater amplification. In *On Equanimity*, Seneca says that those who behave restlessly are like fidgety sleepers, who find it impossible to sleep, because they cannot locate just the right spot or position on a bed. 'By repeatedly altering the condition of their life,' he adds, 'restless people arrive finally at that condition in which novelty-shrinking old age, not dislike of making a change, has caught them.'[112]

A modern example of human restlessness is competitive eating.[113] Competitive eating is a relatively new sport and it is, unsurprisingly, most popular in the United States.

> The sport of competitive eating has risen in stature in the past several years and the IFOCE [International Federation of Competitive Eating] offered more than $230,000 in purses at its

events in 2005. Television exposure also has increased significantly. The IFOCE produced a one-hour live broadcast of the Nathan's Famous contest for ESPN and a three-hour elimination tournament on ESPN called the Alka-Seltzer U.S. Open of Competitive Eating.[114]

The sport's most dominant competitive eater is Japan's Kobayashi Takeru, who held the record of 53¾ hot dogs in 12 minutes at the 2006 Annual Nathan's Coney Island Hot-Dog Eating Contest, a contest that he has dominated since 2001, though he weighs a mere 132 pounds.[115] Other records include 83 vegetarian dumplings in eight minutes (Hong Kong, 2005), 100 steamed pork buns the very next day in 12 minutes, 97 Krystal Hamburgers in eight minutes (World Hamburger Eating Contest, 2006), 17.7 pounds of cow brains in 15 minutes and 20 pounds of rice-balls in 30 minutes.[116]

There are also other 'colourful' characters in the sport, like 'Super' Paul Barlow of Atlanta. Barlow vaunts that he is happy to eat competitively for reasons other than money. He states, 'It's fun, filling, and I still get free T-shirts!'[117]

Restlessness also manifests itself in fickleness and continual preparation for future events. Seneca states, 'A fool, with all his other faults, has this also: He is always getting ready to live.'[118] Always getting ready for tomorrow, he never enjoys the present.

> Consider individuals. Survey men in general. There is none whose life does not look forward to the next day. 'What harm is there in that?' you ask. Infinite harm. Such persons do not live, but are preparing to live. They postpone everything. Even if we paid strict attention, life would soon get ahead of us, but as we are now, life finds us lingering and passes us by as if it belonged to another. In this manner, though it ends on the final day, life perishes every day.[119]

Seneca adds in *Letter* XXXII: 'Do you wish to know what it is that makes men covet the future? No one has [yet] found himself.'[120]

In addition, long-term planning is foolish, as the future is guaranteed to no one. 'Let us order our minds as if we had come to the very end. Let us postpone nothing. Let us balance life's account every day . . . One who daily puts the finishing touches to his life is never in want of time.'[121]

A specific type of long-term planning cherished by the self-discontent is travel. In *Letter* XXVIII, Seneca describes the malaise of a weary traveller, who is burdened because his longed-for trip has not taken his mind off his troubles.

> Are you surprised . . . that after such long travel and so many changes of scene you have not been able to shake off the gloom and heaviness of your mind? You need a change of soul rather than a change of climate . . . Socrates made the same remark to one who complained. He said, 'Why do you wonder that travelling the world does not help you, given that you always take yourself with you?'[122]

The difficulty is that a mere change of place does little to settle an unsettled mind. A mind at peace with itself can find comfort and seclusion among the noisiest places and in the presence of the most rancorous people. An unsettled mind, in contrast, will be ill-at-peace in any place. 'What advantage is there in crossing the sea and going from city to city? To escape your troubles, you do not need another place, but another being [*alius*].'[123] One is reminded, in *On the Road*, of Jack Kerouac's character Dean Moriarty – the man who was 'beat' itself. Moriarty travelled the country and 'dug' everything from prostitutes and weed to Mexican insects and sunsets, and all of these things at 80 miles per hour.

At best, travel affords the irritated a temporary and an inadequate respite from self-discontent.

> What benefit has travel of itself ever been able to give anyone? No restraint of pleasure, no bridling of desire, no checking of bad temper, no quashing of the wild assaults of passion, and no opportunity to rid the soul of evil. Travelling cannot give us judgment or shake off our errors. It merely holds our attention for a moment by a certain novelty, as children pause to wonder at something novel.[124]

Aurelius states that one can travel quite easily and at any time by retreating within oneself. That is the best and the easiest way to find equanimity and renewal, yet it is a retreat that is only possible for one with a tranquil soul.[125]

Another example of the irritation of self-discontent is the person for whom war gives meaning to life that peace cannot give. Without war, these restive types revel in lust or drunkenness. They fail to realize that peace and liberty are within the grasp of all men alike and are not the privilege of any few.[126]

One remedy for irritation is rest – real rest – the peace of mind contemplation affords. Contemplation, for the Stoics, relieves the mind of servitude and frees it from greed and meanness.

If you devote yourself to contemplation, you will have escaped all your aversion toward life. You will not long for night to come, because you are weary of the light. You will not be burdensome to yourself or useless to others. You will attract many to friendship and those who gather around you will be the most excellent.[127]

A second remedy for irritation is meaningful activity – for example, occupation in practical affairs, the management of public affairs, and the duties of citizenship.

For whenever a person aims to make himself useful to his fellow citizens and all mortals, he gets practice and does service at the same time. When he has placed himself in the very midst of active duties, he serves to the best of his ability the interests of the public and individuals.[128]

Overall, restlessness is the symptom of expectancy – the hope that tomorrow will be better than today. Expectancy is often the effect of two emotions – distress, the feeling that some ill is present, and appetite, the feeling that some good is lurking on the horizon to replace the ill. Seneca says, 'The greatest hindrance to living is expectancy, which depends upon tomorrow and wastes today. You dispose of what lies in the hands of Fortune. You let go of what lies within you.'[129] To avoid such waste of life, 'Let us ply the spur [addamus calcar]', Seneca says, as the time for living and acting is now. If something is worth attaining, it is foolish to wait for tomorrow, for tomorrow is granted no one.[130]

Khreiai *for 'Rest and Restlessness'*

■ 'Diligence does not make people restless; false conceptions of things makes them insane.'[131]

- 'To my thinking, the primary indication of a settled mind is the ability to remain in one place and to linger with oneself'[132]

REST AND RETIREMENT: BENEFITING OTHERS

Related to the forward-looking perspective of travellers is the forward-looking perspective of those with one eye on retirement (*quies*). It is safe to assert that most people look forward excitedly to retiring, so that they can be in complete control of what they do and when they do it.

Retirement is a sticky issue for the Stoics, as the Stoic cosmopolitan ideal is one of fullest participation in public activities and fullest participation would seem to rule out leisure, which seems to be prominently a selfish ideal. Here Stoics and Epicureans are especially at odds. While the Epicureans advocate withdrawal from society, except in case of emergency, the Stoics advocate full participation, except in prohibitive situations. Seneca himself notices the tension between retirement and what appropriate action seems to demand in his treatise *On Leisure*.

Surely you Stoics say, 'We shall participate in affairs till the very end of life. We shall never cease to work for the common good, to help each and every person, and to give help even to our enemies, when our hands are feeble with age. We grant no exemption from service because of one's years . . . We hold very strongly that there should be no leisure before death and that, if circumstances permit, we take no leisure for death itself.'[133] Seneca gives a provisional reply that is twofold. First, it is sometimes right to seek retirement from public affairs, even from one's youth, in order to contemplate truth. Second, one who has devoted a life to public service has earned a life of contemplative leisure in his final years.[134] Of these, the second seems reasonable, but the first condition needs a fuller justification.

Retirement before advanced age seems patently to violate Zeno's principle of engaging in public affairs, if there is nothing to prevent you from doing so.[135] Seneca agrees, 'It is required of a person that he should benefit other humans – many, if he is able; if not many, a few; if not a few, those nearest; if not those nearest, himself.' Yet a Stoic will never involve himself in affairs that are corrupt beyond repair, when he lacks a capacity to improve such affairs or if he is hampered by ill health.[136]

The paradox of retirement exists only when one fails to grasp that each human for the Stoics belongs not to one, but two commonwealths: one local and one cosmopolitan. Seneca states plainly that some amount of time must be spent in leisure in order to do service to the greater commonwealth of gods and humans. Without contemplative activity, which for Stoics is a form of practical wisdom, no one bears witness to the magnificence of the gods, and that is not a local crime, but one of cosmological scale.

> We are able to serve, even in leisure, the greater commonwealth – I am inclined to think even better in leisure – so that we may inquire what virtue is and whether it is one or many; whether it is nature or art that makes men good; whether this world, which embraces seas and lands and the things that are contained in the sea and land, is a solitary creation or whether deity has created many systems of the same sort; whether all the matter from which everything is formed is continuous and compact or disjunctive and a void is intermingled with the solid; what deity is – whether he idly gazes on his handiwork or directs it and whether he encompasses it without or pervades the whole of it – whether the world is eternal or is to be counted among the things that perish and are born only for a time. What service does he who ponders those things do for deity? He keeps the mighty works of deity from being without a witness [*sine teste*].[137]

Thus, virtue and invincibility require active participation in both commonwealths.

Often retirement comes of necessity. Seneca considers, for instance, someone who states that the best life is one of ship-sailing, but then adds that there is no place nearby where one can safely sail a ship, without likelihood of shipwreck. What this person is really saying is that the best sort of life is one in which it is practically impossible to engage. Similarly, if participation in stately affairs is the best life, but no state exists nearby that is not corrupt, then the best practicable life for one may be that of withdrawal from stately affairs.[138]

A key to gainful retirement is equanimity. To achieve equanimity, one must at some point in one's life acclimate oneself to one place and cease off wandering around. Otherwise, retirement will be disquieting and burdensome.[139]

One must also embrace quietude without interruption. Quietude is a remedy for restive souls, and remedies that are most effective are like curative medicines: They must be taken without interruption.[140] Thus, retirement enables one to quash desire by not allowing desire an outlet for display. 'You can make us cease to desire by making us cease to display. Ambition, luxury and violent passion need a stage upon which to act. You will cure all of these by seeking retirement.'[141]

Finally, if one must retire, it is best to do so quietly. There is no need to boast of or advertise one's retirement. 'There is no need to write on oneself "Philosophy and Retirement". Give it some other name. Call it "Valetudinarianism", "Feebleness" or "Idleness". To pride oneself of leisure is idle ambition.'[142]

Khreiai *for 'Rest and Retirement'*

- 'Nature has bestowed on us an inquisitive disposition and, being aware of her own skill and beauty, it has made us spectators of her mighty display.'[143]
- 'Nature intended me . . . to be active and to have leisure for contemplation . . . I do both, as even the contemplative life is not void of action.'[144]

NOTES

1 James Dao, 'Instant Millions Can't Halt Winners' Grim Slide', *The New York Times*, 5 December 2005, 1A, 20a.
2 Seneca, *Benefits*, V.xii.6.
3 Paul Tharp, 'Lottery Raises Issues of Cents and Sensibilities', *New York Post*, 14 November 1997.
4 Charles T. Clotfelter and Philip J. Cook, *Selling Hope: State Lotteries in America* (Cambridge, Mass.: Harvard University Press, 1989), p. 122.
5 Seneca, *Providence*, IV.10.
6 Seneca, *Good Life*, XXII.2–3.
7 E.g., D.L., VII.122 and Cicero, *Ends*, III.xxii.75.
8 Seneca, *Benefits*, V.iv.3–4.
9 Seneca, *Epistles*, XVII.12.
10 Seneca, *Epistles*, CXV.17.
11 Seneca, *Epistles*, XIX.7, CXIX.7.
12 Seneca, *Equanimity*, VIII.1.
13 Seneca, *Epistles*, LXXXVII.31–2.
14 Epictetus, *Discourses*, IV.ix.4–5.

15 Seneca, *Epistles*, CX.14–20.
16 Seneca, *Epistles*, CXV.11.
17 Seneca, *Epistles*, CXVIII.6.
18 Seneca, *Equanimity*, VIII.7.
19 Seneca, *Epistles*, CXIX.5–6.
20 Epictetus, *Discourses*, III.xxiv.17–19.
21 Cicero, *Duties*, I.viii.25.
22 Cicero, *Duties*, III.xiv.57.
23 Cicero, *Stoic Paradoxes*, 51.
24 Seneca, *Epistles*, LXII.3.
25 Seneca, *Benefits*, I.viii.1–2 and ix.1.
26 Seneca, *Good Life*, XXIV.1.
27 Seneca, *Benefits*, I.vi.1.
28 Seneca, *Benefits*, I.v.2 and *Epistles*, LXXXI.6
29 Seneca, *Epistles*, LXXXI.19.
30 Seneca, *Benefits*, VI.xxi.2.
31 I.e. that one's very life is saved or that one is freed so that one may act as one wishes.
32 Seneca, *Benefits*, I.xi.2–4, II.xi.1, xxxv.3.
33 Seneca, *Benefits*, I.xi.5, II.xxvii.4. To be offered up voluntarily, not because of compulsion. Cicero, *Duties*, I.ix.28.
34 Seneca, *Benefits*, I.xi.5–6.
35 Seneca, *Benefits*, I.xii.1.
36 Cicero, *Duties*, I.xiv.42.
37 Cicero, *Duties*, I.xv.47–xvi.51.
38 Seneca, *Epistles*, LXXXI.10.
39 Seneca, *Benefits*, II.ii.2.
40 Seneca, *Benefits*, II.1.2.
41 Seneca, *Benefits*, IV.xxxvi.3.
42 Seneca, *Benefits*, II.xviii.8, V.ix.1.
43 Seneca, *Benefits*, I.vi.2, I.xv.6.
44 Seneca, *Benefits*, IV.xiv.4, VI.vii.2.
45 Seneca, *Benefits*, I.xiv.1.
46 Seneca, *Benefits*, II.xvii.2.
47 Seneca, *Benefits*, IV.xxx.3.
48 Seneca, *Benefits*, VII.xix.9.
49 Seneca, *Benefits*, II.xxii. At II.xxxi.1, he says that glad reception is *full* payment. The discrepancy is resolved at II.xxxiii.3, where he states that cheerful acceptance repays the benefit in full, but not one's indebtedness, which is something independent of one's acceptance.
50 It is otherwise from the perspective of the recipient. The object given is independent of gratitude, and its debt can only be repaid by a similar act of giving back. Again, intention is everything. 'You are unjust, if you require me to pay in fact when you see that I have not failed in intention.' There would be no obligation to return a benefit, if there should be no power to reject it. Seneca, *Benefits*, III.xxxv.1, VII.xiv.6 and II.xviii.7.
51 Seneca, *Epistles*, LXXXI.28–31. The causes of ingratitude are many. See Seneca, *Benefits*, II.xxvi.1–xxviii.4, and III.iii.1–4.

52 Seneca, *Benefits*, II.xxiii.1.
53 Seneca, *Benefits*, II.xviii.3.
54 Seneca, *Benefits*, VII.xix.3.
55 Seneca, *Benefits*, II.xv.3.
56 Seneca, *Benefits*, II.xvi.2.
57 Seneca, *Benefits*, I.i.13.
58 From the poet Rabirius and ascribed to Mark Antony. Seneca, *Benefits*, VI.iii.1.
59 Seneca, *Epistles*, CXXII.3.
60 E.g. the story of Lucius Piso. Seneca, *Epistles*, LXXXIII.14–19, 26.
61 Also with the sense of 'proud' or 'arrogant'.
62 More literally, a 'lazy fat'.
63 Seneca, *Epistles*, CXXII.4.
64 Seneca, *Epistles*, LXXXIII.18.
65 Seneca, *Epistles*, CVIII.15–16.
66 A digging tool, somewhat like a pickaxe.
67 Seneca, *Anger*, II.xxv.2–4.
68 Seneca, *Epistles*, LXXXII.2–3.
69 Epictetus, *Discourses*, III.xxvi.21–3.
70 Epictetus, *Discourses*, I.xxiv.9–10.
71 Seneca, *Epistles*, XC.14, 16.
72 The great Roman general and citizen, most noted for his brilliant victory over the Carthaginian Hannibal at Zama in 202 BC. Seneca, *Epistles*, LXXXVI.
73 Seneca, *Epistles*, XIX.10.
74 Epictetus, *Discourses*, III.xiii.21.
75 Plutarch, *Lives: Pyrrhus*, XIV.1–8.
76 Seneca, *Epistles*, XCIV.62–3.
77 Seneca, *Epistles*, CXIX.7.
78 Seneca, *Benefits*, V.vii.5.
79 Plutarch, *Equanimity*, 466d.
80 Seneca, *Epistles*, LXXIII.2–3.
81 Seneca, *Epistles*, LII.11.
82 Cicero, *Duties*, I.xix.65.
83 Cicero, *Duties*, II.xii.43.
84 Seneca, *Epistles*, CII.11–13.
85 Seneca, *Epistles*, CII.17.
86 Seneca, *Equanimity*, I.13.
87 Seneca, *Anger*, II.xxxiv.1.
88 Seneca, *Benefits*, VII.vii.5.
89 More literally, 'having a good flow to one's life'.
90 Epictetus, *Discourses*, IV.iv.2–5.
91 Epictetus, *Discourses*, IC.iv.6–13.
92 Seneca, *Epistles*, II.3–4.
93 Seneca, *Equanimity*, IX.6–7.
94 Seneca, *Equanimity*, IX.4.
95 Seneca, *Epistles*, LXXXIV.1–2.
96 Aurelius, *Meditations*, XI.29.

97 Cicero, *Duties*, III.x.43.
98 Seneca, *Epistles*, IX.8.
99 Understanding 'as many as possible' to mean as many as one's particular condition will allow for progress toward invincibility.
100 Seneca, *Epistles*, IX.15.
101 Cicero, *Ends*, III.xxi.70.
102 A reference to Stoic cosmic cyclicality.
103 Seneca, *Epistles*, IX.17.
104 Seneca, *Epistles*, XI.9.
105 Seneca, *Epistles*, XLVIII.2–3.
106 Cicero, *Duties*, II.viii.30.
107 Seneca, *Epistles*, XCIV.40
108 Seneca, *Benefits*, II.xv.1.
109 Seneca, *Epistles*, III.2.
110 Seneca, *Shortness of Life*, XII.3.
111 Seneca, *Equanimity*, II.6–7.
112 Seneca, *Equanimity*, II.6.
113 Seneca, *Shortness of Life*, XIII.1.
114 http://en.wikipedia.org/wiki/Competitive_eaters.
115 4 July 2004.
116 http://en.wikipedia.org/wiki/Takeru_Kobayashi. Recently eclipsed by Joey Chestnut in 2007 with 66 hotdogs.
117 http://en.wikipedia.org/wiki/Competitive_eating.
118 Seneca, *Epistles*, XIII.16.
119 Seneca, *Epistles*, XLV.12–13.
120 Seneca, *Epistles*, XXXII.4.
121 Seneca, *Epistles*, CI.8–9.
122 Seneca, *Epistles*, XXVIII.1–2. See too *Epistle* CIV.7 and *Equanimity*, II.13–14.
123 Seneca, *Epistles*, CIV.7
124 Seneca, *Epistles*, CIV.13.
125 Aurelius, *Meditations*, IV.3.
126 Seneca, *Epistles*, LXXIII.5–8.
127 Seneca, *Equanimity*, III.6.
128 Seneca, *Equanimity*, III.1.
129 Seneca, *Shortness of Life*, IX.1.
130 Seneca, *Epistles*, XCVIII.14.
131 Seneca, *Equanimity*, XII.5.
132 Seneca, *Epistles*, II.1.
133 Seneca, *Leisure*, I.4. French translators render *otium* (of the Latin *de Otio*, which I translate here as *On Leisure*) as *disponibilité*, which means 'availability'. That gets at the notion that complete retirement from the affairs of gods and mortals was anathema to Stoics.
134 Seneca, *Leisure*, II.1–2.
135 Seneca, *Leisure*, III.2.
136 Seneca, *Leisure*, III.3–5.
137 Seneca, *Leisure*, IV.2.
138 Seneca, *Leisure*, VIII.3–4.

139 Seneca, *Equanimity*, II.9.
140 Seneca, *Epistles*, LXIX.1–3.
141 Seneca, *Epistles*, XCIV.71.
142 Seneca, *Epistles*, LXVIII.3.
143 Seneca, *Leisure*, V.3.
144 Seneca, *Leisure*, V.8.

CHAPTER 5

THE HEROIC COURSE

'Live not to avoid death, but rather to pursue life.'

Democritus

It is characteristic of a Stoic sage that his every action is faultless – that all of his actions are not only appropriate (*kathekonta*), but also right (*katorthomata*). Thus, everything a sage does, from eating and sleeping to fighting in a battle and conducting affairs of state, is perfect and without reproach.

Yet perfect wisdom, as complete equanimity, seems to be an unreachable ideal. It is hard to find, Epictetus notes, even someone aspiring to this ideal.

Show me a man who though sick is happy, who though in danger is happy, who though dying is happy, who though condemned to exile is happy, and who though in disrepute is happy. Show him to me! By the gods, I would then see a Stoic! Still you cannot show me a man completely so fashioned. Show me then at least one who is becoming so fashioned and has begun to tend in that direction. Do me this favour. Do not begrudge an old man the sight of that spectacle that to this very day I have never seen.[1]

Epictetus' pessimism notwithstanding, the impossibility of total wisdom does not mean it is vain to strive for it, any more than it is vain for someone, say, to strive for total health, even though that is impossible. Thus, I take sagacity to be a reasonable archetype for a Stoic apprentice, who strives to act to the best of his ability with perfection in mind. An apprentice strives to make all of his acts appropriate insofar as circumstances and his capacities allow.

As we have seen, for Stoics appropriate acts do not come to us naturally, but need coaxing through exercise and education.

Someone asked, 'How, then, shall each of us become aware of what is appropriate to his own person?' How does it come about that, when the lion charges, the bull alone is aware of his own prowess [*paraskeues*] and rushes to defend the whole herd? . . . Yet a bull does not become a bull at once, any more than a man becomes noble, but a man must undergo a winter's training.[2] He must prepare himself and must not plunge recklessly into what is inappropriate for him.[3]

Like a well-trained athlete, who keeps in mind the voice of his trainer when he trains or competes, an apprentice ought to keep in mind precepts and doctrines that guide right-intended human actions and act to the best of his ability in all situations.[4]

As virtue for Stoics is knowledge and vice is ignorance, proper education requires removal of ignorance and athletic training is a suitable model. A trainer seeks to get an athlete as close to perfection as he can, without expectation that it will ever be had.

HERCULES AT A CROSSROADS

Training, both through schooling in principles and through life's experiences, ultimately makes a Stoic sage immune to life's unexpected turns and reversals. He is so conditioned to act in the right manner over time that virtue literally becomes part of his physical make-up. Stones thrown upward can do no other than fall back to the ground. So it is, Epictetus says, with a well-disposed man (*ho euphues*). The more one beats him back, the more he inclines towards those ends to which Nature disposes him.[5]

Following the ideal of perfectionism, an apprentice does not train himself to weed out vices gradually; rather he seeks the complete elimination of vices, for vices, contrary to what Aristotle says, can never be tamed.[6] 'For if one has vices, they will grow, and as they grow, they will hamper him. Just as a large and complete cataract wholly blinds the eyes, so a medium-sized cataract dulls vision.'[7] Thus, for canonical Stoicism, there is a perfectibility of the soul that does not exist for the body. No athlete, for instance, can ever expect to throw the discus perfectly. He can aspire to perfection and hone his skills so that he gets ever closer to it, but he never will attain it. It is otherwise with the soul. For a Stoic sage, there was a point to one's ethical development where one has made a leap: One has gone from progressing toward wisdom to having wisdom.

The invincibility that Stoic perfectionism promises is an invincibility that I and critics, like Cicero and Plutarch, find gratuitous and indefensible. Consequently, one must either abandon all hope of practicable Stoic ethics or adopt a less demanding form of it. It is, I have been arguing, sensible to abandon perfectionism for progressivism – to take invincibility as an ideal to be approximated, not reached. Instead of invincibility as a way of life, Stoic invincibility should be taken as an archetype for life. Perfectionism should be discarded in favour of progressivism.

To instantiate progress toward virtue, one must have the right sort of training. A Stoic blames no one when things go awry; he merely meets the challenge of Fate. He is invincible, among other reasons, because he faces what fortune puts in his path and never retreats. 'Just as an enemy is more dangerous to a retreating army, so every trouble that fortune brings attacks us all the harder when we yield and turn our backs.'[8] So skilful is he that Seneca likens a Stoic to a feral animal tamer, who puts his hand into a lion's mouth, gets kissed by a tiger and commands an elephant to kneel.[9]

The right sort of life, then, is not one that shuns adversity and seeks prosperity, but one that meets courageously and without complaint all challenges that come its way. The right sort of life seeks not to shun, but meet, duty. The ideal is Herculean.[10]

It is more in agreement with Nature to emulate the great Hercules and undergo the greatest toil and trouble for the sake of aiding or saving the world, if possible, than to live in seclusion – not only free from all care, but revelling in pleasures and abounding in wealth, while excelling others also in beauty in strength. Thus, Hercules denied himself and underwent toil and tribulation for the world and, out of gratitude for his services, popular belief has given him a place in the council of the gods.[11]

Though a son of Zeus, Hercules was given few conveniences in life and suffered greatly most of the time. 'Son of Zeus that I was,' says the ghost of Hercules to Odysseus in Homer's *Odyssey*, 'my torments never ended, forced to slave for a man [Eurystheus] not half the man I was.'[12]

Xenophon[13] tells us the story, originally told by Prodicus in the fifth century BC, about Hercules' choice. When at the crossroads of his youth, he retired to a solitary desert to consider what to do with his life. Soon he saw two goddesses. One had a noble, modest air, graceful countenance and a natural, easy beauty. She wore bright white raiment and her eyes were cast down to the ground. The other had a florid complexion and beautiful looks, complemented by make-up and smug self-assurance. She wore numerous colours in her dress to supplement her beauty, and her eyes were cast on herself and her shadow. This goddess rushed up to Hercules and proposed a life of ease, quiet and sensual gratification. She promised him sumptuous meals, beds of roses, perfumes, beautiful people and pleasing music. Her name was Pleasure (*Hedone*). Afterwards, the other goddess walked up to Hercules with a distinctly different offer. Asserting that nothing of value could be had without much pain and long labour, she offered a life of tumult – though one deeply involved in the affairs of gods and men. Her name was Virtue (*Arete*). Pleasure chimed in, before Virtue had finished her proposal, and stated that the path to Pleasure is short and easy, whereas the path to Virtue is steep and difficult. Virtue retorted that the easy path involved eating before one was hungry, drinking before one was thirsty and sleeping before one was tired. Such was the choice before Hercules. He chose Virtue.

Hercules endured and succeeded in 12 labours (*agones*) – six local and six worldly – and thus earned his rightful place, through suffering and sweat, among the immortal gods. He became the world's first athlete (*athletes*[14]). Epictetus says:

> Zeus did not give much to Hercules, though he was the son of Zeus, but someone else [Eurystheus] was king over Argos and Mycenae, while Hercules was ordered to suffer labours and discipline. Eurystheus, such as he was, was not king over Argos or Mycenae, for he was not even king over himself. Yet Heracles was ruler and leader of all the land and sea, purging them of injustice and lawlessness and introducing justice and righteousness, and all that he did naked and by himself.[15]

The Herculean ideal neatly illustrates one key feature of Stoic invincibility: Invincibility does not imply invulnerability. One overcomes and conquers not by avoiding wounds or not feeling those that one receives, for a Stoic certainly does get wounds and does feel them. Rather, a Stoic overcomes by not having wounds influence his magnanimity and equanimity.

> A Stoic receives some wounds [*ictus*], but those that he receives he overcomes [*evincit*], heals [*sanat*], and conceals [*comprimit*]. The lesser things he does not even feel and he does not use against them his accustomed virtue of bearing hardship, but he either fails to notice them or counts them worthy of a smile.[16]

Overall, one can and ought to find inspiration in the labours of Hercules, when one confronts adversity. Following Epictetus, one might ask: 'What would Hercules have been had he said, "How am I to prevent a great lion, a great boar, or savage men from appearing?" What do you care for that? If a great boar comes forth, your struggle will be greater. If wicked men appear, you will clear the world of them.'[17]

Finally, what makes the pursuit of virtue such a Herculean task? It is because virtue itself involves not only achievement, but also achievement through right use of reason, which is most difficult to cultivate. 'Along the whole path of life, reason must be our guide. All of our acts, from the smallest to the greatest, must follow her counsel.'[18]

Khreia *for 'Hercules at a Crossroads'*
■ 'The Stoics regard Fate as . . . Hercules . . . because his power is invincible.'[19]

THE ATHLETIC PARADIGM: WINNING BY ENDURANCE

For Stoics, the only cure for wickedness is therapy for the soul, of the sort that is similar to that of the body when the body is unwell. The Stoic mind is not substantially different from the body – it too is corporeal – and it needs to be trained to become excellent. Seneca states, 'The mind must be exercised both day and night, for it is nourished by moderate labour and that form of exercise need not be hampered by cold or hot weather, or even by old age.'[20]

Yet the Stoic aim is not mere wisdom, but practical wisdom. Therefore, wisdom is not merely schooling; it is training for life's exigencies, which requires exposure to hardships – though not artificial exposure.

No proof of virtue is ever mild. If we are lashed and torn by Fortune, let us bear it [*patiamur*]. It is not cruelty but a contest [*certamen*], and the more often we engage in it, the stronger we shall become. The strongest member of the body is the one that is kept in constant use. Struggling with Fortune, we should offer ourselves to her in order that we may be hardened by her. Gradually she will make us a match for her. Thus, persistence in the face of danger will bring about contempt for danger.[21]

Ultimately, it is for hardship that an apprentice has trained. Writes Epictetus, 'What, then, ought a man to say to himself at each hardship that befalls him? "It was for this challenge that I kept training [*egymnazomen*]; it was to meet this challenge that I used to practise".'[22]

Stoics, like Cynics, were fond of likening training for hardship to an athlete's training for a contest (*askesis*). In such passages, one finds additional confirmation for the Peak-Performance Model of virtuous activity, which implies, in keeping with the Principle of Stoic Progressivism, that progress toward virtue is a unique form of contesting for a prize, where many winners are possible and competitors strive to help each other along the way. Epictetus says:

Those who are engaged in the greatest contest [*agona*] ought not to flinch, but to suffer the blows [*plagae*]. The contest before us is not in wrestling or pancratium, in which, whether a man succeeds or fails, he may be worth a great deal or only a little – yes, by Zeus, he may even be extremely happy or miserable. It is the contest for good fortune and happiness themselves.[23]

A Stoic then is intimately involved in the greatest contest – life.

In the contest of life, unlike the Olympic Games, one does not have to wait every four years to compete; the contest occurs each second of every day. However many times a person gives in to fortune, he may always enter back in the contest and challenge fortune once again. Victory comes with persistence itself. As Hannah Jelkes says in Tennessee Williams' *The Night of the Iguana*, 'Endurance is something that spooks and blue devils respect. And they respect all the tricks that panicky people use to outlast and outwit their panic.' Once victory is had, it is as though one had never given in.[24]

What blows do athletes receive on their faces and all over their bodies! Nevertheless, through their desire for fame, they endure every torture and they suffer such things not only because they are fighting, but also in order to be able to fight. Their training [*exercitatio*] is itself torture. So, let us also be victorious in all our struggles, as the reward is not a garland, a palm, or a trumpeter who calls for silence at the proclamation of our names, but rather virtue, equanimity and peace – won for all time, once Fortune has been vanquished in any combat [*certamine*].[25]

Bodies, as professional athletes show us, can be trained to withstand blows and kicks all day long, while they are scorched by the sun, burnt by dust and drenched in blood. 'If that can be done, how much easier might the mind be toughened so that it could receive the blows of Fortune and be unconquered [*invictus*], so that it might struggle to its feet again after it has been laid low and trampled?'[26]

Taking the analogy further, before an athlete can compete, he must first pick a particular sport and that makes all the difference in the type of activities in which he thereafter engages. Distance running involves diet, walking, rubbing and exercise of a particular sort. Sprinting involves training and preparation of a different sort. So too does pentathlon. It is the same with the sciences or arts. Each science requires unique training, through selection of an appropriate standard, if it is not to be done randomly. Choosing the wrong standard will result in failure.[27] This is how a progressor chooses to live: according to the right standard.

A Stoic bathes as a faithful person, eats as a self-respecting person and similarly, whatever the subject matter may be with which he has to deal, he puts into practice his guiding principles [*proegoumena*], as a runner does when he applies the principles of running and a voice-trainer does when he applies the principles of voice-training. That is a person who, in all truth, is making progress [*prokopton*] and that is a person who has not travelled at random.[28]

Adversity in life is comparable to having a rugged training partner in wrestling or pancratium. If an athlete is serious about competing to the best of his ability, he will willingly add the most stiff-necked and challenging training partner. A rugged training partner makes one rugged, through sweat, and best prepares one to become, as it were, an Olympic victor.[29] 'What good does a wrestling companion do for an athlete? He does the greatest good. So also does one who abuses me, because he prepares me for living. He exercises my patience, dispassion and gentleness.'[30]

Overall, a Stoic's manner of victory over fortune in life is unique. He is like an athlete who succeeds at the games, not by overwhelming an opponent, but by enduring and wearing him out.

> In the sacred games many have won the victory by wearing out the hands of their assailants through stubborn endurance [*obstinata patientia*]. Consider a Stoic to be in this class of men, who by long and faithful training have attained the strength to endure and tire out any assault of an enemy.[31]

Epictetus adds that the excellent man (*ho spoudaios*) is invincible (*aettetos*), because he only competes in the realm of moral choice, which exacts that one not hold on to things unneeded for virtue.[32]

At the end of the day, apprenticeship in Stoicism is very forgiving. Only rational planning and persistent effort toward virtue matter. As when one gets thrown in wrestling, one needs to continue to wrestle with the aim of no longer getting thrown.[33] Peak performance, through eliminating non-appropriate acts, is a matter of unending persistence in right-minded activity, and he who persists wears the olive crown.

Khreiai *for 'The Athletic Paradigm'*

- 'Such a person, who no longer puts off being considered among the best persons, is some sort of priest or minister of the gods. He uses what is settled within him and keeps his person unstained by pleasures, invulnerable [*atroton*] to all pain, and beyond the touch of all insolence.'[34]
- 'It is not shameful not to attain [*consequi*], provided that you keep striving [*sequaris*].'[35]

WHAT WOULD SOCRATES HAVE DONE?

The development of Stoic thought – like Cynicism and Platonism – was markedly affected by the life of Socrates. While the Cynics focused on Socrates' deeds and made Socratic hardihood and simplicity keys to a virtuous life, Plato and his followers focused on Socrates' words and made the acquisition of knowledge the key to a virtuous life. Stoics, so to speak, split the difference. For Stoics, the good life was a simple life whose chief ambition was the pursuit of knowledge.

Expressed best in Plato's *Apology*, what set apart Socrates from other human beings was his dogged belief that no business was more pressing each day than the improvement of his own soul. The picture Plato fashions of Socrates here and elsewhere is striking. Socrates has a single-minded devotion to the pursuit of moral truth, so much so that he neglects all other pursuits – even things such as family and wealth.[36] In such single-minded devotion to the pursuit of truth, Socrates is portrayed as exhibiting the very virtues he says he does not possess, though he ceaselessly pursues: courage, justice, wisdom, devotion to the gods and self-control. Socrates' manner of living, Plato tells us in *Apology*, is god-directed.

Unlike philosophers prior to him, Socrates gave up an early interest in the study of nature, because of confusion on such issues examined by the celebrated nature-philosophers (*physiologoi*) of his day. Sitting in jail and in the middle of a discussion on the immortality of the soul with friends just prior to his death, Socrates tells his friends of his special frustration with Anaxagoras, who mentioned in one of his books that it was Mind (*Nous*) that was the cause of all material arrangement in the cosmos.[37] That delighted Socrates at first, for it seemed uncommon sobriety to posit that there must be some directive principle that arranges and regulates all things for the best. Socrates' optimism was quickly dashed, because Anaxagoras gave no regulative role to Mind. Instead, just like many others of or prior to his time, he merely talked of the causal force of air, water, ether or other seeming absurdities. With his hopes of obtaining a suitable, mind-directed grasp of the working of the cosmos dashed, Socrates turned his philosophical focus exclusively toward one single query: How ought a person, whose sole concern is to live the best possible life, live?

Despite always claiming to know nothing throughout his life, Socrates never wavered from his commitment toward a plain and honest lifestyle, aimed at knowing. In *Apology*, Plato states that Socrates' manner of living came about because of a queer response of the Delphic oracle to a question posed by Socrates' friend Chaerephon. Chaerephon asked the priestess, 'Is anyone wiser than

Socrates?' The oracle responded bafflingly, 'No one is wiser than Socrates', and that pronouncement was, for Socrates, a sufficient goad for a lifestyle aimed at clarifying its meaning. Thus, Plato relates, Socrates sought out the very best minds in Athens to prove the literal meaning of the oracle wrong. In doing so, however, Socrates came to recognize that he was not inferior to those others, when it came to wisdom. He at least realized that he knew nothing, while those others thought themselves wise in a good many things about which, when questioned, it was evident they knew nothing. Socrates, then, was wiser than them at least insofar as he had a full grasp of his ignorance, while they professed to have knowledge, without actually possessing it. Furthermore, they took part in affairs where their ignorance was sure to do them, others and their city damage.

For Socrates, grasping the truth about oneself – apprehending that human knowledge was nothing next to that of the gods and that all of one's life was a continued and cooperative quest for self-understanding – was a necessary condition for activities that involved instruction of others. The Stoics agreed. Epictetus, who refers abundantly to Socrates, says that Socrates' renowned quest for self-understanding should be that of every person:

> What does Socrates say? 'As one man rejoices in improving his own farm and another his own horse,' he says, 'I rejoice every day in following the course of my own improvement' . . . Who among you, then, makes that purpose of Socrates the purpose of his own life? Why, if you did, you would have been glad even to be ill, to go hungry, and to die.[38]

Still, since Socratic self-knowledge is necessarily a cooperative venture, it entails public conversation on ethical issues – Socratic dialectic (*elenchos*). Socratic dialectic is practised as much to improve the soul of one's interlocutor as it is to improve one's own soul. To illustrate, Socrates used to satisfy himself not with the verdict of the many, but with the verdict of his interlocutor, whom he generally left dumbfounded and perplexed (*aporia*), regarding the success of dialectical discussion on any topic. Epictetus states:

> How did Socrates act? He used to force the man who was arguing with him to be his witness and never needed any other witness.

That is why he could say, 'I can dispense with all the others and am always satisfied to have my fellow-disputant for a witness, and the votes of the rest I do not take, but only that of my fellow-disputant.' He used to make the consequences that followed from the concepts so clear that everyone realized the contradiction in which they were involved and gave up the battle.[39]

He adds that Socrates always conversed on any topic without using terms of insolence or abuse, though he absorbed such terms from others so as to put an end to strife.[40]

In the passage below, Epictetus refers to evidence of Socrates' uncommon restraint in Plato's *Symposium*, where the strikingly handsome Alcibiades recalls his many failed attempts to seduce the older, physically unappealing philosopher.

Go to Socrates and mark him as he lies down beside Alcibiades and makes light of his youthful beauty. Consider how great a victory he once won and knew it himself, like an Olympic victory, and what his rank was, counting in order from Hercules, so that by the gods one might justly greet him with the salutation, 'Hail, astonishing man!' He was victor over something more than these rotten boxers and pancratiasts and the gladiators, who resemble them.[41]

Not allowing his relationship with Alcibiades to have an erotic component, as was customary at that time, Socrates won a victory over his own lustful impulses and put his concern for Alcibiades' moral welfare ahead of the fulfilment of his own desires.

Epictetus sums the life of this godlike figure in the following striking passage:[42]

Take Socrates and observe a man who had a wife and children, but regarded them not as his own, who had a country – as far as it was his duty and in the way in which it was his duty – friends, and kinsmen – one and all subject to the law and to obedience to the law. That is why, when it was his duty to serve as a soldier, he was the first to leave home. That is why he ran the risks of battle most ungrudgingly . . . When he had to speak in defence of his life, he did not behave as one who had children or wife, did he? No, he spoke as one who was alone in the world. Yes, and when he had to drink the poison, how did he act? . . . He did not care, he says, to save his paltry body, but only what is increased and preserved by justice and what is decreased and destroyed by injustice . . . It is impossible to save such a man by dishonour, but he is saved by death, not by fleeing from prison.[43]

Because Socrates – putting divine affairs ahead of human ones – has treated everything other than the pursuit of knowledge as inferior to the pursuit of knowledge, he was in effect the first Stoic. As he showed by willingly going to his death – when sentenced by the Athenian jurors for, among other things, corrupting the young – for Socrates, even life was answerable to virtue.

Consequently, when one is faced with a trying situation from which one would rather shrink, one ought to ask oneself before shrinking, 'What would Socrates have done?'[44] It is quite likely that the answer to that question will at once be the appropriate act in the specific situation.

Khreia *for 'What Would Socrates Have Done?'*

■ 'When you are about to meet someone, especially someone who seems to be distinguished, put to yourself the question, "What would Socrates or Zeno have done in those circumstances?", and you will not be at a loss about the occasion.'[45]

EDUCATION: SAVING THE 'SHIPWRECKED MARINERS'

Martha Nussbaum, in her book *Cultivating Humanity*, argues persuasively that American liberal education is changing quickly to meet the needs of ever-increasing diverse populations of students – ethnic and racial minorities, gays, lesbians, women and non-Western peoples.

Today's teachers are shaping future citizens in an age of cultural diversity and increasing internationalization . . . As citizens we are also increasingly called upon to understand how issues such as agriculture, human rights, ecology, even business and industry, are generating discussions that bring people together from many nations . . . The new emphasis on 'diversity' in college and university curricula is above all a way of grappling with the altered requirements of citizenship, an attempt to produce adults who can function as citizens not just of some local region or group but also, and more importantly, as citizens of a complex interlocking world.[46]

With the world increasingly becoming a global community of nations, she argues for Stoic cosmopolitanism of a sort as an educative ideal for the twenty-first century. She lists four reasons. First, Stoic cosmopolitanism entails the 'examined life' – critical reflection on oneself and one's traditions that requires logical reasoning skills, testing for consistency, factual correctness and accurate judging. Second, Stoic cosmopolitanism entails a capacity to see oneself connected by ties of recognition and concern to all other humans, however distant they may be. Third, Stoic cosmopolitanism entails narrative imagination, the ability to put oneself in the 'shoes' of any other person, however different they are. Last, Stoic cosmopolitanism entails scientific understanding.[47] That means, as Lawrence Becker states, 'following the facts' – getting the facts about one's physical and social world as well as about one's position in it before one deliberates normatively about the right course of action.[48] Nussbaum's educative ideal nicely captures the essence of Stoic thinking.

For Stoics, as it is for Aristotle, early education must be in the form of habituation toward the right sorts of behavioural patterns in generic circumstances. I say 'behavioural patterns' simply because circumstances, ever unique, do not allow for a neat application of rules to scenarios. The best one can hope for is to teach standard behavioural patterns, consistent with precepts and doctrines, to certain scenarios in early life to groove correct, reason-based action in later life.

Nonetheless, the very notion of what one aims to do with one's life will depend in large part on one's capacities and natural inclinations. In early youth, most of us are ignorant of our capacities and inclinations. Cicero writes:

> Above all, we must decide who and what manner of person we wish to be and what calling in life we would follow, and those are the most difficult problems in the world. It is in the years of early youth, when there is the greatest weakness of understanding, where each person decides his calling in life shall be that to which he has taken a special liking. Thus, he becomes engaged in some particular calling and career [*genere cursuque*] in life before he is fit to decide intelligently what is best for him.[49]

Being forced to decide too early and without the proper application of reason to one's circumstances, one errs in blindly following the advice of parents or in being swayed by current popular opinion.

In order to apply reason correctly to circumstances, one must be aware of the many hats each person wears in his life. Everyone, Panaetius states in Cicero's *On Duties*, is endowed with two per-sonae. First, everyone has a universal persona (*communis*), insofar as each is a human being and not a brute. Second, everyone has a particular persona (*singulis*), which distinguishes each person in terms of physical prowess, personal appearance and character.[50] Later Cicero adds two more personae for Panaetius. There is, third, that which chance (*casus*) or circumstance (*tempus*) imposes and, fourth, that which everyone takes on by his deliberate choosing (*nobismet ipsi iudicio nostro accommodamus*).[51] Correct application of reason is a matter of reconciling chance with each particular persona through choices aimed at self-discovery – that is, through following Nature.

Since reason is the sole psychical faculty for Stoics, it follows that an all-important part of one's moral education is training in logic – specifically argument (*epikheiretike*) and persuasive reasoning (*pithanologike*).[52]

'Logic bears no fruit' . . . If one should grant that, it is enough to say in defence of logic that it has the power to discriminate and examine everything else and, as one might say, to measure and weigh them. Who says that? Only Chrysippus, Zeno and Cleanthes? Well does not Antisthenes[53] say it? Who wrote, 'The beginning of education is the examination of words?' Does not Socrates, too, say the same thing? About what does Xenophon write, that he begins with the examination of words, asking about each, 'What does it mean?'[54]

Ultimately, Stoic apprentices need logic to discriminate between true and false impressions so that they may assent only to those that are true. Moral decision-making presupposes that. Furthermore, logic teaches the intellect to do well what it is naturally suited to do. In short, 'This is the nature of the intellect [*dianoia*] – to agree to what is true, to be dissatisfied with what is false and to withhold judgment about what is uncertain.'[55]

We must emphasize, however, what has been often mentioned

already: Stoic education is training for living and not training for its own sake. It is not enough to practise arguing in textbook fashion; one must be able to use such textbook knowledge in everyday life. Otherwise, argument is useless. Epictetus states that those who have taken in the principles of any school, without having fully absorbed them, are generally those who are most eager to spew them out peremptorily. In that, they differ not at all from someone, with a weak stomach, who cannot keep down his food. Undigested principles are like vomit – foul and unfit for human consumption.[56] Elsewhere he adds:

> We are fiery and fluent in school, and if some little problem . . . comes up, we have sufficient skill to think through it. Yet drag us into practical application and you will find us to be wretched ship-wrecked mariners [*talanes nauagous*]. Let a disturbing thought [*phantasia taraktike*] come to us and you will find out what we have been practising and toward what we have been training. Thus, due to lack of practice, we always pile things up and make them out to be greater than they are.[57]

In short, education enables a Stoic to prepare suitably for and to handle everyday-life situations, instead of creating insurmountable problems out of them.

As there are limits to reasoning abilities and to what one needs to know, there are limits to education. Once one grasps what there is worth grasping for appropriate acts in the textbooks, then it is time to stop reading and begin living, and Stoic right living is much less difficult than textbooks on logic make it out to be. Aurelius illustrates:

> Is the cucumber bitter? Throw it out. Are there brambles in the path? Go around them. That is all you need to know. There is nothing more. Do not demand to know why such things exist. Anyone who grasps the world will laugh at you, just as a carpenter would, if you seemed shocked at finding sawdust in his workshop, or a shoemaker would, if you seemed shocked at finding scraps of leather left over from his work.[58]

Throughout the educative process, one must never lose sight of the fact that education is preparation for living and is not to be confused with living itself. Thus, there are definite limits to education. At best, education gives one preparation for maintaining solidity of character in face of the many reversals of fortune that ought to be expected. Epictetus reminds us that we are not educated to change the fundamental principles (*hypotheseis*) of things, but to harmonize judgement (*gnomen*) with what happens.[59]

To begin training aright, one ought to begin one's 'winter's training' first. Seeds need to be buried and hidden for a season and gradually, but surely, they produce fruits over many seasons. Thus, one ought to train in such a manner that others are initially unaware of who one is and what one is doing. Slowly others will come to know who one is and that one has been all the while studying philosophy.[60]

Overall, one is educated to be as invincible as is possible – unshaken and firm in one's soul – such that one remains the same person even in states of sleep, slight inebriation and melancholy.[61]

Khreiai *for 'Educating "Shipwrecked Mariners"'*

- 'People exist for one another. You can instruct or endure them.'[62]
- 'The first thing that philosophy undertakes to give is fellow-feeling with all human beings – that is, sympathy and sociability.'[63]
- 'Instruction [*to paideuesthai*] consists precisely in learning to desire each thing just as it happens.'[64]

TEACHER AS PHYSICIAN: TOWERING ABOVE FORTUNE

Medicine and philosophy were known as 'sister sciences' in Greco-Roman antiquity insofar as medicine was the science of the body and philosophy was the science of the soul. Aristotle labels both 'sciences' (*technai*), but includes philosophy (literally, ethics) among political sciences, whose good, the best condition for cities and the persons in them, is internal, while he relegates medicine to the productive sciences, whose good, manufacture, is something external to the practice. Nonetheless, the goals of each are strikingly similar: While medicine aims at restoring or maintaining physical harmony within bodies, philosophy aims at restoring or maintaining harmony within souls. Thus, it is not surprising that ancient philosophers, Stoics included, were fond of comparing the two. In this section, I look at the Stoic tendency to speak of educators as physicians of the soul.

The first similarity between Stoic ethics and medicine is the recognition that those who lack virtue lack psychical health just as those who are physically unwell lack physical health. As psychical illness is a matter of ignorance, a Stoic 'physician' (*medicus*) needs to be especially tolerant of the non-virtuous.

> And so a Stoic is kindly and just towards errors. He is not the foe, but the reformer of those who have gone astray [*peccantium*] and, as he goes out each day, he will think: 'I shall meet many who are addicted to wine, many who are lustful, many who are ungrateful, many who are greedy, many who are agitated by the frenzy of ambition.' He will view all those things in as kindly a way as a physician views the sick.[65]

Once a Stoic recognizes psychical illness in another, his behaviour to that other will be just like a physician to his patient.

> A Stoic's mindset towards all men is that of a physician towards his patients. He does not scorn to touch their private parts, if they need treatment, to view the body's refuse and discharges or to endure violent words from those who rage in delirium. A Stoic knows that all who strut about in togas and in purple, as if they were well and strong, are for all their bright colour quite unsound and, in his eyes, they differ not at all from the sick, who lack self-control.[66]

Just as correct perception of things guides him in everyday life, so too does the correct diagnosis of a student's psychical illness help him be a better educator of that student. Cicero writes, 'In encountering danger we should do as doctors do in their practice. In light cases of illness, they give mild treatment. In cases of severe sickness, they are compelled to apply risky and uncertain remedies [*periculosas curationes et ancipites*].'[67]

Overall, the Stoic manner of educating is not gentle, but heroic, as the aim is cure of a sick soul and cure often requires difficult, radical measures. The correct course is not the quickest or the easiest, but the one best suited to cure a patient's ignorance.

> Other philosophers, using gentle and persuasive measures, are like the intimate family doctor, who commonly tries to cure his

THE STOICS: A GUIDE FOR THE PERPLEXED

patient not by the best and quickest method, but as he is allowed. The Stoics, having adopted the heroic course [*virilem viam*], are not so much concerned in making it attractive to us who enter upon it, as in having it rescue us as soon as possible and guide us to that lofty summit that rises so far beyond the reach of any arrow so as to tower high above all Fortune.[68]

Aspiring towards virtue, one must be careful in selecting the right teachers. Seneca says that teachers are at fault for teaching their students the art of debate, not the art of living, while students are at fault for coming to their teachers to develop their cleverness, not their character.[69] Thus, an apprentice will look for those who wish to make him a better person, not a clever speaker or debater.

If not wit and cleverness, what should one learn from teachers? One goes to learn general principles (*theoremata*), Epictetus tells us. One also learns to systemize one's concepts – to organize facts under preconceptions (*prolepseis*) and to revise one's preconceptions, if needed. Let us return to medicine by way of analogy. Everyone has the concept 'healthy', because of having a preconception of it, before he visits a physician. Yet upon visiting a physician, he finds diverse and more precise uses of the term. To a physician, 'healthy' can mean 'abstain from food', 'give nourishment', 'cut a vein' or 'use the cupping glass', among other things. Similarly, everyone has the concepts 'good' and 'wicked', on account of having a preconception of them, before he goes to school. Yet to a Stoic, 'good' and 'ill' can mean different things under different circumstances.[70] Thus, education is a prefatory attempt to apply Stoic principles to the vagaries of everyday-life situations to generate right-intended activity. Teachers must teach so that students act on what they learn.[71]

For students to act on what they learn, they must first have a proper disposition for learning. A student must come into a lecture hall with the right attitude and leave with the right attitude. As it is with physical remedies, psychical remedies take time and are painful. A student is, according to the teacher-as-physician analogy, a patient.

The schoolhouse of a philosopher is a hospital. You ought not to walk out of it in pleasure, but in pain. You are not well when you come in . . . Am I then to sit down and recite to you little notions [*noematia*] and little mottoes [*epiphanematia*], so that you will go out with words of praise on your lips? . . . Was this what Socrates, Zeno or Cleanthes used to do?[72]

Teachers too must have a proper disposition. A Stoic teacher, if he is not to corrupt, must be authentic. Epictetus adds that whoever teaches in one manner and lives in another is no better than a seasick pilot in a storm. In fact, he is worse, for the storm of life is incomparably greater than any sea-storm.[73]

Last, should a teacher advertise and invite others to a lecture? As a physician of the soul, advertising and inviting are absurd. What physician invites those who are ill to come to him? Illness itself, Epictetus says, is the proper invitation.[74]

Khreiai *for 'Teacher as Physician'*

■ 'Whenever you see a man looking pale, just as a physician judging from the complexion says, "This man's spleen is affected and this man's liver is affected," so too do you say, "This man's desire and aversion are affected. He is not getting along well. He is feverish."'[75]

■ 'Who among us did not use terms "healthy" and "diseased" before Hippocrates was born?'[76]

STOIC 'CURATIVES'

With a Stoic teacher assuming the role of physician of the soul, education in Stoic principles is a sort of philosophical or cognitive therapy for the psychically ill. Cure requires schooling in Stoic principles and, as a first step, an unbiased attitude, when being schooled. Epictetus says:

People say, 'Nobody gets any good from going to school.' Well, who goes to school with the expectation of being cured? Who with the expectation of submitting his own judgments for purification? Who with the expectation of coming to a realization of what judgments he needs? Why, then, are you surprised if you carry back home from your school precisely the judgments you bring to it? You do not come with the expectation of laying them aside, correcting them or getting others in exchange for them.[77]

Seneca agrees. Showing up to school is not sufficient for progress. For there are those who attend the lectures of the wise, yet they learn nothing. These are likened to 'squatters' (*inquilini*). They come to listen, but not to learn. Squatters come to have a lounge for their leisure and regard the words of philosophers as mere delights for the ear. They care not at all for reflection or remediation.[78] They are there to see and be seen.

The first steps of progress toward virtue require more than flattery toward those nearer to it. One has to desire a cure for one's illness and be receptive to teachers. Cure requires developing the rational faculty to have a thorough grasp of one's own capacities and a correct apprehension of the circumstances in which one is to act. Thus, Stoic training for virtue and for the elimination of emotion are principally cognitive. On the one extreme, cognitive therapy involves *khreiai* – short, easy-to-recite apothegms designed to reinforce key doctrinal points. On the other extreme, it involves training in Stoic argument that is designed to anchor principles through demonstrative reasoning.

The teacher, as physician, has at his disposal certain rational remedies, which I call epistemological and ethical 'curatives'.[79] In this section, I take a closer look at some of these curatives.

Epistemological Curatives

First, there are epistemological curatives, which comprise doctrines, precepts, *khreiai*, reminders or exhortations aimed at right action through seeing the world as it really is.

Test impressions

The first duty of a Stoic apprentice, Aurelius says, is to discriminate between impressions.

> Make for yourself a definition or description of every object presented to you, to see what sort of thing it is in its own naked substance, complete and entire, and tell yourself its proper name and the names of the things that comprise it and into which it will disintegrate. Nothing so elevates your mind as examining systematically and truly everything that comes before you in life. Always look at things to see at once what kind of cosmos you live in, what sort of service each performs in it, what value each has in relation to the whole and what value the whole has for people

who are citizens of this lofty city, to which all other cities are as families.[80]

One must be especially on guard when impressions seem to convey emotive content of some sort. Epictetus gives the example of anticipating a pleasant experience. When some future event seems to be pleasant, one ought not to let oneself be carried away by gleeful anticipation. Instead, one ought to delay and bring to mind the anticipated enjoyment of that pleasure as well as the regret you will likely have soon after the enjoyment. One ought also to consider the gratification one will have on account of refraining from the pleasure. If one must act on the pleasure, act so as not to be overcome by its seductiveness. In such a manner, one can win a victory over it.[81]

Overall, proper testing of impressions will enable a person, in time, to judge correctly the worth of each object. 'It is essential to remember to have concern for each action according to its own worth and proportion.'[82]

See things in their proper context
Another epistemological exercise is to get in the habit of seeing things not in isolation, but in their fullest context. That involves seeing them within the larger context of Nature itself or having a non-provincial or cosmological perspective. Aurelius states:

> If a person has a feeling for and deeper insight into the things produced in the cosmos, there is hardly one of their characteristics that will not seem to him to be of a sort to give him pleasure. He will look at the gaping jaws of living wild beasts with as much pleasure as at those that painters and sculptors depict in imitation; and in an old woman and an old man he will perceive a certain ripeness and handsomeness; and will look on the attractive loveliness of young persons with chaste eyes. Many such beautiful things will show themselves, not pleasing to every person, but to him who has become truly at home with Nature and her works.[83]

When one see things as products of divine intelligence, the most seemingly vulgar things – the lion's jaw, poisons and thorns – are recognizably beautiful.[84]

For our purposes, since I have adopted an agnostic stance toward

Stoic pantheism, seeing things in their proper context means seeing things in the largest context possible – that is, adopting as much of a god's-eye or holistic perspective as a situation allows. A holistic perspective gives one pause before one hastily forms judgements about other people, and requires each to see things from as many different perspectives as are reasonably warranted. That is not so much viewing them from some 'higher perch', but putting oneself in the shoes of another, what Nussbaum labels 'narrative imagination', before judging a situation.

For example, when one puts oneself in the shoes of another with whom one disagrees – perhaps, someone from a different cultural perspective – one gets a deeper appreciation of the other perspective as well as one's own. Seneca gives the example of a man's 'perception' that others are much more fortunate than he is. By putting oneself in the shoes of those deemed more fortunate, a person may come to find that those who seem most happy because of good fortune may be the most pitiable of all.[85]

Avoid evaluative judgements on indifferents

Epictetus warns that people too hastily pass judgement on matters on which judgement should not be passed. If someone takes a bath quickly, one ought not to say that he bathes badly, but that he bathes quickly. If someone drinks a great deal of wine, one ought not to say that he is a drunkard, but that he drinks a great deal of wine. Epictetus' point is that one cannot be in a position to evaluate another's actions, unless he knows perfectly well the mindset of that other and his situation.[86] Without knowing the particulars of another's situation and the reasoning behind his actions, such judgements are more of a sign of the judger's moral instability than a valid critique of the person being judged.

For a Stoic, one who is psychically well disposed will pass judgement only on things on which judgement ought to be passed – things within the province of moral choice (*prohairesis*) – and not on things merely assumed to be good or ill.[87]

How is one to refrain from judging things outside of moral choice – the Stoic indifferents? In Book IV of his *Discourses*, Epictetus gives an exercise. One must turn his attention first to his most trifling 'possessions' and then progressively toward his most cherished 'possessions' and practise treating each in turn as something disowned.

One must attend to this practice from morning until evening. Begin with the most trifling things – the ones most exposed to injury, like a pot or a cup – and then advance to a tunic, a paltry dog, a mere horse and a bit of land. Proceed then to yourself – your body and its members, your children, wife and brothers. Examine these things from every angle and cast them away from you. Purify your judgments [*katheron ton dogmata*], as something that is not your own may be attached to them or may have grown with them and give you pain, when it is torn loose.[88]

If it proves too difficult to refrain from forming judgements of some sort on indifferents, the next best thing is to practise postponing judgements, which works especially well with anger.[89]

Follow Nature
Progress toward invincibility, at one point, Seneca describes as a continually successful retreat from the things that are against Nature (e.g. pain) and a continually successful forward movement toward those things that are in agreement with it (e.g. health and toleration of pain).

We are [naturally] attracted by things such as riches, pleasures, beauty, ambition and other alluring and pleasing objects. We are [naturally] repelled by toil, death, pain, disgrace or lives of greater frugality. We ought therefore to train ourselves so we may avoid fear of the one and a desire for the other. Let us fight in the opposite direction: Let us retreat from things that seduce us and set out against things assailing us.[90]

Aurelius bids us to consider the world as a flood that sweeps away, in its current, all persons equally. In such a world, 'little men', like statesmen and philosophers, would doubtless still be preoccupied with their 'large affairs', like affectation and reputation. Yet, in such a flood, how far removed would such affairs be from those of Nature.[91]

Wish for what you have
For Stoics, one ought not to seek what one does not have, but to be content with what one has. That is especially evident in Epictetus' thinking – particularly in the *Handbook*. He states, 'Do not seek to

have things happen as you want them to happen, but want them to happen as they do happen, and your life will go well.'[92] Again, 'Wish to have happen only what does happen and wish for the person to win who actually does win, as that way you will not be disappointed.'[93]

Aurelius endorses this sentiment, when he says all things that happen come about justly.[94] He illustrates the point later in his *Meditations* with the following proscription:

> Think less of what you do not have than of what you do have. Of the things you have, choose the best, and then reflect how eagerly you would have laboured for them if you did not have them. At the same time, however, take care that you do not, through being so pleased with them, accustom yourself to so overvalue them as to be distressed if you should ever lose them.[95]

Right self-judgement
Another epistemological curative is to practise the right self-judgement – one that squares with reality. The right self-judgement entails self-knowledge. An important step in that direction is not to concern oneself with satisfying the image others have of oneself, but with one's own self-image. To set the right self-image, Epictetus says, one must first wish to appear inwardly beautiful in the sight of deity. It is also critical to withdraw from the society of fools and enter the society of those striving to be virtuous so that one may model one's actions after good persons.[96]

Right self-judgement also depends critically on a proper assessment of one's own capacities concerning the things that are within and outside of moral choice.

> You can be invincible [*aniketos*], if you never enter a contest where victory is not up to you. When you see some person treated more honourably than you, possessing great power or otherwise enjoying great repute, be cautious that you are never carried away by the external impression and judge him to be happy. If the true nature of the good is one of the things under our control, there is no place for envy or jealousy, and you yourself will not wish to be a praetor, senator or a consul, but one who is free [*eleutherios*].[97]

Practise silence

No words spoken, Plutarch tells us, have ever done anyone the same service as have words unspoken, since words spoken cannot be recalled and forgotten, but words unspoken may be spoken at some later date, if circumstances require. Moreover, people often regret having said something that cannot be taken back, but seldom regret having held their tongue.[98]

It is incumbent upon Stoic apprentices to practise silence. For those who know, actions are the best educators. For those who are still ignorant, there can be great harm in speaking on topics that are not fully digested.

> At a banquet, do not say how a person ought to eat, but eat as a person ought to eat . . . If talk about some philosophical proposition arises among non-philosophers, for the most part, be silent, as there is great danger in your spewing out what you have not digested . . . Sheep do not show how much they have eaten by bringing their fodder to the shepherds, but they digest the food inside themselves, and outside themselves they bear wool and milk. So, in your case, likewise do not display principles to non-philosophers, but let them see the actions that come from those principles, when they have been digested.[99]

Ethical Curatives

Next, there are ethical curatives, which comprise doctrines, precepts, *khreiai*, reminders or exhortations aimed at right action through improved psychical equilibrium.

Use–disuse

Epictetus gives the principle of use–disuse as a general strategy for strengthening desirable activities. The rational faculty, like bodily muscles, must be exercised to be strengthened.

> Every skill [*hexis*] and capacity [*dynamis*] is built up and strengthened by corresponding actions – walking by walking, running by running. If you wish to be a good reader, read. If you wish to be a good writer, write. If you, engaged in some other activity, should give up reading for thirty straight days, you will know what happens. Similarly, if you lie in bed for ten days, get up, and

try to take a rather long walk, you will see how wobbly your legs are. In general, if you want to do something, make a habit of it; if you do not want to do something, refrain from doing it and accustom yourself to something else instead. The same thing holds true in the affairs of the mind as well.[100]

If one's governing principle is swayed by a desire for wealth, one must apply a remedy to restore it to its original state of indifference. Acting on that desire bruises one's soul. Continued activity in that direction turns bruises into wounds. To free oneself from a base activity, one must keep track of the days one has been free of such activity and, after 30 days or so, give thanks to deity.[101] Thus, someone may gradually weaken a bad habit and eventually annihilate it. In this manner, a Stoic exercises his mental capacities to improve and strengthen them.

Flee from strong impressions
A rule for apprenticeship in Stoic philosophy early in one's apprenticeship is to shun temptations. Trying to master temptations without having internalized the right precepts, one runs a great risk of losing a battle that has not rightly begun.

> Train oneself to use wine with discretion, not with a view to heavy drinking . . . but first for the purpose of achieving abstention from wine . . . And then some day, if the occasion for a test really comes, one will set down a plan at a proper time to discover whether one's sense-impressions are still as overwhelming as they previously were. First, however, one must flee far away from impressions that are too strong. A pretty wench is not a fair match for a young beginner in philosophy.[102]

Live authentically
To attain equanimity, it is essential that people speak consistent with their actions and act consistent with their words. Epictetus considers a common phenomenon, even today – a teacher who busies himself with arguments at school and yet leaves his words behind when he leaves the school.[103]
Seneca has a similar outlook to that of Epictetus:

Philosophy teaches us to act, not to speak. It requires every person to live according to his own standard [*legem suam*]. It requires that his life should not be at odds with his words and that his inner life should be united and not out of harmony with all his actions. This, I say, is the greatest duty [*maximum . . . officium*] and the greatest evidence of wisdom – that deed and words should be in agreement, that a man should be equal to himself and always be the same person under all conditions.[104]

As we have seen in Chapter 2, authenticity is merely a commitment toward being the same person in public as in private.

Prepare for the future
For Stoics, the worst life of all may not be one of unlimited misfortune, but one of unlimited prosperity. Still, a life of good fortune is desirable, if only because overall it may make the exercise of virtue easier.

One of the greatest difficulties with the having of good fortune is the notion that good fortune, without warning, may not only cease, but also reverse itself. In times of reversal of fortune, perceived goods, the Stoic conveniences, may likely be a bane. What use is a plethora of fine things, when disaster strikes suddenly? 'No man can swim ashore and take his baggage with him,' Seneca reminds us.[105] That is why a Stoic prepares, when things are going well, for harsher days. When food is abundant, he readies for scarcity. When there is peace, he hardens himself for war. In times of wealth, he prepares for poverty. 'That', Seneca says, 'is anticipating [*praeoccupare*[106]] the arrows of Fortune'.[107]

Ill-fortune anticipated is a blow that is softened.[108] Thus, a Stoic is no more surprised by a reversal of good fortune than he is when a fig tree produces figs, when a doctor has ill patients or when a helmsman has a wind that blows against him.[109]

Nothing ought to be unexpected by us. Our minds should be sent forward in advance to meet all problems, and we should consider, not merely what is likely to happen, but what can happen. What does Fortune, when she has so willed, not drag down from the very height of its prosperity? What is there that she does not more violently attack the more brilliantly it shines? . . . No time is exempt. In the midst of our own pleasures, the causes of suffering spring up. The best preparation is practice in growing accustomed to a life devoid of luxuries. Hence, self-sufficiency requires a good-humoured stomach, willing and readied to endure rough treatment.[110]

Winnow one's thoughts

Aurelius states, 'The things that you often think about determine the quality of your mind. Your soul takes on the colour of your thoughts.' One who continually indulges himself with perverse and debased thoughts in the privacy of his own home is in essence a perverse and debased person, whether he acts on those thoughts or not. Colour the soul, Aurelius adds, with thoughts that elevate one's mind, not those that disgrace it.[111]

Aurelius' words are well stated. One should practise avoiding malicious and self-important thoughts so that one may be proudly transparent to others. In such a way, if others ask one what one is thinking at a certain time, one can readily tell them one's thoughts, immediately and honestly, and they will know from the response that one is non-indulgent, unselfish and forthright, which is, of course, just being authentic.[112]

Be patient

To make progress in virtue, one must exercise patience. A person must wait for things to come to him without rushing toward them.[113] After all, nothing he needs is outside him. What he needs, he already has in abundance. He must not hope for inconveniences to pass quicker than they must pass. He must not hope that conveniences stay longer than they must stay. The exercise of patience is succinctly summed in Epictetus' own saying: 'Bear and tolerate' (*anekhou kai apekhou*).

Treat each day as the last day

Stoic therapy prepares a person for life by asking him to begin without delay what is worth doing. If one must act courageously on a particular day, one must not delay the activity and first indulge oneself in pleasure, as a recompense for the difficulties ahead. Delay in matters that are imminently worth pursuing may prove costly, for no one is guaranteed another day of life.

Thus, let us, omitting diversions along the way, strive with all our soul. Let us struggle with a single aim, unless we grasp too late the speed of quick-flying time, whose course we cannot delay, when we are left behind. Let every day, as soon as it comes, be welcome as being the best and let it be rendered our own.[114]

To prepare for each day, Aurelius advises that each person begin at daybreak to ready himself mentally for unexpected rigours of what lies ahead. Each will encounter numerous others who do not know goodness from evilness and who will test one's patience, due to their ignorance.[115]

Virtuous living is, thus, efficient living, because no one is guaranteed another day. Seneca sums, 'Let us order our minds as if we had come to the very end. Let us postpone nothing. Let us balance life's account every day . . . One who puts the finishing touches to his life every day is never in want of time.'[116]

Take daily inventory
Finally, the best way to assure oneself of living efficiently and progress toward invincibility is to keep a daily journal of one's moral progress. Seneca, in a practice that is Pythagorean in origin, relates that it was his habit, prior to going to sleep each night, to take moral inventory of his day.

> The soul should be summoned to give an account of itself every day. Sextius had this habit, and when the day was over and he had retired to his nightly rest, he would put these questions to his soul: 'What bad habit have you cured today? What faults have you resisted? In what respect are you better?' Anger will cease and become more controllable, if it finds that it must appear before a judge every day.[117]

Epictetus says roughly the same thing, when he bids each person to remember who he is, where he intends to go, and what his duties are along the way.[118] Aurelius also took daily inventory of his life. His *Meditations* was written as a diary while he was on campaign in the Germanic countries.

SIGNS OF PROGRESS: THE CONTEST IS NOW

Plutarch, no real friend to Stoicism, tells a story of a difficult day in the life of the philosopher/beggar, Diogenes the Cynic. As the story goes, the Athenians were making merry on the day of a public festival. There was theatre, feasting, laughter and drinking all the night. Diogenes, huddled in a corner somewhere, could not sleep. He wondered why he too was not making merry and how he had stumbled into his difficult and strange way of living. Such thoughts disturbed him, until he shortly saw a mouse making a feast of some crumbs of bread left behind from his last meal. When reflecting on the two lives, the soft life of the revellers and that of the mouse, he gained his composure and convinced himself that the life he had chosen, the life of the mouse, was preferable. Plutarch concludes that self-doubting is an integral part of moral progress (*prokope*). Yet one can be sure one is making moral progress, he adds, when such fits of self-doubting become increasingly infrequent.[119]

How can one measure progress? Seneca offers an analogy related to motion. One indifferent to virtue is moved around in many directions by external factors, yet it is otherwise for a progressor and a sage. A sage has so mastered his emotions that external events do not move him at all. A progressor, striving for virtue, has a bobbing-like motion without a change of position.[120]

> The difference, I say, between a man of perfect wisdom [*consummatae sapientiae virum*] and another who is progressing in wisdom [*alium procedentis*] is the same as the difference between a healthy man and one who is convalescing from a severe and lingering illness, for whom 'health' means only a lighter attack of his disease. If the progressor is not cautious, there is an immediate relapse and a return to the same old trouble; but a Stoic sage cannot slip back or slip into any more illness at all. Health of the body is a temporary matter that a physician cannot guarantee, even though he has restored it ... In contrast, the mind, once healed, is healed completely.[121]

We may now return to the question: Why did the Stoics believe in invincibility as a state qualitatively distinct from all other states of psychical being, if the ideal was never realized? Moreover, how, one might ask, does a process of incremental addition make one invincible, if invincibility is a qualitative state of soul and progress is quantitative?

Seneca responds to those questions with an analogy involving wine and honey. Each has the same quality, indistinguishable to taste, no matter how much the quantity is reduced or enlarged. In addition, he uses the helpful analogy of an archway's keystone.

> There are other things, however, that change by the last addition after many increments. There is stamped on them a new character, different from the old one. One stone makes an archway – the stone that wedges the leaning side and holds the arch together by its position in the middle. Why does the last addition, although very slight, make a great deal of difference? Because it does not increase; it fills up.[122]

In *Consolation of Helvia*, he merely says succinctly, 'Reason lays low the vices all together, not one at a time. It conquers completely and all at once.'[123] The Stoic all-or-nothing reply to such questions smacks of Kant.

As it is very probably a humanly unrealizable demand that one so master his emotions that he is completely unmoved by things not up to him, I have been arguing for invincibility not as perfectionism, but as progressivism – not as an ideal to be achieved, but as an archetype to be approximated. I focus now on keys for progress towards virtue.

One important key for progress is the capacity to take counsel from experts and the willingness to be admonished by well-intentioned teachers.

> The second best form of virtue is to be willing and able to take advice [*moneri*]. The horse that is docile and obedient can easily be turned one way or another by a gentle movement of the reins. For a few people, the mind is the best governor of itself. Next best are those who return to the right path, when they are admonished. They must not be deprived of their guide.[124]

Having a willingness to be advised and admonished, of course, implies that one must be careful in selecting the appropriate teachers. An apprentice should look for those who seek to make him a better person, not just a clever speaker or debater. Teachers should look for willing and sincere pupils.[125] A willing pupil should undertake philosophy with the aims of bettering his soul and increasing his happiness.[126]

Another key to progress toward virtue and invincibility, like the key to athletic success, is practice. One should study philosophy daily and both look for and measure one's progress each day. 'He who studies with a philosopher should take away with him some one good thing every day. He should return home daily a sounder man or on the way to becoming sounder.'[127] He can measure the results of such exercise by keeping a daily log.

What are the signs that someone is making progress? Epictetus lists several. A progressor never talks about himself as a person who has amounted to something or knows anything. He praises no one and, if someone praises him, he laughs quietly at him who has praised him, since he does not take the praise to heart. He censures no one. If someone censures him, he does not respond in like manner. He goes around like an invalid, mindful not to move any of his parts that are healing before they have healed.[128]

> Make up your mind, before it is too late, that the right thing for you to do is to live as a mature person who is making progress, and to let everything that seems to you best be for you a law that must not be violated. If you meet anything that is laborious, sweet, held in high-repute, or held in no repute, remember that now is the contest and here, before you, are the Olympic Games. It is impossible to delay any longer. Whether progress is lost or made depends on a single day and a single action.[129]

Plutarch says that a progressor gives favours without telling others. He speaks candidly among dishonest persons. He declines showy invitations by the rich or public officials. He scorns bribes. He does not drink, when he craves drink. He does not give in to the affections of a handsome youth or beautiful girl. He treats all of his faults seriously. Most importantly, he does all things silently and because they are worth doing, not because of public opinion.[130]

Khreiai *for 'Signs of Progress'*

- 'Apply reason to difficulties. It is possible for hard things to be softened, for narrow things to be widened and for serious matters to weigh down much less those who bear them with skill.'[131]
- 'It is enough for me, if every day I reduce the number of my vices and correct [*objurgare*[132]] my mistakes.'[133]

NOTES

1 Epictetus, *Discourses*, II.xix.22–5. See also IV.xii.19.
2 The sign of a dedicated soldier would be that he trained for soldiery during the off-season for war – the winter.
3 Epictetus, *Discourses*, I.ii.30–2.
4 Epictetus, *Discourses*, I.iv.18–22.
5 Epictetus, *Discourses*, III.vi.10.
6 Seneca, *Epistles*, LXXXV.9.
7 Seneca, *Epistles*, LXXXV.5.
8 Seneca, *Epistles*, LXXVII.17.
9 Seneca, *Epistles*, LXXXV.41.
10 Epictetus, *Discourses*, III.xxii.57.
11 Cicero, *Duties*, III.v.25.
12 Homer, *The Odyssey*, XI.620–33. Trans. Robert Fagles (New York: Penguin Books, 1997).
13 Xenophon, *Memorabilia*, II.i.13.
14 From *athlein*, meaning 'to contest for a prize', 'to labour' or 'to combat'.
15 Epictetus, *Discourses*, III.xxvi.31–2.
16 Seneca, *Firmness*, X.4.
17 Epictetus, *Discourses*, IV.x.10.
18 Seneca, *Benefits*, II.xviii.2.
19 Seneca, *Benefits*, IV.viii.1.
20 Seneca, *Epistles*, XV.5.
21 Seneca, *Providence*, IV.12.
22 Epictetus, *Discourses*, III.x.7.
23 Epictetus, *Discourses*, IV.iv.31.
24 Epictetus, *Discourses*, III.xxv.3–4.
25 Seneca, *Epistles*, LXXVIII.16.
26 Seneca, *Epistles*, LXXX.2–3.
27 Epictetus, *Discourses*, III.xxiii.2–3.
28 Epictetus, *Discourses*, I.iv.20–2.
29 Epictetus, *Discourses*, I.xxiv.1–2.
30 Epictetus, *Discourses*, III.xx.9–10.
31 Seneca, *Firmness*, IX.5.
32 Epictetus, *Discourses*, III.vi.5–7.
33 Epictetus, *Discourses*, IV.ix.15.
34 Aurelius, *Meditations*, III.4.
35 Seneca, *Benefits*, V.v.4.
36 Epictetus, *Discourses*, III.xxiii.21–2.
37 Plato, *Phaedo*, 97a–100a.
38 Epictetus, *Discourses*, III.v.14–18.
39 Epictetus, *Discourses*, II.xii.5–6.
40 Epictetus, *Discourses*, II.xii.14–15.
41 Epictetus, *Discourses*, II.xviii.22–3.
42 For the impact of Socrates on Epictetus' thought, see A.A. Long, *Epictetus: A Stoic and Socratic Guide to Life* (Oxford: Oxford University Press, 2002), esp. pp. 67–96.

43 Epictetus, *Discourses*, IV.i.159–65. See also Aurelius, *Meditations*, VII.66.
44 See also Plutarch, *Progress in Virtue*, 85b.
45 Epictetus, *Handbook*, 33.
46 Martha Nussbaum, *Cultivating Humanity: A Classical Defense of Reform in Liberal Education* (Cambridge, MA: Harvard University Press, 1997), p. 6.
47 Martha Nussbaum, *Cultivating Humanity*, pp. 9–11 and chapters 1–3.
48 Lawrence Becker, *A New Stoicism* (Princeton, NJ: Princeton University Press, 1998), chapter 5.
49 Cicero, *Duties*, I.xxxii.107.
50 Cicero, *Duties*, I.xxx.107.
51 Cicero, *Duties*, I.xxxii.115–17.
52 Epictetus, *Discourses*, I.viii.7.
53 Mentor of Diogenes the Cynic.
54 Epictetus, *Discourses*, I.xvii.10–12.
55 Epictetus, *Discourses*, I.xxviii.1–2.
56 Epictetus, *Discourses*, III.xxi.1–3.
57 Epictetus, *Discourses*, II.xvi.20–1.
58 Aurelius, *Meditations*, VIII.50.
59 Epictetus, *Discourses*, I.xii.17.
60 Epictetus, *Discourses*, IV.viii.35–40.
61 Epictetus, *Discourses*, II.xvii.33.
62 Aurelius, *Meditations*, VIII.59.
63 Seneca, *Epistles*, V.4.
64 Epictetus, *Discourses*, I.xii.15. See also I.xxii.9–10.
65 Seneca, *Anger*, II.x.7.
66 Seneca, *Equanimity*, XIII.2.
67 Cicero, *Duties*, I.xxiv.83.
68 Seneca, *Firmness*, I.1.
69 Seneca, *Epistles*, CVIII.23.
70 Epictetus, *Discourses*, II.xvii.5–13.
71 Seneca, *Epistles*, CVIII.35–6.
72 Epictetus, *Discourses*, III.xxiii.30–2.
73 Seneca, *Epistles*, CVIII.35–6.
74 Epictetus, *Discourses*, III.xxiii.27.
75 Epictetus, *Discourses*, II.xiii.13.
76 Epictetus, *Discourses*, II.xvii.8.
77 Epictetus, *Discourses*, II.xxi.25–7.
78 Seneca, *Epistles*, CVIII.5–8.
79 In ancient medicine, regimen included alimentary habits as well as habits of exercise.
80 Aurelius, *Meditations*, III.11. See also Epictetus, *Discourses*, I.xx.7.
81 Epictetus, *Handbook*, 34. Seneca argues that anger, a radically different sort of emotion, can be softened by merely looking at oneself in a mirror, when angry. Seneca, *Anger*, II.xxxvi.1–3.
82 Aurelius, *Meditations*, IV.32.
83 Aurelius, *Meditations*, III.2.

84 Aurelius, *Meditations*, VI.36a.
85 Seneca, *Epistles*, CXXIV.24 and *Benefits*, V.xii.6.
86 Epictetus, *Handbook*, 45.
87 Epictetus, *Discourses*, III.iii.18–19.
88 Epictetus, *Discourses*, IV.i.111–13. See also *Discourses*, III.iii.14–16 and Aurelius, *Meditations*, VI.41.
89 Seneca, *Anger*, III.xii.4.
90 Seneca, *Epistles*, CXXIII.13.
91 Aurelius, *Meditations*, IX.29.
92 Epictetus, *Handbook*, 8.
93 Epictetus, *Handbook*, 33.
94 Aurelius, *Meditations*, IV.10.
95 Aurelius, *Meditations*, VII.27.
96 Epictetus, *Discourses*, II.xviii.19–21.
97 Epictetus, *Handbook*, 19.
98 Plutarch, *Talkativeness*, 505f and 514e–f.
99 Epictetus, *Handbook*, 46.
100 Epictetus, *Discourses*, II.xviii.1–5.
101 Epictetus, *Discourses*, II.xviii.8–13. Incorrectly labelled a principle of reinforcement by Sorabji. One's sacrifice to the deity is an offering of gratitude, not a reward. Richard Sorabji, *Emotion and Peace of Mind: From Stoic Agitation to Christian Temptation* (Oxford: Oxford University Press, 2000), p. 216.
102 Epictetus, *Discourses*, III.xii.10–11.
103 Epictetus, *Discourses*, IV.i.138–43.
104 Seneca, *Epistles*, XX.2.
105 Seneca, *Epistles*, XXII.12.
106 This can also mean 'to prevent'.
107 Seneca, *Epistles*, XVIII.11.
108 Seneca, *Epistles*, LXXVI.34.
109 Aurelius, *Meditations*, VIII.15 and 20.
110 Seneca, *Epistles*, XCI.
111 Aurelius, *Meditations*, V.16.
112 Aurelius, *Meditations*, III.4.
113 Epictetus, *Handbook*, 15.
114 Seneca, *Epistles*, CVIII.27.
115 Aurelius, *Meditations*, II.1.
116 Seneca, *Epistles*, CI.7–8.
117 Seneca, *Anger*, III.xxxvi.1–2.
118 Epictetus, *Discourses*, IV.xii.15–16.
119 Plutarch, *Progress in Virtue*, 77e–78a.
120 The sense of *commoveo* here indicates especially lack of motion with respect to passion. Seneca, *Epistles*, XXXV.4.
121 Seneca, *Epistles*, LXXII.6. Cleanthes said the state of virtue entails its continual exercise – that is, it cannot be lost, once found. Chrysippus thought otherwise. D.L., VII.127–8.
122 Seneca, *Epistles*, CXVIII.16.
123 Seneca, *Helvia*, XIII.3. See also Seneca, *Epistles*, CXVIII.17.

124 Seneca, *Benefits*, V.xxv.4–5.
125 Seneca, *Epistles*, CVIII.23.
126 Seneca, *Epistles*, CVIII.35–6.
127 Seneca, *Epistles*, CVIII.4.
128 Epictetus, *Handbook*, 48.
129 Epictetus, *Handbook*, 51.
130 Plutarch, *Progress in Virtue*, 81a and 85e.
131 Seneca, *Equanimity*, X.4.
132 Also, meaning 'reprove'.
133 Seneca, *Good Life*, XVII.3.

BIBLIOGRAPHY

ANCIENT SOURCES

Aristotle, *Nicomachean Ethics*, trans. H. Rackham, Loeb Classical Library (Cambridge, MA: Harvard University Press, 1990).

Arrian, *The Campaigns of Alexander*, trans. Aubrey de Selincourt (New York: Penguin Books, 1971).

Aurelius, Marcus, *Meditations*, in *Marcus Aurelius and his Times*, ed. Irwin Edman, trans. George Long (Roslyn, NY: Walter J. Black, Inc., 1945).

—*Meditations*, trans. C. R. Haines, Loeb Classical Library (Cambridge, MA: Harvard University Press, 1999).

Cicero. *Academics*, trans. H. Rackham, Loeb Classical Library (Cambridge, MA: Harvard University Press, 2000).

—*On Divination*, trans. William Armistead Falconer, Loeb Classical Library (Cambridge, MA: Harvard University Press, 1992).

—*On Duties*, trans. Walter Miller, Loeb Classical Library (Cambridge, MA: Harvard University Press, 2001).

—*On Ends*, trans. H. Rackham, Loeb Classical Library (Cambridge, MA: Harvard University Press, 1994).

—*On Fate*, trans. H. Rackham, Loeb Classical Library (Cambridge, MA: Harvard University Press, 1966).

—*Paradoxes of the Stoics*, trans. H. Rackham, Loeb Classical Library (Cambridge, MA: Harvard University Press, 1966).

—*Tusculan Disputations*, trans. J. E. King, Loeb Classical Library (Cambridge, MA: Harvard University Press, 1966).

Curtius Rufus, Quintus, *The History of Alexander*, trans. John Yardley (New York: Penguin Books, 1984).

Diogenes Laertius, *Lives of Eminent Philosophers, Vol. II*, trans. R. D. Hicks, Loeb Classical Library (Cambridge, MA: Harvard University Press, 1991).

Epictetus, *Discourses, Vols. I–II*, trans. W. A. Oldfather, Loeb Classical Library (Cambridge, MA: Harvard University Press, 2000).

—*Meditations*, trans. Gregory Hays (New York: The Modern Library, 2002).

Plutarch, *Greek Lives*, trans. Robin Waterfield (New York: Oxford University Press, 1998).

—*Moralia VI, Control of Anger*, trans. W. C. Helmbold, Loeb Classical Library (Cambridge, MA: Harvard University Press, 2005).

—*Moralia VI, On Talkativeness*, trans. W. C. Helmbold, Loeb Classical Library (Cambridge, MA: Harvard University Press, 2005).

—*Moralia VI, On Tranquility of Mind*, trans. W. C. Helmbold, Loeb Classical Library (Cambridge, MA: Harvard University Press, 2005).

—*Moralia XIII, Vol. II, Against the Stoics on Common Conceptions*, trans. Harold Cherniss, Loeb Classical Library (Cambridge, MA: Harvard University Press, 2004).

—*Moralia XIII, Vol. II, On Stoic Self-Contradictions*, trans. Harold Cherniss, Loeb Classical Library (Cambridge, MA: Harvard University Press, 2004).

—*Moralia XIII, Vol. II, The Stoics Talk More Paradoxically than the Poets*, trans. Harold Cherniss, Loeb Classical Library (Cambridge, MA: Harvard University Press, 2004).

Seneca, *Letters, Vols. I–III*, trans. Richard M. Gummere, Loeb Classical Library (Cambridge, MA: Harvard University Press, 2000–2).

—*Moral Essays, Vols. I–III*, trans. John W. Basadore, Loeb Classical Library (Cambridge, MA: Harvard University Press, 1998–2001).

Sextus Empiricus, *Against the Mathematicians, Vols. I–II*, trans. Rev. R. G. Bury, Loeb Classical Library (Cambridge, MA: Harvard University Press, 1961).

GENERAL WORKS

Annas, Julia, *The Morality of Happiness* (Oxford: Oxford University Press, 1993).

Becker, Lawrence, *A New Stoicism* (Princeton, NJ: Princeton University Press, 1998).

Berlin, Isaiah, 'Two Concepts of Liberty', in *Four Essays on Liberty* (Oxford: Oxford University Press, 1969), pp. 118–72.

Bobzien, Susanne, *Determinism and Freedom in Stoic Philosophy* (Oxford: Oxford University Press, 1998).

Bracht Branham, R. and Goulet-Cazé, M.-O. (eds), *The Cynics: The Cynic Movement in Antiquity and Its Legacy* (Los Angeles: University of California Press, 1996).

Brennan, Tad, *The Stoic Life: Emotions, Duty, and Fate* (Oxford: Clarendon Press, 2005).

Cooper, John, 'The Emotional Life of the Wise', *The Southern Journal of Philosophy*, XLIII (2005): pp. 176–218.

—'Eudaimonism, the Appeal to Nature, and "Moral Duty" in Stoicism', in *Aristotle, Kant, and the Stoics*, ed. Stephen Engstrom and Jennifer Whiting (Cambridge: Cambridge University Press, 1996), pp. 261–84.

Engberg-Pedersen, Troels, 'Discovering the Good: *Oikeiosis* and *Kathekonta* in Stoic Ethics', in *The Norms of Nature*, ed. Malcolm Schofield and Gisela Striker (Cambridge: Cambridge University Press, 1986), pp. 145–83.

Frede, Michael, 'On the Stoic Conception of the Good', in *Topics in Stoic*

Philosophy, ed. Katerina Ierodiakonou (Oxford: Oxford University Press, 1999), pp. 71–94.

Freud, Sigmund, *Civilization and Its Discontents*, trans. James Strachey (New York: W. W. Norton & Company, 1989).

Gass, Michael, 'Eudaimonism and Theology in Stoic Accounts of Virtue', *Journal of the History of Ideas*, 61 (2000): pp. 19–37.

Hadot, Pierre, *La Citadelle intérieure: Introduction aux 'Pensées' de Marc Aurèle* (Paris: Fayard, 1992).

Hicks, R. D., *Epochs of Philosophy: Stoic and Epicurean* (New York: Russell & Russell, Inc., 1962).

Holowchak, M. Andrew, 'Carrying One's Goods from City to City: Seneca on Friendship, Self-Sufficiency, and the Disdain of Fortune', *Ancient Philosophy*, XXVI.1 (2006): pp. 93–110.

Inwood, Bran, 'Rules and Reasoning in Stoic Ethics', in *Topics in Stoic Philosophy*, ed. Katerina Ierodiakonou (Oxford: Oxford University Press, 1999), pp. 95–127.

Irwin, T.H., 'Permanent Happiness: Aristotle and Solon', in *Aristotle's Ethics*, ed. Nancy Sherman (New York: Rowman & Littlefield Publishers, Inc., 1999), pp. 1–34

Jackson-McCabe, Matt, 'The Stoic Theory of Implanted Perceptions', *Phronesis*, 49.4 (2004): pp. 323–47.

Kraut, Richard, 'Aristotle on the Human Good: An Overview', in *Aristotle's Ethics*, ed. Nancy Sherman (New York: Rowman & Littlefield Publishers, Inc., 1999), pp. 79–104.

Krueger, Derek, 'The Bawdy and Society: The Shamelessness of Diogenes in Roman Imperial Culture', in *The Cynics: The Cynic Movement in Antiquity and its Legacy*, ed. R. Bracht Branham and M.-O. Goulet-Cazé (Berkeley: University of California Press, 1996), pp. 222–39.

Lapidge, Michael, 'Stoic Cosmology', *Phronesis*, 18 (1973): pp. 161–85.

Lin Yutang, *The Wisdom of Laotse* (New York: The Modern Library, 1976).

Long, A. A., *Epictetus: A Stoic and Socratic Guide to Life* (New York: Clarendon Press, 2002).

—'Stoic Eudaimonism', in *Proceedings of the Boston Area Colloquium in Ancient Philosophy, Volume IV*, ed. John J. Cleary and Daniel C. Shartin (Lanham, NY: University Press of America, 1986), pp. 77–101.

Nietzsche, Friedrich, *On the Genealogy of Morality*, trans. M. Clark and Alan Swensen (Indianapolis: Hackett Publishing Company, Inc., 1998).

Nozick, Robert, *Anarchy, State, and Utopia* (New York: Basic Books, Inc., 1974).

Nussbaum, Martha, *Cultivating Humanity: A Classical Defense of Reform in Liberal Education* (Cambridge, MA: Harvard University Press, 1997).

Obbink, Dirk, 'The Stoic Sage in the Cosmic City', in *Topics in Stoic Philosophy*, ed. Katerina Ierodiakonou (Oxford: Oxford University Press, 1999), pp. 178–95.

Porter, J. I., 'The Philosophy of Aristo', in *The Cynics: The Cynic Movement in Antiquity and its Legacy*, ed. R. Bracht Branham and M.-O. Goulet-Cazé (Berkeley: University of California Press, 1996), pp. 156–89.

Sedley, David, 'The Stoic–Platonist Debate on *Kathekonta*', in *Topics in*

Stoic Philosophy, ed. Katerina Ierodiakonou (Oxford: Oxford University Press, 1999), pp. 128–52.
Sellars, John, *Stoicism* (Berkeley: University of California Press, 2006).
Sherman, Nancy, *Stoic Warriors: The Ancient Philosophy behind the Military Mind* (Oxford: Oxford University Press, 2005).
Sorabji, Richard, *Emotion and Peace of Mind: From Stoic Agitation to Christian Temptation* (Oxford: Oxford University Press, 2000).
Striker, Gisela, 'Following Nature: A Study in Stoic Ethics', in *Essays on Hellenistic Epistemology and Ethics* (Cambridge: Cambridge University Press, 1996), pp. 221–80.
—'Origins of the Concept of Natural Law', in *Essays on Hellenistic Epistemology and Ethics* (Cambridge: Cambridge University Press, 1996), pp. 209–20.

INDEX

gain; 159–62
Galen 8
general principles 210
glory 174
Goncharov, Ivan 175
good(s) 29–32, 54, 60, 96, 106,
 110–11, 125, 132, 142, 158,
 161, 186, 200
 Aristotle on 29–30
 Stoics on 30–2
good life 77–80, 114
Gorky, Maxime 122
Grief 142–5
Gyges 100

Hadot, Pierre 64n. 24
happiness 26, 30, 52, 60–1, 78, 79,
 81, 82, 94, 110, 115, 149, 161,
 178, 180, 193, 198, 223
hardihood 200
hardship 169, 197–8
Hecato 35, 54, 65n. 60
Hegesias of Cyrene 122, 155n. 118
Hemingway, Ernest 126
Herculean thesis 14, 19
Hercules 135, 172, 196–7, 203
Herillus of Carthage 7
Herodotus 91
heroism 193–228
Hierocles 75
Hippocrates 211
Hippolytus 92
homologia 39–45, 107
hunger 135
hyperbole 61–2

illness 132
impressions 212–3, 216
Impugnity, Principle of 130
impulse 24
inconveniences 34, 47, 103, 123–6,
 151, 220
indifference see *apatheia*
indifferents 32–4, 66n. 71, 103–4,
 180
indifferents thesis 13–4, 19
intellect 206
intention 90, 91

invincibility 5, 6, 19, 21, 48, 51, 62,
 72, 78, 80, 96, 109–16, 124,
 126, 127, 128, 134, 141, 142,
 143, 151, 181–2, 187, 195, 196,
 215, 216, 221, 222, 223
invulnerability 19, 48

judgment 214–6
Julian 2
Jupiter see Zeus
justice 37, 54, 58, 141, 179, 201

Kant, Immanuel 80, 83, 98, 118n.
 88, 223
Kerouac, Jack 184
khreiai 57–8, 212
knowledge 24, 53, 62–4, 89, 124,
 194, 201, 202, 204, 207, 216

lazy argument 45–7
Leonidas 77
liberty 87
Livius 176
logic 206
Lucillius 39, 49, 58, 101, 125, 159,
 170, 171, 176
Lysamachus 148

Manes 161
Marcinko, Richard 3
Master Argument 67n. 120
medicine 208
metaphysics 13
metriopatheia 11–13
Mill, John Stuart 101
Mindyrides 169
misfortune see adversity
moral choice/judgment/worth 34, 35,
 54, 60, 68n. 124, 124, 136, 214
moral progress 37
moral right 28

naturalism, two types of 38
nature 6, 8–9, 14, 20, 33–4, 35–8,
 39, 40, 41, 42, 44, 47, 58, 62,
 73, 79, 84, 96, 102, 103, 106,
 110, 112, 115, 123, 125, 128,
 130, 135, 141, 143–4, 149, 152,